Glastonbury and the Grail

ALSO BY JUSTIN E. GRIFFIN

The Grail Procession: The Legend, the Artifacts, and the Possible Sources of the Story (McFarland, 2004)

The Holy Grail: The Legend, the History, the Evidence (McFarland, 2001)

Glastonbury and the Grail

Did Joseph of Arimathea Bring the Sacred Relic to Britain?

Justin E. Griffin

McFarland & Company, Inc., Publishers
Jefferson, North Carolina, and London

LIBRARY OF CONGRESS CATALOGUING-IN-PUBLICATION DATA

Griffin, Justin.
    Glastonbury and the Grail : did Joseph of Arimathea bring the sacred relic to Britain? / Justin E. Griffin.
      p.   cm.
    Includes bibliographical references and index.

    ISBN 978-0-7864-6582-8
    softcover : acid free paper ∞

    1. Grail — Legends — History and criticism. 2. Joseph, of Arimathea, Saint. 3. Glastonbury (England) — Church history. I. Title.
PN686.G7G746 2013
398'.352—dc23   2012043087

BRITISH LIBRARY CATALOGUING DATA ARE AVAILABLE

© 2013 Justin E. Griffin. All rights reserved

No part of this book may be reproduced or transmitted in any form or by any means, electronic or mechanical, including photocopying or recording, or by any information storage and retrieval system, without permission in writing from the publisher.

On the cover: the Santo Caliz of Valencia (photograph courtesy of Janice Bennett) and the view from the top of Glastonbury Tor (photograph courtesy of Sophie Morse)

Manufactured in the United States of America

McFarland & Company, Inc., Publishers
  Box 611, Jefferson, North Carolina 28640
    www.mcfarlandpub.com

For my wife Donna Griffin, without whose love, support, and perseverance none of this would be possible. I dedicate this book and all my work to you, with all my love and all my heart.

Contents

Acknowledgments	ix
Preface	1
Introduction	5
PART I: GLASTONBURY	11
1. The Legends of Glastonbury	12
2. History in a Timeless Place	22
3. The Second Golden Age	32
PART II: KEY PLAYERS	53
4. Joseph — Nobilis Decurio	54
5. Recreating Joseph's Wattle Church	67
6. The Prophecy of Melkin	86
7. The Mystery Tomb of "J.A."	107
PART III: THE WRITTEN RECORD	151
8. John Leland — The King's Antiquarian	152
9. Glastonbury's Warrior Monk	166
10. The Book of the Grail	188
11. England to France, Spain to Germany	200
PART IV: THE CASE FOR GLASTONBURY AND THE HISTORICAL GRAIL	225
12. Making a Case for Glastonbury	226
13. The Historical Grail	252
Bibliography	271
Index	273

Acknowledgments

I have been very fortunate to have many friends and make many more who have made an impact on my study. To them go my thanks.

Thanks first to my wife, Donna, for her patience and kindness, and to my dear friends Timothy Watson, Elizabeth Ridley, and Leslie Johnson for providing support and proofing my many drafts. Thanks also to my colleague, John Koopmans, who has been my sounding board, tome of knowledge, magnifying glass, and most of all friend even in times when life interrupted. My most humble thanks to those who kindly lent me their knowledge and at times their ears during my research. Thanks to Doctor James Carley for indulging my questions, and to both Janice Bennett and Michael Hesemann for bringing new light to the study of the Santo Caliz in Valencia and the Monastery of San Juan de la Pena.

Thanks to all the wonderful people at Glastonbury who have both made me feel welcome and proven to be such invaluable help in learning about the abbey, the town, and the surrounding areas that make Somerset a land of mystery and magic. Thanks to Francis Thyer, who has been my lifeline to Glastonbury for many years, as well as to all the good people who care for Glastonbury Abbey. You have all been very kind and tolerant of a distant Yank's infernal, endless requests for information.

My thanks also go to theose who dedicate themselves to preserving Britain's sacred landmarks and historic treasures, such as the good people at Wells Cathedral, the British Library in London, St. John the Baptist Parish Church, and most especially Neill Bonham and the Glastonbury Antiquarian Society. Thank you to Rex Harrison and Roberto Abizanda for allowing me to use their wonderful photos of the tympanum at St. Mary's Church in Stoke sub Hamdon and the arched chapel of San Juan de la Peña, respectively.

Finally, I would like to extend a special word of thanks to a dear friend in Poole, Sophie Morse. I must honestly say that Sophie has a truly artful eye as a photographer, not only in beautiful, majestic stills, but also in the most incredible 360-degree panoramas of Glastonbury Abbey and many other places around England. Her photos have allowed me to virtually revisit the land I love so well both for further study and for pure pleasure.

Thank you all. I feel most privileged to have worked with you on this project.

Preface

Soon after I began studying the legend of the Holy Grail, I found that the town of Glastonbury in England stood at the very heart of the matter, both in history and in story. I knew that one day I would have to go there in order to truly understand. In October of 2008, I found myself standing in the Glastonbury Abbey Museum looking out a window onto the Lady Chapel. A gentleman at Glastonbury named Francis Thyer, now retired, allowed me the rare opportunity to spend some time among the ruins after everyone else had gone. Holding a skeleton key in my hand that opened a great iron gate, my own private entrance that night, was a surreal experience that I have difficulty expressing even today. However, because I asked politely, I feel that this *grande dame* of Britain's past entrusted me with a few of her secrets.

The legend of the Holy Grail has been relegated to the "Speculation" and "New Age" sections of bookstores for far too long, and it was my goal upon beginning my research to challenge that. I felt there was a seed of truth, a single mote of history, lying at the heart of this well-known but little-understood legend. To bring this core of truth to light, I realized that demonstrating the existence of the Holy Grail as an historical artifact relied on proving that Joseph of Arimathea not only was a historical character but was in fact present in Britain in the first century a.d. Therefore, I began looking for evidence that would place Joseph at Glastonbury *outside* the realm of fiction.

As impossible as this may sound, I soon found such evidence. As time passed, more and more evidence presented itself, pointing to one conclusion. Although it is ultimately impossible to prove beyond a shadow of a doubt that Joseph of Arimathea was at Glastonbury in the first century, there is an abundance of very credible circumstantial evidence suggesting this tradition was accepted as fact since a time long before the traditional medieval birth of the Joseph/Grail legends. The "Prophecy of Melkin," first recorded in the fifteenth century and considered a mere fabrication, appears to have influenced this tradition and possibly that of King Arthur as long ago as the eighth century. A stone crypt now sitting in a local parish church is known to have been part of a shrine to Joseph once held in Glastonbury Abbey, and can be traced back to at least the fifteenth century, suggesting the discovery of St. Joseph's final resting place. Finally, literary evidence from the thirteenth century alludes to a chapel containing Joseph's relics that stood for centuries before the height of the medieval Arthurian mania.

To demonstrate the likelihood that Joseph truly did build the wattle church, the nucleus around which the great medieval abbey grew, it became clear that I had to bridge the gap between two widely divided aspects of the legend: the early origins of the church's history and the romances, stories, and histories that were later written about it. Through books such as *Glastonbury Abbey: Myth and Archaeology* and *The Architectural History of Glastonbury Abbey*, I discovered much about the abbey's past. Forgotten doorways, footprints of lost architectural features, and secrets hidden in the landscape point to a history long forgotten, yet in its way very telling. Turning then to the invaluable works written by authors of the time such as William of Malmesbury and John Leland as well as modern scholars like James P. Carley, I was able to see how the legend developed over time from a forgotten tradition to a foundation of national identity. Yet all the while, standing on either side of a great chasm, these two facets of the Grail legend were joined only by a text allegedly written by Melkin in the sixth century.

Like the Grail, these few lines of nearly inscrutable Latin have been written off as myth with no place in scholarship. However, when I began finding suggestions that this text was known by several different sources, in several different time periods, I knew the bridge had finally been built. All that remained was to walk from one side to the other. Once that was done, the concept that Joseph indeed travelled to Britain, built a church to his fallen Lord, and perhaps carried some important religious artifact with him along the journey ceased to be the stuff of fairy tales and became all quite feasible. However, one question remained: How did the simple, nearly forgotten story of an ancient immigrant from Israel become the sweeping saga of popular culture that it has become today? At the heart of this question lies a book: One book given to Chrétien de Troyes by his patron, Phillip of Flanders, holds all the necessary answers.

If one were to ever ascertain the true nature of the fabled sourcebook used to create the first European story of the Grail, *Le Conte del Graal*, it could be possible to learn not only what the Grail was, but where it came from and when. Again Glastonbury offers a wealth of information. Although the exact sourcebook may never be found, it is possible to trace the migration of the Grail story from France back to Glastonbury through the interconnectivity of those who played a part in its creation. We find an intriguing character named Henry of Blois, abbot of Glastonbury in the twelfth century, who may have introduced the English tales of Joseph and his enigmatic relic to his relative across the channel, Henry of Champagne. However, like Chrétien's story itself, this picture of the Grail's evolution is incomplete. To take the final step toward understanding not only the historical nature of Joseph of Arimathea at Glastonbury but that of the Grail itself, one must venture even further. From its journey from first century Jerusalem to Somerset in Britain, and on to France in the twelfth century, it becomes necessary to reach further east to Germany and then west to Spain.

It has been said that truth is stranger than fiction. In the case of the Holy Grail at Glastonbury — the ancient Isle of Avalon — this statement couldn't be more true, and considering how strange and utterly fantastic the Grail stories can be, that's quite a statement. Although I cannot say this is the truth of the Grail Legend, I can say with reasonable certainty that the theory outlined herein successfully separates itself from the fantasy of the Grail romances while answering many questions regarding what the Grail is, what it is not, and how the story began and progressed. I propose that the Grail is exactly what it is claimed to be: a vessel that once held the blood of Jesus Christ. Further, I propose that it is any vessel that once contained this type of blood relic. In that sense, there was not one Grail but at least six, possibly seven. To further muddle the issue, I suggest that although the Grail story began in Britain, its growth and dissemination were thanks to troubadours in France, Germany, and Spain, drawing in no small part on the appearance and story of another grail, called the *Santo Caliz*.

Just as nature eventually overtakes the creations of man, man with time overtakes a simple history with his imagination, creating an entity wholly and fundamentally different from its origins. With only minor echoes of its former self, fact is eventually conflated, making it nearly impossible to see anything but the ornate housing into which it is framed. However, if one has the mindset of a student rather than a teacher, a careful investigator can begin to part the gold from the rock, the face from the caricature, and the true relic from the reliquary.

Introduction

As odd as it may seem to us now, there was a time, very long ago, when man lived by passion, not reason. By passion, I mean neither lust nor abandon, nor do I mean whim or folly. In using the word "passion," I mean living by all the intangibles which, although still dear to us, have been reserved for use in our private lives, while our society has centered itself on the pursuit of reason. Now that a working definition of passion has been established, I shall attempt to more clearly define the word "reason."

We've all heard of the Dark Ages and may have wondered what exactly the term means. Some have theorized that the Dark Ages were in fact dark, likely due to a meteorite impact releasing dust into the atmosphere, causing literal darkness throughout Europe. As interesting as this theory may sound, it is generally agreed that the term "Dark Ages" means simply a time for which the light of historical knowledge is regrettably dim. This was a time after the fall of the Roman Empire when wars, power struggles, and misery were commonplace in daily life. For this reason, there were no elaborate histories or illuminated accounts that would today help us better understand this tumultuous period.

Following this time of darkness was a period of brilliance appropriately called the Renaissance, meaning "rebirth." This was an age as full of wonder and advancement as the Dark Ages were of despair and stagnation. For that reason, the mindset during the Renaissance was to cast off the very things that were hallmarks of the Dark Ages in order to fully appreciate the joy that rebirth brings. This goal reached its pinnacle during what is known as the Age of Enlightenment, during which time reason was king. Gone were the days when the church ruled daily life; fear and superstition were replaced by science and verifiable fact. Now, man was in control of his own destiny.

Therefore, the word "reason" could be defined as being justified by verifiable fact, or in a word, proof. Presenting proof has been the litmus test by which all science, and indeed all theories, must be judged, and rightfully so.

Without some degree of proof, there can be no certainty that a thing, whatever that thing may be, is true or false. However, using the word "proof" can be somewhat scattershot. After all, what exactly is proof, and who determines its validity?

To demand proof is a bit like someone from the United States referring to themselves as "an American"—while true, it is more a statement of ideal than actuality. The further clarification of being a "North American" would be required to make it a fact, but the phrase doesn't roll off the tongue quite so easily. Skepticism is the qualifying characteristic of the modern mind. Reason demands proof, but in so doing asks for something nearly impossible. In essence, you are inviting someone into your home when there is in fact no door.

In a word, there is no such thing as "proof." There can be no proof, either in science or in any other endeavor of knowledge. There can be only "evidence." There can be strong evidence or weak evidence, and there can of course be evidence to refute a claim. However, no matter the quality or quantity of evidence for or against a theory, there can be no irrefutable proof. Even in the irrefutable world of physics and mathematics proof is elusive. For centuries, Newtonian laws of motion were accepted as the undeniable manner in which the universe worked. Then along came an unassuming man who would later upset the proverbial apple cart. Albert Einstein introduced a small but significant addendum to this universal truth of physics with his theory of relativity, stating that at very high speeds, Newtonian physics no longer apply.

In 1907, workers digging in a gravel pit discovered some curious pieces of bone and presented them to amateur antiquarian and paleontologist Charles Dawson, knowing his predilection for old bones. Finding them intriguing, he began his own dig in the gravel pits, some time later asking the assistance of Arthur Woodward from the British Museum. In 1912, Dawson found two broken pieces of skull and nearby, half a jawbone. Upon examination, Dawson and Woodward were surprised to see that the reconstructed skull resembled a modern, if somewhat small, human skull, while the jaw looked more like that of a primate, most likely a chimpanzee.

This skull, supposedly representing a creature called "Piltdown Man," was presented as evidence of the long-sought-after "missing link" between ape and man. As early as 1915, scholars researching the skull began to question the artifact, concluding the jaw came from an ape. In 1923, Franz Weidenreich discovered not only that the jaw was that of an orangutan, but that the teeth appeared to have been filed down. His claim that the skull was a hoax did not meet with agreement until nearly forty years later.

In 1953 Oxford University professor Kenneth Oakley discovered that the reconstructed skull was fabricated from a roughly medieval human skull artificially aged with chromic acid, a 500-year-old orangutan jawbone, and fossilized chimpanzee teeth that had been filed down to present a more human appearance. Although the forgery was almost immediately discovered, the scientific community did not acknowledge this as anything other than hard proof of a "missing link" for nearly four decades. For all that time the skull was nearly iconic, staunchly defended by scholars despite claims to the contrary.

Understanding that the topic of evolution is hotly debated, these examples merely serve to show that "proof" is largely a matter of opinion. Whether it turns out to be a hoax, inconclusive, or apparently true, something that today is called definitive proof might be a quaint story told by college professors in a hundred years to demonstrate how far knowledge has come. Of course we don't have to look that far back to see examples of "proof" found to be lacking. Take for example an artifact from a different field of archeological endeavor.

In the 1980s, the Israel Museum paid over $500,000 to an anonymous seller for a curious object — a 4 centimeter high, partially broken carving of a pomegranate made of ivory. What made this otherwise unremarkable artifact of such great value was that just under the neck of the carving, there was a Hebrew inscription reading, "belonging to the Temple of the Yahweh, holy to the priests." Another curious feature was that it had a small socket in the bottom, suggesting that the curious piece was only a part of a larger whole. Said to have originated from the Temple Mount, these features suggested that it was a decorative headpiece to a scepter used by priests in the Temple of Solomon, making it the only archeological proof that the temple ever truly existed. It was given pride of place in the museum and was heavily researched by scholars for years, most of whom argued for its authenticity.

Some years later, another object allegedly from the Temple Mount surfaced. Called the Joash Tablet, this blackened stone slab featured an inscribed text describing repairs done to the temple. The artifact was offered for sale by a private collector and was chased around Israel's antiquities trade for years before anyone had the opportunity to examine it. When experts finally inspected it, it showed all the signs of being authentic — the stone itself appeared genuine, and its patina was found to be of the right time in ancient history. It exhibited signs of being subjected to fire, containing tiny traces of gold embedded in the surface from the lavish decorations inside the rich temple. Authorities rejoiced, calling this unquestionable proof of Solomon's Temple.

It was only after another artifact of biblical interest was found to be hoaxed that these two pieces of "proof" were called into question. The James Ossuary, a legitimate first-century funerary bone box, was made famous by the inscription carved into its side. It read, "James, son of Joseph, brother of Jesus." Investigators immediately became suspicious and upon investigation found not only that the second part of the inscription, the "brother of Jesus" portion, had been copied from other disparate originals and in a different hand than the first portion, but that the patina on the forged portion of the inscription was easily removed, revealing fresh carving marks underneath.

Since the owner of the James Ossuary had been the same as of the Joash tablet, namely Oded Golan, researchers descended on the tablet, and like the ossuary, the patina in the lettering was found to be quite easily removed with a wooden stick. As part of the investigation of this epic hoax, an entire forgery ring was discovered that called into question the legitimacy of any artifact not found *in situ* (in archeological context) that had been purchased in the past several decades.

Since the Ivory Pomegranate had been purchased in the same manner, it fell under the scrutiny of the Israel Museum as well. Under in-depth microscopic investigation and date testing, this honored relic also turned out to be a hoax. Although the ivory proved to be ancient, in fact much older than Solomon's Temple, the inscription appeared to have been carved only recently, stopping just short of the broken edge. Although there is still some debate over whether or not the Ivory Pomegranate is a fake, the piece has been removed from exhibition.

At the time of this writing, the criminal trial surrounding the Joash Tablet and the James Ossuary has ended. During the trial, many experts suggested these carvings might actually be authentic, despite other expert testimony asserting them to be hoaxes. The debate over these artifacts, and many others that have come under the same clinical scrutiny, will no doubt rage on for decades to come. Whatever the outcome, it is likely that these pieces will never again be viewed objectively.

My goal in speaking about these matters is not to open a debate about evolution, Biblical history, or any other topic about which people love to argue. True scholarship does not content itself with what it already knows and accepts. It questions, digs, and learns from whatever it may find, surprising or not, comfortable or not.

My point is that history, and by extension archeology, is not a mathematical equation. It cannot be proven; it cannot be solved. Unless we as researchers were there to see the event happen, there is no way of proving its truth. As I said previously, there is only evidence of varying quality leading toward some conclusion.

Trying to find fact and good, reliable evidence is difficult enough, as we have seen. Trying to find fact and evidence behind a legend is many times more so. It makes what would otherwise be evidence good enough to support a thesis inherently suspect. In fact, the Middle Ages were famous for forged artifacts and fabricated evidence. So how would one proceed in searching for evidence to support the idea of Joseph of Arimathea and the Holy Grail being anything other than the objects of fiction?

Simply put, judge all available evidence objectively, independent of the legendary status or taint of storytelling ascribed to the subject matter. With the understanding that there is no proof that cannot be refuted or that fully satisfies a true skeptic, judge whatever accounts are available on both the veracity of related accounts — perhaps other works by the same person — and the context in which the source has been introduced.

I would counsel readers not to dismiss or discount any author, any account, or any evidence offhand because it doesn't match preconceived opinion. I cite the example of Heinrich Schliemann, the man who, using only Homer's *Iliad* and some knowledge of history, is credited with finding the city of Troy. Although later archeological research of the site demonstrated that his discoveries were not fully as he thought, it did prove to be the location of the historical Troy — found nonetheless thanks to his efforts and his faith in the truth behind a legendary story.

Although many modern archeologists claim Schliemann's clueless discovery was due less to Homer than to a fortuitous combination of educated guesswork and luck, one must remember that many of the greatest finds in early archeology were made using these same tools. As the modern writer may take ideas from some inspiration, the writers of our greatest legends needed something to inspire their sagas. Taken simply on these merits, finding history in the legend of the Holy Grail and the traditions of Glastonbury becomes much less fanciful.

The question ceases to be whether or not Joseph of Arimathea, striking his flowering hawthorne staff into the earth, brought the sacred chalice, the Holy Grail, to Britain to be later found by the renowned King Arthur, who lies there buried on the Isle of Avalon. The true question becomes, did a man from Israel travel to England and found a church there? This is the question that I have tried to answer and to find evidence to support. This is my case for Glastonbury.

Part I

Glastonbury

The small town of Glastonbury in Somerset is today known more for its annual musical festival than most anything else. Second to that, Glastonbury is known as the center of the Arthur and Grail legends in England. The abbey around which the medieval town grew is responsible for much of the town's tourism today, just as it was over a thousand years ago. This is a place where Neo-paganism and Christianity brush shoulders and vie for visitors' pounds.

To understand the tortured history of Glastonbury is to understand the Holy Grail itself. Here legend and history mix in a stew that is both succulent and bitter. One can never fully separate one flavor from another so as to recreate it once one returns home. It must be experienced to be fully appreciated. In this section we will begin our investigation of the Grail by learning more about its origin at the Last Supper and Crucifixion. We will then move on to see how the legendary figure of Joseph of Arimathea could have given rise to Glastonbury's current acclaim.

Chapter 1

The Legends of Glastonbury

During the early to mid–1990s, there was a rather quirky television series called *Northern Exposure*, set in a remote Alaskan town. There was usually some light moral set in an odd story line that left you pondering. One episode in particular sticks in my mind as being quite profound, and something I had never realized before then. The basic plot was as follows. A member of the local Native American Eskimo tribe was trying to find out more about the collective culture of the white man by asking people to tell stories that had been passed down to them. Most had either some uninteresting story, meaningful only to them, or no story to tell at all. In the end, the fellow retired in frustration to another of the tribe, a young man who was completely enthralled by motion pictures, and expressed his confusion about why he was having such difficulty finding any insightful stories.

Never removing his eyes from the black and white drama playing out on his television screen, the young man told his elder that perhaps his answer could be found in this movie, or maybe it was more like what this character said in some other movie, etc. It was at that moment when the other man realized the truth of his failure. The stories illustrating the collective culture for his neighbors were to be found on the silver screen. We take our cultural insights, at least to some degree, from the movies. Of course it was not always thus. An age ago, people who made history took their inspiration from the popular media of their day, such as books, magazines, or even comic books.

Like travelers and scholars did at the turn of the twentieth century, reading epic tales of adventures in the wilds of Africa or the bleak dunes of Egypt, many a modern archeologist can trace their love of antiquity, or have at least likened themselves to, one particular cinematic hero from the 1980s — Indiana Jones. Although I claim to be no great scholar, and can't really call myself a world traveler, I must admit my passion for the Grail legend began with Indiana Jones and his quest to find the hallowed relic. In fact, as I sit writing this first chapter, I do so looking at a calendar my wife Donna made for me, which

1. The Legends of Glastonbury

includes a picture of me standing framed in a set of sarsen stones at Stonehenge, looking more than a little conspicuous in my brown leather coat, fedora-styled hat, and military surplus haversack slung over one shoulder.

With the full eagerness and passion that image would entail, I began my investigation into the Grail some twenty years ago by reading Malory's *Morte d'Arthur*—the Arthur legend. Quickly learning the depth of literature and related topics involved, it didn't take me long to run across one name that would forever alter the direction of my research. Glastonbury has been called the seat of all Arthurian legend, and the place from which the classic story likely sprang. Although it has been debated what role the abbey played in the development of the lore surrounding Arthur and the Grail, it cannot be disputed that these subjects are now inexorably intertwined.

Like any good legend, there are many variations one may encounter while reading about Glastonbury and Arthurian Legend. However, the basic framework common to all can be summarized as follows. At the crucifixion of Jesus around A.D. 30, Joseph of Arimathea asked for the body to be taken down and handed over to him. Pilate agreed, the body of Jesus was taken down, and hasty funeral preparations began since the Sabbath was fast approaching, during which time a Jew was not allowed to touch anything ritually unclean such as a dead body.

As the story of the Passion goes, Jesus's body remained in a sealed tomb for two days while Roman soldiers stood guard and the disciples kept a low profile to avoid a similar fate. On the third day, some women who were among His followers went to the tomb to do a more proper job of preparing the body for what would be one year spent in the tomb, donated by Joseph, while the remains decomposed to bone, after which time they would be relocated to another tomb and left in an ossuary box. What the women found was an empty tomb; they had no idea what had become of the body. Joseph was surely among those to whom the women came with the news that apparently their master's body had been stolen by the Romans. At that point, some among them went to the tomb to see for themselves that it was actually empty.

A separate account from the apocryphal Gospel of Nicodemus, also known as the Acts of Pilate, states that Joseph was then suspected of stealing the body from under the nose of the Roman guards and was imprisoned. According to this gospel the Spirit of God, possibly Jesus Himself, visited Joseph while he was incarcerated and soon allowed him to escape. Found some time later in his home, he was going to be arrested again, but instead he was banished — set adrift in a ship with no sails and no rudder or oars.

Bridging the account from an apocryphal text to pure legend, Joseph and some number of followers allegedly traveled to other parts of what is now western Europe. Many stories tell of Joseph and his party landing in Gaul, what is now France, later continuing to the isle of Britain. Some say certain members of his company remained in France, and some accounts claim Joseph came to southern England by way of Scotland. Although the particulars of this journey will likely never be known, the main point of this mini–Exodus story is that Joseph and some others eventually made their way to Britain, allegedly first seeing their new home amid the marshy Somerset landscape from atop Wirral, or Wearyall Hill, just to the southwest of the present Glastonbury Abbey.

Once there, their first order of business was to provide for the necessities of life. Some claim Joseph had been there before and knew the local people of the region, gaining their support in the new environment. Others claim Joseph and his companions were alone and had to fend for themselves. Once their means of survival had been established, they set out to achieve the goal with which they had left their homeland in Israel, that being to begin a ministry there in that remote corner of the known world. Since gatherings were held in homes and in other inauspicious places in the early Christian church,

The view from the top of Glastonbury Tor, 512 feet in height, is dizzying to say the least. Following the footpath straight out into the distance, the finger of land called Wearyall Hill, the site where Joseph landed and planted his thorn staff in the ground, can be seen. Where the flat Somerset Levels meet the slopes up to its summit, one can see the outline of the shore that once separated the Isle of Avalon from the marshes beyond (photograph courtesy Sophie Morse).

In December 2010, the famous "Holy Thorn" Tree that stood atop Wearyall Hill for centuries was vandalized, leaving nothing but a bare trunk. This was actually the second time the tree was cut down, previously destroyed as an act of iconoclasm. As with the first vandalism, the tree was cared for and resurrected by the local townspeople. In fact, the first signs of rebirth can be seen coming from the top of the tree. Glastonbury Tor stands in the distance, giving us today a glimpse of what Joseph and his followers saw when they arrived in Glastonbury (photograph courtesy Sophie Morse).

it is doubtful that they wanted to build a grand place of worship. The glory that Glastonbury could later boast no doubt started from much humbler origins.

Over time, either as a further act of devotion or just to accommodate the souls they had converted, they constructed some form of church building. According to tradition, the building was made of wattle and daub, making it a crude shack or hut. Then, after Joseph's death, the remains of the original church, or Ealde Cirche as it has been called, was discovered by later emissaries of the pope. Eventually erected on the site was the great church of Glastonbury Abbey, the ruins of which can still be seen and visited today. Unfortunately, what remains today tells of a painful history, including a catastrophic fire, murders, and finally the dissolution and destruction of what was once one of the greatest churches in all of Christendom.

This story forms the basis of what has become the Glastonbury Tradition, and is partly why the great abbey reached such a height of wealth and acclaim — upheld by centuries of early church writers and popes. Visitors to the abbey today can see accounts and illustrations of this tale proudly displayed in the museum alongside archeology from the site's past. Although the town of Glastonbury has a definite mystical flavor, the abbey stands on its own merits. There is certainly a vast wealth of history and archeology to be explored there, even by the amateur enthusiast, and most everyone is happy to share their knowledge with anyone interested. However, another tradition related to Glastonbury is somewhat downplayed, if not in the gift shops.

If the legend of Joseph of Arimathea would seem difficult to substantiate, the legend of the Holy Grail is even more steeped in lore and shrouded in mystery, having as many different variations as there are people who recount it. Although the term "Holy Grail" has become more synonymous with Monty Python than it has been considered in a historical context, there was a time when the idea of the sacred chalice was taken seriously, literally inspiring quests for religious artifacts throughout Europe. Like the legend of Joseph, the traditional story of the Grail seems fairly straightforward on the surface.

The classic retelling of the legend begins at the foot of the cross at the time of Christ's death. Tradition states Joseph of Arimathea donated his own tomb, into which Jesus's body was to be placed. However, certain funerary rites needed to be performed before the tomb could be sealed. One of these rites was to collect the blood from the body since the blood was seen as "the seat of the soul." This meant collecting blood issuing from any wounds on the body as well as any blood that had been spilt.

As a result, either Joseph or Mary Magdalene collected some of Jesus's blood that ran down the cross as He remained nailed to it, and collected more later while they prepared the body in the tomb. The legend claims the vessel used to catch His blood was the very same from which all drank at the Last Supper, just days before, during which time Jesus gave His admonition to remember that night, and his impending sacrifice, inspiring the rite that would become the Eucharist, or communion. Thus in some Grail literature, the chalice is referred to as the cup of the Last Supper. The cup then finds its way back into the hands of Joseph of Arimathea and goes with him on his journey to Britain, where he founds the first Christian church.

Moving forward through time about five centuries, Arthur enters the story during the Dark Ages. To aid his mission to unite the fractured kingdom of Britain, his friend and confidant Merlin tells the king that the Holy Grail, now lost for many years, must be found, and that with it shining as a beacon in the dark time, he would bring men together and cleanse their sins, beginning a golden age in which mankind could rejoice and enjoy a better life. All his knights of the Round Table rode out in the name of the quest and found a great many adventures to test both their mettle and their souls. Many died during their trials, and most others who survived failed to achieve their quest. Gawain proved too worldly; Lancelot, the best among them, failed due to his love for Queen Guinevere. Ultimately only one would accomplish the quest, and in finding the Grail, return the world to the paradise Arthur had imagined.

However, as all worldly paradises are, Arthur's golden age was short lived. Either through wars fought over Guinevere or by the sins of excess, the king was brought low, and the Grail left his high court, again becoming lost — waiting to be found by one who is worthy. Some texts even mention some poor individual who later went out looking for the lost relic. Usually becoming either irredeemably mad or a repentant hermit, he spends his years in service to the Lord, waiting for the next knight to ride through his woods on the quest, willing to impart his wisdom to the new adept in hopes that the Grail would one day be returned to the world. Although the Grail has been thought to be many things, from a Celtic horn of plenty to an alchemical transmutation table, this version of the legend, the Christian branch, has become the most common and most recognizable among them.

Students of medieval literature can glean a great many things by dissecting and scrutinizing a medieval romance such as this, but typically very little history can be taken from a work of fiction. Usually only insights into the mind of the author can be taken from such fantastic tales. The reader must often imagine the original audience's viewpoint to fully appreciate and understand the narrative. As a result, the Arthur and Grail stories has been broken down in several different ways, some claiming mere recapitulation, while others claim something of more personal benefit that can be harvested from the mysteries presented therein.

The most common view of the Arthurian saga, especially when it comes to the Grail, is that it is descended from the Celtic oral tradition of the warrior hero and his interactions with the unseen world. In fact, the manuscript that first brought the story of the Grail to the medieval mind and high court of France, *Le Conte del Graal*, written by Chrétien de Troyes, parallels almost exactly a fifteenth-century Welsh story found in the *Mabinogion* called *Peredur*. It is easy to agree with this assessment when one reads the opening sequence of those texts. Both stories open by introducing the hero, Peredur in the Welsh, Perceval in the French, explaining how his mother has kept him from the world of knighthood due to the deaths of other knights in his family.

One day while he is hunting in the forest he loves so dearly, he sees a group of knights in the forest, their armor dazzling him in their brilliance. Inquiring about what exactly they are, angels or demons, he learns about knighthood despite his mother's efforts. He tells his mother about seeing the knights and she immediately forbids him to follow after them or to seek this course in life. Nevertheless, Perceval leaves her mourning alone in the woods to become a knight. It isn't long after this that the stories of Peredur and Perceval diverge, following the tones expected in a Celtic tale and a courtly European tale, respectively.

However, this text isn't the only reason for this theory. The Arthurian tradition was set down by other works such as *Culhwch and Olwen* and *Spoils of Annwn* in which Arthur performs such deeds as fighting giants, venturing into the underworld, and bringing back magical cauldrons of plenty to the British Isles. Modern Arthurian scholars such as Jessie Weston and Roger Sherman Loomis have made quite convincing cases for the idea that the Grail appears to have its origin in Celtic mythology. While Celtic ties are undeniable, this explanation alone fails to yield the understanding that a full investigation demands.

One may wonder how a pagan Celtic story would find its way to a Christian high court in France. The twelfth century was not a time to relate a story about worshipping a severed head on a platter. Therefore, Chrétien's *Conte del Graal* became a story of chivalry, shining knights on white steeds, and the relics depicted within touched the Christian heart of the audience: a bleeding lance and a chalice. The aura of sanctity demonstrated that these were objects of the greatest holiness, and the virgins who ushered them into the Fisher King's banquet hall demonstrated their purity. As a result of the dazzling spectacle, Perceval fails to perform the one act that would make these relics his and restore the health of the wounded Fisher King. He fails to ask a question.

The rapid acceleration Perceval encounters in becoming a knight makes him something of a hollow hero. Had he acquired the Grail at this early stage, it would suggest that it takes very little to be deemed worthy of these precious treasures. Therefore when Perceval fails to demonstrate his naïve state, suggesting he is guilty of the sin of pride, it becomes clear that although he is worthy to witness the Grail, he is not yet worthy to possess it. Indeed, before Perceval again witnesses the Grail, he will have endured much and proven himself worthy in his actions as well as his spirit.

This sort of high moral tale was fairly common in the middle ages, serving as an ideal for which all men and women should strive. It has been said that the concept of chivalry was created to rein in the brutal and self-serving principles that transitioned the Dark Ages into the Middle Ages. Killing was a way of life, feuding and warring for land was the way one progressed, and women were considered property if they were considered at all. In addition to strength and prowess at arms, chivalry became an implied code of conduct for all nobles, emphasizing courtesy, kindness to the weak, honor, and above all respect for women.

It becomes clear how the quest for the Grail became viewed as the ultimate depiction of chivalry. While other medieval tales showed how to be honorable in court, here was a tale that suggested if one followed the ideals of chivalry to its greatest extent, even in the wilds of heathen lands, it would mean ultimately being judged worthy by none other than God Himself. Therefore when Perceval is gifted the opportunity to witness the Grail procession, an opportunity not granted to even the iconic Lancelot, it is clear Perceval is meant to win the Grail, but he must first earn it by testing the very code he had left his innocent woodland home to pursue.

It is this journey to sanctity, this pathway to enlightenment, on which modern Grail writers have focused for their inspiration. While the key to reaching the end of the quest and thereby the Grail is still to undergo ordeals, achieve learning, and finally be judged by the creator, the focus of the quest has changed. Subjecting oneself to trial as a means to reach the Grail is no longer the objective. The trial has become the goal — the Grail as a physical object is now rejected in favor of making the Grail a spiritual ideal to pursue.

The concept of the Grail as a spiritual path has spawned a veritable New Age industry at Glastonbury. With the nearby Chalice Well and Glastonbury Tor, the quest for enlightenment and healing of the spirit has become big business, second only to the annual Glastonbury music festival. This latest incarnation of the area's mysterious nature has in a way overshadowed the rich history that greets you around every corner. However, there is one example of Glastonbury's mysticism that can be used to shed more light on its legendary past.

John of Glastonbury makes reference to the writings of an alleged sixth-century Welsh bard in his *Chronicle of Glastonbury Abbey*, written in the last half of the fourteenth century. Known as the "Prophecy of Melkin," the text details in curious terms the circumstances and whereabouts of Joseph of Arimathea's burial.

> The Isle of Avalon, eager for the death of pagans, at the burial of them all will be, decorated beyond the others in the world with the soothsaying spheres of prophecy, and in future will be adorned with those who praise the Most High. Abbadare, powerful in Saphat, most noble of pagans, took his sleep there with 104,000 men. Among these Joseph of Arimathea received eternal slumber in the marble tomb, and he lies on a divided line next to the oratory's southern corner where the wickerwork is constructed above the might and venerable Maiden, and where the aforesaid thirteen spheres rest. Joseph has with him in the sarcophagus two white and silver vessels, full of the blood and sweat of the prophet Jesus. Once his sarcophagus is discovered, it will be visible, whole and undecayed, and open to the whole world. From then on, those who dwell in the noble island will lack neither water nor the dew of heaven. For a long time before the day of judgment in Josaphat these things will be openly declared to the living. Thus far Melkin [*Chronicle of Glastonbury Abbey*, Carley, p. 55].

If the claims of John of Glastonbury and later John Leland are to be believed, this is the first written account of Joseph of Arimathea and the Grail in Britain at Glastonbury. This account will be presented again and better treated in a later chapter, but for now it serves as an introduction to two other Glastonbury legends that are much more controversial and ultimately impossible to substantiate.

Some scholars making a close examination of the reference above have suggested that the translation is not entirely accurate. They claim that instead of being read as, "he lies on a forked line close to the southern corner of the chapel with prepared wattle for the powerful venerable Maiden," it should read, "he lies on a forked line close to the southern corner of the chapel with prepared wattle *above* the powerful venerable Maiden." In other words, their claim is that the Virgin Mary was buried somewhere beneath the original wattle church constructed in Joseph's time.

This claim gains credibility when one recalls the well-known "Jesus/Maria" stone still visible on the southern wall of the Lady Chapel; however, the building of the Lady Chapel would also seem to discredit the claim. When the site of the Norman building was being prepared, there surely would have been a written account of such an auspicious burial being discovered, especially if this tradition existed at that time. Since no such reference has ever been found, there exists virtually no evidence to support the idea that Mary was buried at Glastonbury. One may wonder where the notion of the Virgin Mary coming to England ever originated.

The traditions of Glastonbury as outlined above deal only with Joseph of Arimathea, the foundation of Glastonbury Abbey, and to a small extent the Holy Grail. However, there is one other part of the story that is perhaps best known from William Blake's "Jerusalem." It begins, "And did those feet in ancient time walk upon England's mountains green." The feet in question belong to none other than Jesus Himself, specifically during the time called the "lost years of Jesus"— the years between His teaching in the temple as a boy and His baptism by John the Baptist. This legend states that Jesus traveled to England during metal trade expeditions with his uncle, Joseph of Arimathea, and perhaps spent some years living there and ministering to the local Britons.

Although there is in truth nothing impossible or for that matter unfeasible about this story, there exists virtually no accepted evidence to support the claim that either Jesus or Joseph ever stepped foot on British soil. Many would say that the very idea is preposterous. However, as we have already discussed, the lack of proof does not mean the lack of evidence. Remember, our goal in this investigation is not to determine whether the good Saint Joseph brought the most holy Grail from the foot of the cross to England so that the great King Arthur could later discover it to bring his failing kingdom back from the brink. We simply want to know if there is any evidence that a man from Judea could have traveled to Britain in the first century A.D., carrying with him a vessel of some kind, out of the realm of fantasy and into the light of history. In fact there actually is some evidence supporting the story, although the evidence deals exclusively with Joseph, not Jesus. However, since making an argument that the Holy Grail was an actual, historical object hangs more on the presence of Joseph of Arimathea at Glastonbury than Jesus, presenting evidence to support the latter will comprise the remainder of this text.

Chapter 2

History in a Timeless Place

In October of 2008, my wife and I had the chance to take a long-awaited trip to Great Britain. Seeing it as a once-in-a-lifetime venture, we tried to see and do as much as possible, taking a guided tour of Scotland as well as touring on our own. We saw the beautiful, stark, misty vistas of the Scottish Highlands and the bustling streets and sidewalks of London. Of our trip, I remember two things the most, one of which I've already mentioned in passing: first, getting to walk among the great monoliths of Stonehenge, and second, at long last having the opportunity to visit Glastonbury Abbey. Like Stonehenge, the town of Glastonbury is both a beautifully quiet and unassuming place and a centuries-old place of pilgrimage. Both seem to be remarkable sites dropped into otherwise unremarkable landscapes, but in truth it only seems that way to one inexperienced in the expansive histories of the land and the context into which they have been placed.

I had the pleasure of speaking to Glastonbury Abbey's deputy custodian, Francis Thyer, a gentleman with whom I previously had corresponded via e-mail. Stepping just outside the Welcome Center and sitting on a bench facing the magnificent Norman structure known as the Lady Chapel, he began to tell me something of the abbey's history. He answered my questions, which usually led to more questions, and volunteered information that I not only had never known, but likely never would have, had I not been there. In fact, it would not be an overstatement of fact to say that I could have spent the next five to ten years in research and still never have learned half of what I took away from my visit. Without question, Glastonbury Abbey is as enigmatic as it is majestic. It is very much like a gilded illuminated manuscript whose author is unknown but has become famous by its many elaborators.

Glastonbury's history is best described by a plaque on a wood cross erected just north of the Lady Chapel. The inscription reads, "The Cross. The gift of Queen Elizabeth II marks a Christian sanctuary so ancient that only legend can record its origin." If one wishes to learn of Glastonbury's origin, it is true that mostly what one has to work with is legend. Church fathers agreed for centuries that it was the oldest church in Christendom, and it is still considered the oldest church in the British Isles. The oldest written record dates back to the second century, but other evidence suggests an earlier foundation by none other than the man of legend, Joseph of Arimathea. However, before investigating the possibility that this legend might have its foundation in history, it is necessary to first learn more about Glastonbury before the church.

The Somerset landscape surrounding modern Glastonbury has changed much in the past two thousand years, and not just socially or religiously. The lush green fields that surround the abbey and Glastonbury Tor are a fairly recent attribute. Around the time when Joseph allegedly brought the Grail to Glastonbury, it was an island in a sea of marsh land, the closest connection to land being in the direction of Ponter's Ball to the east. Although modern land elevations would suggest Glastonbury was more of an isthmus than an island, modern fieldwork and deposition are likely to blame for this appearance. The truth is that this area, for at least most of the season, was separated from the nearest land as an island.

Referred to as the Isle of Avalon in folklore, the clutch of hills peaked by the impressive 512-foot-high Glastonbury Tor stood alone in a dark sea, surrounded by reeds and other growth making it seem all the more inaccessible and forbidding. Such mountains in the ocean surely appeared as otherworldly to the ancient mind as the image of it would seem to us now, likely becoming the place of ritual and burial, creating the notion of Avalon as the Celtic underworld. A land of the dead amid thick swamp would seem a place no one would want to settle; however, ancient Britons were well used to taming such challenging environs as this.

There is ample evidence that early nomadic tribes were present on what would have been the dry land at the time, but the area was not truly settled until Neolithic peoples first made an effort to survive by controlling their surroundings. While the people of this age are more famous for creating sites such as Avebury and Stonehenge further to the east, their most lasting contribution is the clearing of land for use in farming. The wood and brush that was abundant at the time would have been used to build shelters, later becoming the well-known roundhouses, as well as going into their more ceremonial constructions. However, Neolithic ingenuity has no greater example than the wooden trackways that were common to the Somerset Levels.

> The trackways were made of planks, poles or rails, secured by pegs or other timbers. The oldest is the Sweet Track, discovered in 1970. This is made of ash, oak and hazel, with pegs of hazel, holly, alder, ash and elm; the whole is packed with peat. Thanks to the precision now made possible by tree-

ring dating, exact dates can be given for this and other trackways. The Sweet Track is dated to the winter of 3807–3806 B.C.; it was thus nearly 6,000 years old. The evidence shows that it was all constructed in one operation. The timber (4,000m [13,000ft] of plank, 2,000m [6,500ft] of heavy rails and 6,000 pegs) had to be felled, split and prepared before being carried to both ends of a line 1,800m (6,000ft) long. It is estimated that the whole track could then have been completed by ten people in a few days in the spring of 3806 B.C. [Rahtz and Watts, pp. 24–25].

Trackways were something between a bridge and a road, allowing people to traverse watery expanses that would otherwise have required the use of a boat. This of course allowed Neolithic man to travel not only farther, but with more goods, linking settlements for trade and expansion. These trackways were not merely utilitarian, however. Passing across the glassy surface of the surrounding dark waters, it made what they saw as sacred much more accessible.

During excavations along many of these trackways, numerous artifacts such as broaches and clasps, weapons and tools, and objects made from semi-precious stones have been discovered. Many of these objects are not only of exceptional quality but also show no signs of use and often ritual breakage (rendering the objects useless to mortal man). Found both in large enough quantities and in locations to suggest they were not merely dropped, these were prized items, archeologists say, cast into the water as tribute to their gods. However, these trackways not only allowed these early people an easy way to practice their rituals; they made it possible to go to sacred sites seen as a place where their world touched the next — places such as their underworld of Avalon.

Although the trackways were a feat of ancient ingenuity, dwellers of ancient Glastonbury were not content to merely cross the marshy expanses. The growing population and need for natural resources spawned a new engineering project. Centuries after the Neolithic earthworks and trackways, settlements were built in the wetland marsh itself by building up artificial land platforms. This provided more land on which to build shelter and rich soil on which to plant crops. There were several of such marsh complexes, but the most famous in the region, the Glastonbury Lake Village, was found near the end of the nineteenth century. Since its discovery, much has been discovered about the people who built the structure, and how exactly they used it. Originally portrayed by artist's reconstructions as a proper village on the water, it has since been discovered that it started small, being used for different types of production in different areas, and most likely seasonally — inhabited in the dryer summer months, and abandoned during the winter.

A great deal of archeological material has been found, suggesting that the Glastonbury Lake Village was slowly expanded over time into a fortified settlement large enough for dozens of families to remain there permanently. Life continued on the Lake Village for well over 100 years until rising flood levels apparently forced its residents to leave, eventually rendering the structure uninhabited by the middle of the first century B.C. Although this would be considered a relatively short period of habitation by archeological standards, it does demonstrate that the people who lived in the sodden landscape around ancient Glastonbury made the land their own and were content to stay.

Roughly 100 years after the Lake Village was left behind, life again changed for the people who lived in the area. Roman occupation of Britain began in the first century A.D. and continued until the invasion of Rome in A.D. 410, at which time distant provinces such as Britain were abandoned to take care of matters closer to home. One of the most famous examples of Roman presence in this part of England is the city of Bath, some twenty miles away from Glastonbury. Although the bath complex is the only Roman ruin visible to the modern visitor, building remains can be found for miles in every direction under the current city streets. This site demonstrates the high status and luxurious living that was possible for Romans even this far from their cultural center.

Although Glastonbury cannot boast such a remarkable and highly visible representation of Roman occupation in Britain, some evidence has been found to suggest there was a Roman presence on Wirral Hill and on the abbey grounds. In addition, an archeological study of the well just outside the southern wall of St. Joseph's Crypt suggested it might have been used in Roman times.

> In September 1991 and June 1992, in an attempt to resolve some of these problems, the well was examined to determine the nature of its structure. The rim, or well-head, now has a thick coating of calcite accretion but removal of part of this showed that it was of segmented stones, of oolitic limestone. Below this, at water level, the stonework of the well has been partly dissolved away by the movement of the water. The water (c.60cm [24in] deep) was bailed out and at the base was mud and rubble with hundreds of coins of 1960 and later. This layer was removed down to a depth of c.1.50 (5ft) or more and it was seen that the shaft of the well (65–66cm [25–26in] in diameter) was lined with skillfully laid pieces of Lias limestone. The overall appearance was very similar to that of Roman wells excavated in the area [Rahtz and Watts, pp. 108–109].

It seems clear that Glastonbury was not itself a Roman center, but there does appear to be evidence that Romans were in that area in the first century A.D., and that it was located along paths that linked larger cities. If it is true that the well outside St. Joseph's Crypt was used by Romans, it would demonstrate that those passing through may have found cause to linger in the area in which the ruins of the once great abbey now stand. In fact, it has been suggested that this site may have centered on the use of this well.

The earliest evidence for Christianity in Somerset roughly follows the time period in which it came to the rest of the Roman world. In the fourth century, Emperor Constantine first banned persecution of Christians and later converted to Christianity himself (although some claim an earlier date, saying he followed his mother, Empress Helena, in his beliefs as early as in his childhood). Similarly, the earliest evidence for Christianity being present in the areas around Glastonbury has been dated to the fourth century. It was only a short time later in the fifth century that St. Patrick allegedly visited Glastonbury, leading to the creation of one of the more famous and most highly contested documents produced at the abbey.

The famous Charter of St. Patrick, which outlined the saint's time spent at Glastonbury, speaks of the church's earliest days. Supposedly written in the thirteenth century by the monks at Glastonbury Abbey, it outlines how St. Patrick happened upon the existing church at Glastonbury and was told of its foundation. The account tells of the missionaries Phagan and Deruvian, who had been sent by Pope Eleutherius at the behest of King Lucius to Christianize the pagan people of Britain. Although this thirteenth-century text has been claimed to be outright propaganda to bolster the abbey's claims of an ancient foundation, it does make one rather interesting statement that should be noted:

> And so they made me their head, though I did not desire it; for I was unworthy to untie the thongs of their sandals. While we thus led a monastic life according to the norm of the honourable fathers, the brothers showed me written documents of Sts Phagan and Deruvian, in which it is recorded that twelve disciples of Sts Philip and James had built that ancient church, at the instruction of archangel Gabriel [*Chronicle of Glastonbury Abbey*, Carley, p. 63].

This passage from the Charter of St. Patrick states that "twelve disciples of St. Philip and St. James had built that Old Church," which means that followers of Philip and James, two of the twelve apostles of Jesus, constructed the original wattle church at Glastonbury. Although strictest history credits King Ine of Wessex with the founding of the church at Glastonbury, unofficial credit goes to saints Phagan and Deruvian, who were sent in the second century, and purportedly built the wattle church then. The claim made by the charter does not of course make the claim true, but its correlation with another earlier history written at Glastonbury does give rise to an interesting idea.

In 1125, William of Malmesbury wrote *Gestis Regum Anglorum Libri Quinque*, or *The Acts of the Kings of England*. This history claimed, as previously stated, that the monastery at Glastonbury was founded by King Ine around A.D. 728. A few years later, then-abbot of Glastonbury Henry of Blois invited William to write a book detailing the long history of the abbey. As a result, William wrote *De Antiquitate Glastoniensis Ecclesiae*, or *The History of Glastonbury Abbey*, completed around 1135. Sadly, it would appear his original work was expanded upon and elaborated by monks at Glastonbury whose alterations throw the history into question. However, scholars comparing the expanded copy of William's work with a later edition of his *Gestis Regum Anglorum Libri Quinque*, revised after his time spent at Glastonbury, have largely separated William's account from the later additions.

Much of the legendary history of Glastonbury Abbey has come from these later, elaborated versions of William's *De Antiquitate Glastoniensis Ecclesiae*. However, a passage from William's original version does render up some quite illuminating information that corroborates the much later Charter of St. Patrick:

> There are numerous documents of no small credit, which have been discovered in certain places to the following effect: "No other hands than those of the disciples of Christ erected the church of Glastonbury." Nor is it dissonant from probability; for if Philip the Apostle, preached to the Gauls, as Freculphus relates in the fourth chapter of his second book, it may be believed that he planted the word on this side of the Channel also. But, that I may not seem to balk the expectations of my readers by vain imaginations, I shall leave all doubtful matter and proceed to the relation of substantial truths [*King Arthur's Avalon: The Story of Glastonbury*, Ashe, p. 42].

It must be here remembered that William of Malmesbury is a credible historical writer of his time and, by his own words, not a person who delves into the conjectural. Although it is commonly held that medieval texts were written according to the views and whims of their patrons and commissioners, it should be remembered that William not only chose to exclude some of the apparently more fantastic claims from his sources but also that whatever he saw while writing this commissioned history, it was convincing and potent enough to prompt him to alter a previous, non-commissioned work regarding the history of the abbey.

From this passage, we learn two things. First, he says the documents from which this claim originated are of "no small credit," which from a source such as him is quite a statement. Any historian in any age who seeks to state a truthful account of a place's origins must endeavor to separate what is likely from what is unlikely, then set out to prove all that seems likely to determine what can be verified and entered as true history. This brings us to our second point taken from the above citation. The mere mention of these others sources shows that although he could not verify them enough to cite, they were weighty enough to at least mention.

William states, "that I may not seem to balk the expectations of my readers by vain imaginations, I shall leave all doubtful matter and proceed to the relation of substantial truths." It has been said in other treatments of Glastonbury Abbey's legendary history that William himself doubted the tradition that Joseph of Arimathea founded the church there. However, this passage would seem to indicate that, although he himself found the notion plausible, he was forced to exclude it from the fact-based history he was attempting to recreate. When he refers to these sources as "doubtful," it would be more likely that he merely means that these sources were called into question because he could not himself substantiate or verify their factuality. Considering the fact that what William tells us about the content of these sources is somewhat vague and lacking in particulars, he simply chose to omit the accounts because they offered no specific information he could use in building his history.

The simple fact that William mentions this at all alludes to information that he could not allow himself as a scholar to set forward. Apparently there did exist information that claimed the wattle church, which he was able to see for himself before the fire of 1184, was not built by or for the second-century saints Phagan and Deruvian, but by someone prior to their arrival. Indeed there are other references that claim the two missionaries arrived to find a group of monks already at Glastonbury who presented them with documents referring to their foundation and were able to show them what remained of the original wattle church which, as legend states, would have been around one hundred years old by that time.

Very little is known of what took place on the site until the eighth century, when Saxon king Ine of Wessex built his stone church just east of the old wattle church. This time period can be cut into two very different sections: the time during which Rome was the power in the land, and the beginning of the Dark Ages after Rome withdrew from this remote outpost. During Roman occupation, this site likely changed little. It is unlikely that the church here received any recognition or stimulus by the governing body during this time. Constantine, the first Christian emperor of Rome, only legalized Christianity by the Edict of Milan in A.D. 313. Christianity wasn't declared the official religion of Rome until A.D. 380 by Theodosius, long after Constantine's death.

After the fall of Rome and its subsequent withdrawal from the lands of Britain, the times of anarchy and war that define the Dark Ages were surely hard on the tiny church at Glastonbury. It is possible that its lack of prominence and wealth is what saved it from the marauders from lands to the north and east. It would be all too easy to envision this tiny wattled construction burning in the wake of a barbarian raid, as was the fate of so many other sites. However, two facts would seem to indicate that this area not only survived, but was possibly protected.

The cemetery at Glastonbury is known as the burial ground for kings and saints. Many accounts speak of the honored burials in close proximity to the wattle church, often called the Old Church. These grave sites were so respected that that during his time as abbot of Glastonbury, St. Dunstan covered over the old cemetery with several feet of earth to seal the graves and protect them from desecration as well as from damage that might have occurred due to future building projects. Further, William of Malmesbury claimed that the wattle church was covered in boards and roofed with lead by Paulinus Archbishop of York in 633 to protect the then-several-hundred-year-old building.

It would seem the church yard that now holds the ruins of the once magnificent abbey remained quite small and simple for about 700 years. After the original wattle church was built, available accounts would indicate that it fell into an early state of disrepair, was reclaimed and re-established, was maintained and protected during the upheaval of the Dark Ages, and was only expanded in the early eighth century by King Ine. One may wonder why a site of such importance did not grow for so many years. Although the times did not allow much development, another possibility is that the monastic community at Glastonbury expanded into another location a short distance away.

Archeological evidence suggests that there was an early, possibly fortified, settlement on top of Glastonbury Tor that eventually became an Anglo-Saxon monastery. The exact nature of this site's habitation is uncertain, but it is clear that this monastery should be viewed as part of Glastonbury Abbey's evolution.

> The new order led to a major expansion of the faith at Glastonbury, which found its expression in the Abbey site. The earliest features there are assigned to the seventh century, but with the possibility of a British foundation before a fully Anglo-Saxon one [Rahtz and Watts, p. 78].

Adjacent to Wirral Hill, a similar situation occurred at the Beckery, another area of high ground that at times of flooding became an island. Evidence suggests an early Anglo-Saxon wooden chapel and an east-west aligned cemetery existed at the summit of the hill as early as the sixth century. When one takes these facts into consideration, the period of dormancy at the site of the Old Church takes on a different perspective. It would seem this site was left undisturbed and unaltered as a place of veneration where the honored dead were laid to rest, while the monastic community at Glastonbury grew, at first, in the surrounding areas.

While these images of a monastery hanging on the edge of a great rock does stir a romantic notion, practicality must always prevail. Eventually the landscape, remoteness and difficulty of access made these sites less attractive for growth, making the site of the wattle church come again into consideration. As the Glastonbury community grew, the open expanse around this site began to change into something more like what visitors to the abbey grounds might see today.

In the eighth century, Glastonbury came under the protection of Christian king Ine, who built a stone church on the site just to the east of the wattle church. Roughly the same size as the old church, archeological excavations and comparison with other churches of the time period have suggested that it would have been in the typical Anglo-Saxon style — rectangular except for one rounded end, with two aisles or side chapels built onto either side of the main building. The construction of this stone church both paid homage to its ancient predecessor and established Glastonbury as a lasting site of worship.

While it appears that King Ine's stone church saw remodeling and additions in later years, the next real change to the site came some 200 years later. Called the most important man in Glastonbury's history, Abbot Dunstan breathed new life into the fledgling monastery. Visitors to Glastonbury Abbey today can see the outline of a small rectangular building to the west of the Lady Chapel, called "St. Dunstan's Chapel," a later chapel built to replace Dunstan's earlier version. He greatly expanded the stone church built by King Ine, adding cloisters and making the entire structure nearly the full length of the fifteenth-century abbey.

As sweeping as these changes were, they would only stand for about 100 years. It is at this point when another defining line is crossed in the history of Glastonbury Abbey — the line between the pre–Conquest (referring to the Norman Conquest of 1066) and post–Conquest lives of the abbey. The first major change to the abbey is a major change indeed. In 1077, then-abbot Thurstin completely demolished the existing Anglo-Saxon stone church and began building another church, this one much larger and in the Norman design.

However, Thurstin's building plans were put on hold a short time later. His tenure as abbot was marked by deep resentment, as he had made drastic changes in tradition that were very unpopular with the monks in residence. Tensions reached their peak when Abbot Thurstin had several monks killed on the high altar, written accounts stating that blood stained the floor and arrows stuck in the cross. Soon thereafter, he was dismissed as abbot. Some thirty years later, Abbot Herlewin demolished the work began by Thurstin and began building an even larger church.

2. History in a Timeless Place

The final stage of construction was completed at the hands of Abbot Henry of Blois beginning around 1125. Being a renowned scholar and builder, Henry was responsible for adding new cloisters, a bell tower, chapter houses, the refectory, an infirmary, outer gates, a brewery, and stables to the vast complex. It was also under his direction that the famous history of Glastonbury written by William of Malmesbury was commissioned, creating the first accepted record of Glastonbury's illustrious past.

According to legend, it is also Henry who is credited for the most tragic event to befall Glastonbury Abbey. In 1184, a fire swept through the length of the abbey, allegedly started by a candle that was to be kept burning at all times, by Henry's order, before a statue of the Virgin Mary. It is this fire that resulted in the destruction of the wattle church that had remained standing for over 1,000 years prior. Along with the famed Old Church, this fire claimed untold numbers of irreplaceable documents held in the abbey's library, and certainly many relics housed on the grounds.

While the tragedy of this fire cannot be overstated, greater even than the Dissolution that would in a few more centuries reduce this place of great sanctity to ruin, it was also the catalyst that would catapult the abbey's history into the realm of legend and world fame. In only two years, the first structure to be rebuilt, the Lady Chapel — built on the exact site of the Old Church — would be consecrated and begin its life as the center of worship on the site. The act of reclaiming and rebuilding the great structure from the ground up again opened the ancient pages holding the history and legends of these hallowed grounds for all who would follow. Although the last remnant of Glastonbury's mythical birth was reduced to cinders, from its ashes would come a new age of discovery. From these discoveries came a golden age to rival that of Arthur himself. From this time would come the tales of the mythic king and the cup of Christ. Though these were but legends, another discovery would be made near the end of the abbey's life that would later serve to unlock the secrets of its mysterious birth.

Chapter 3

The Second Golden Age

Whenever someone visits ruins of any kind, they are in essence looking upon a corpse. The broken arch is a jutting rib, pieces of window frames are jagged teeth, and the excavated footprint of the structure is no more than a chalk outline. However it may have taken place, someone broke the body that once stood where now only the shell remains. No matter how complete the ruin, no matter the wealth of architectural fragments that remain to reconstruct, it is impossible to fully picture the original whole.

Picture the magnificent edifice of Wells Cathedral — its enormity, its elaborate archways, its soaring height. It is the very picture of grace. Now imagine it completely ruined. Where the front entrance once stood is now only a three-foot section of wall. Where the piers of its great choir once towered, nothing remains but a flat stone in the dirt, perhaps a broken stem of a single pillar like a shattered icicle. No more is the vibrant stained glass in the window. If you are lucky, a small fragment of glass may be found, dulled by the acid of the earth in which it rests.

Like a forensic scientist, an archeologist uses the knowledge of reconstruction to make sense out of the scene in which he has found himself. A best effort can be made to discover exactly what happened and when, and eventually an image begins to form of what the scene was like ... just before.

Opposite: This awe-inspiring image gives visitors to Southern England the closest sight we can see today of how Glastonbury Abbey might have looked at its peak of acclaim and power in the sixteenth century. The use of scissor arches at Glastonbury, as here in Wells Cathedral, has always helped form a strong parallel between the two great churches. In addition to the scissor arches, the clock (designed by the fourteenth-century monk Peter Lightfoot) that once stood atop a tower at Glastonbury is now mounted in a wall at Wells (visible just above the crucifix to the lower right). The second oldest in England, this clock was moved here following the Dissolution, and its original wooden mechanism is housed in the London Museum of Science (photograph courtesy Sophie Morse).

Then, moving backwards, it is possible to see how the victim, in this case a building, came to be in its present state of ruin. That is when the sadness creeps in. Comparing the picture of its former beauty, alive and whole, with the lifeless form that is left behind, one is left with the question, "I wonder what it was really like."

Let us now consider the life of Glastonbury Abbey, now a celebrated ruin over which as much speculation has grown as once grew vines and brush. Consider this fact first: Nothing that remains of the abbey is older than 1186. While some of the burials found in the south cemetery are certainly older, nothing of the pre-twelfth-century building remains above ground. Sadly, any part of the oldest structure on the site, the wattle church, was almost surely destroyed completely by the creation of the crypt under the Lady Chapel in the sixteenth century. The Lady Chapel, the oldest part of the reconstruction, is oddly the most intact. The only parts missing from the original are the roof, the floor, two turrets, and the remainder of the very large abbey that once adjoined its eastern end.

Records indicate that a mere two years after the fire of 1184, the Lady Chapel was consecrated and began to see its first use. Although it is unlikely that it was fully complete, it would seem that only the elements of refinement were lacking. According to archeological investigation, the interior of the Lady Chapel once boasted the richest colors and the most elaborate ornamentation of its time. If one had been standing in the chapel around 1189, their surroundings would have been draped in the richest materials, gleaming with colors of reds, blues, greens, black, and white, with gold leaf accents — all very different from the creamy tan of the stone that survives today.

Looking at the exterior, it becomes clear that this was a building meant to mark a special place. The Norman influence is apparent in the upper windows, displaying the typical rounded arches; however, below that is an array of intersecting Norman arches forming shallow peaks. In fact, the Lady Chapel at Glastonbury is known as something of a unique treasure because of this transitional feature, somewhere between Norman and Gothic architecture. The main entry doors on the north and south walls are richly decorated by arches framed in intricate figural carvings, some say depicting the story of the Massacre of the Innocents from the story of Christ's birth.

Taken on its own, set apart from the rest of the abbey ruins, it has the appearance of a highly decorated jewelry box, such as you might find sitting on a Victorian lady's dresser. This likeness was pointed out to me when I first saw the structure in person. A previous visitor to the abbey pointed out that, if seen with the vaulted roof still intact with all four corner towers restored, the building has the appearance of another sort of treasure box very familiar to the medieval monastic mind: a reliquary, a beautifully ornamented box,

Northern exposure of the Norman Lady Chapel at Glastonbury Abbey — once the site of the Old Church, allegedly built by Joseph of Arimathea. Note how the towers at the four corners (only two remaining) combined with the typical medieval A-framed roof would result in an appearance resembling an ornate reliquary casket (author photograph).

usually crusted with gold, silver, and jewels, in which some holy relic or artifact was placed for worship, such as a bone of a saint or an object of great holiness.

If the Lady Chapel at Glastonbury was built in the likeness of a reliquary box, what relic was it meant to contain? It was a bit large for the finger bone of a saint. Likewise, a spur from the crown of thorns would have been quite lost inside it. In fact, the only holy relic that would seem at home inside a reliquary the size of a building would be a building that was itself a holy relic. Considering the speed with which the Lady Chapel was built, the resplendent ornamentation within, and the appearance without, it seems logical that it was built not only to remember the place where the wattled church built by Joseph of Arimathea stood for a thousand years, but to forever seal its remains within the confines of its walls.

Sadly, the sacred remains of the wattle church were not left preserved for posterity. They were destroyed by the relentless march of time. However, the wealth of archeology and history it might have yielded did not fall to the Dissolution. Simple progress and expansion were the culprits. As mentioned previously, the creation of the crypt under the Lady Chapel likely destroyed all evidence of the wattle church that remained. However, this was not the first time the treasured reliquary was encroached upon.

If we recall the inscription on the brass plaque that once marked the eastern boundary of the Old Church, something of significance can be learned about the original chapel:

> And lest the site or the size of the earlier church should come to be forgotten because of such additions, he [St. David] erected this column on a line drawn southwards through the two eastern angles of the same church, and cutting it off from the aforesaid chancel. And its length was 60ft westward from that line, its breadth was truly 26ft; the distance from the centre of this pillar from the midpoint between the aforesaid angles, 48ft [Rahtz and Watts, pp. 43–44].

The plaque clearly states two things: first, that the size of the Lady Chapel corresponded to the exact size of the original wattle church, or more likely, the slightly larger structure it became when it was covered in boards and lead in the seventh century, and second, that the location of the Lady Chapel, given in distances from the post on which the plaque was mounted, corresponded exactly to the location of the wattle church. Needless to say, a fourteenth- or fifteenth-century inscription is usually no aid whatsoever in making any verifiable statements about something originating from the first century. However, one all-important aspect of this inscription gives us an almost certain date pertaining to its creation.

The text on the plaque begins with the statement, "Lest the site or size of the earlier church should come to be forgotten because of such additions." Remember that this plaque went into some detail about the size and location of the original church that once stood on the site, not the Lady Chapel. Some have suggested that the writer of this inscription could simply be passing along a tradition that the Lady Chapel was built to exactly mirror the wattle church. However, this assumption is quite unlikely since there was still a clear memory and written record of the wattle church and the Lady Chapel's original creation. Therefore, if one looks into the history of Glastonbury Abbey's construction and looks for a time when the eastern extent of the Lady Chapel was changed, prompting someone to point out where the eastern wall once stood, an answer can be found in the thirteenth century.

Sometime between 1274 and 1291, during the abbacy of John of Taunton, the eastern wall of the Lady Chapel was demolished to join it to the Galilee, a small chapel which for the first time made the site of the Old Church a small part of a much larger structure. It is quite likely that some saw this act

3. The Second Golden Age

of addition as nothing less than removing the honor once bestowed upon that patch of ground. What had once been set apart had now become just another wing of the Great Church being constructed. Even if we take the latest date of 1291 for the demolition of this wall, it still means that the time between the fire of 1184 and this remodeling was likely only around 100 years. It then becomes unnecessary to rely on tradition regarding the size, shape, and location of the Old Church because this inscription, written within one or two generations' memory, leaves little room for doubt. Understanding the exact nature of the wattle church, built in Joseph's time, will become quite important once we enter into the discussion of Joseph's tomb, which is the subject of subsequent chapters. Curiously enough, something still exists of the eastern wall that once made the Lady Chapel a freestanding monument. Two of the window arches mirrored on the west wall now stand over the well several feet under ground, accessible from the southeast corner of St. Joseph's crypt.

The abbey's journey from the lone Lady Chapel to the imposing expanse it became was not an easy one, to be sure. As much as the speedy reconstruction of the Lady Chapel ushered in Glastonbury's second golden age, the building of the new great church was a testament to what could be called the second dark age of Glastonbury Abbey. Reconstruction started off well enough, with authorization from the king to dedicate all revenues to the effort. It seems when this proved insufficient, the king paid for the construction himself. However, this was all to change in July of 1189 when King Henry II died, removing the largest supplier of building funds.

A new king with an interest in the Holy Land, his subsequent capture and ransom by German king Henry VI, and a string of self-serving abbots reduced the rebuilding effort to a crawl. Life for the monks at Glastonbury was harsh and cruel, and money that could have been used for the new church usually went everywhere but where it should have. Making matters worse, a schism developed between Glastonbury and the powerful church at Wells. Although animosities and discord continued long afterwards, Glastonbury finally found itself independent and seemingly on the road to recovery in 1218.

It would seem that Glastonbury's reputation for being a "hoax factory" began during this time of upheaval. While the corruption of its leadership at that time was well known, the sentiment stems largely from one event that took place in 1190 or 1191. While digging a grave in the old cemetery just south of the Lady Chapel, allegedly between two ancient pyramids which once stood there, monks found a curious and apparently very old burial. Seventeen feet below the surface, they found a hollowed-out trunk of an oak tree containing two bodies. As the story goes, the first body was a male of impressive height and was apparently a warrior, given the evidence of wounds on his body. The second appeared to be female, fine featured, with the remains of long blonde hair clinging to the skull.

Considering the graveyard was known to contain many ancient burials, including those of Celtic warrior-kings, this discovery would have been of little note if not for another discovery within the same burial shaft. At the seven-foot level, a stone slab was found that seemed to indicate it was a grave of some significance. When the slab was lifted, the monks discovered it had a curious metal plaque that had been mounted on the underside, concealing its inscription. When the plaque was removed, it was discovered that it was an inscribed cross of an unusual form.

"Arthur's Burial Cross," as it is known, has become iconic among those interested in Arthurian legends. Its inscription made it immediately clear that the burial was not that of the average ancient chieftain: "HIC IACET SEPVLTVS INCLITVS REX ARTVRIVS IN INSVLA AVALONIA." In English, it can be translated as "Here lies buried the renowned King Arthur on/in the Island of Avalon." There can be little doubt that this cross did in fact exist. Over the next 400 years, several individuals of note bore witness to the fact and wrote about it in their histories, although the text was altered slightly from time to time, sometimes including a mention of Guinevere and in one account Mordred. One of the most notable among these witnesses was John Leland, who visited the abbey in the sixteenth century. Allegedly, the cross adorned a new marble tomb in which the bones had been reinterred, where both remained until the Dissolution. Allegedly, the cross survived and was kept for about 100 years in St. John's Parish church, which stood just outside the abbey precincts. It is said that the cross was housed in the "Reverstry." This probably means the "revestry," now simply called the "vestry," that once stood outside the current Lady Chapel adjoining the old St. Katherine's chapel, where the famous "Joseph of Arimathea" crypt is.

Proving the cross existed is one matter. Suggesting a date for its creation is another entirely. It has been assumed that the cross was yet another medieval forgery and that the discovery of Arthur's grave was nothing more than an attempt to garner revenue to continue with the reconstruction effort. Several factors actually support this supposition. First, Geoffrey of Monmouth in his 1136 *Historia Regum Britanniae*, or "History of the Kings of Britain," used the word "renowned" to describe Arthur, just as the inscription does. Second, Geoffrey also stated that King Arthur's resting place was on the "Isle of Avalon," as does the inscription. However, it is interesting to note that Geoffrey never called Glastonbury "Avalon." It was Gerald of Wales who first made this connection in 1193, after the grave was discovered.

Possibly the most concrete evidence to support a twelfth-century creation can be found not far away in the town of Stoke-sub-Hamdon near Montacute in Somerset. The twelfth-century parish church of St. Mary's has an unusual carving over the main doorway which includes a centaur and the carved word "SAGITARIVS." The style of lettering used for this inscription is nearly identical to that found on the burial cross. While all this evidence certainly seems to point to a twelfth-century date, several factors would suggest otherwise.

Although the inscription on the tympanum at St. Mary's would suggest a style specific to the twelfth century, this lettering style was also common in the tenth century. While the use of the letter "V" in place of the "U" was likely due to a revival in the use of classical Latin for scholarly and ecclesiastic writing, the most unusual feature of the inscription is the similar appearance between the letters "N" and "H" in much the same manner as Arthur's Burial Cross. As evidenced by the Ramsey Psalter, written some time between A.D. 980 and 1000, a capital "N" looks quite similar to a capital "H." Furthermore, it is known that certain shortcuts were used in carving that were not used in

This twelfth-century inscription can be found in the tympanum over the main entrance to the Church of St. Mary in Stoke-sub-Hamdon. The carved word "SAGITARIVS" on the left has led several scholars to use this as a demonstration that the carving on King Arthur's burial cross was a twelfth-century hoax. However, the Ramsey Psalter, dating from the tenth century, also resembles the debated inscription on the cross, suggesting the leaden cross found in the twelfth century came not from this time but from the time of Abbott Dunstan (photograph courtesy Rex Harris).

writing that would make this similarity more pronounced, such as eliminating the sweep into the vertical members.

Similarly fallacious is the notion that the discovery of King Arthur's grave was a publicity stunt. Much has been made of accounts given by Adam of Domerham a century later and then John of Glastonbury that claim white drapes or curtains were put up around the site while the grave was being dug. Some say this is quite an unusual act for the simple burial, suggesting that the monks at Glastonbury were in fact hiding something — perhaps the planting of ancient bones discovered elsewhere or the salting of the grave with the phony lead cross and its fortuitous inscription. Although some have claimed this would have been done to shield the other monks from the traumatic site of having one of their own laid to his final rest, it seems more likely that this was a later elaboration lent to this story for dramatic effect.

Lastly, it would seem logical that such a PR stunt, as it has been called, would have included a formal announcement of the discovery, or the construction of a chapel or sanctuary to exhibit the illustrious remains; or would have resulted in a noteworthy increase in pilgrimage to view such characters of legend. In fact, records indicate that little was done with the bodies until they were formally removed to a new marble tomb before the high altar in the presence of King Edward and Queen Eleanor in 1278. Similarly, there seems to have been no building or marked increase in pilgrimage due to the discovery.

One important aspect of this excavation helps refute the claim that this was a fabrication intended to make the suffering abbey some much-needed money. Varying accounts agree that the stone slab and cross were found at a depth of around seven feet, and that the remains were found about ten feet further down. This would indicate that either the burial was originally made very deep (unlikely considering the cemetery was already known to be dense with burials), or that the original burial was at an average depth and the ground level increased at some later time.

HIC· IACET·SEPVLTVS ·IHCLITVS·
REX ARTVRIVS·
IH IHSVLA ·AVALOHIA

The inscription allegedly found on the leaden cross discovered in King Arthur's gravesite in 1191. Taken from William Camden's 1607 illustration and rearranged into "paragraph" form for comparison (author photograph).

3. The Second Golden Age 41

ad te confugi: doce me facere
uoluntatem tuā quia ds ms es tu ·:
S ps tuus bonus deducet me
in terram rectam propt nom tuū
dne: uiuificabis me inequitate tua ·:,
E duces de tribulatione animā meā:
& in misericordia tua
disperdes inimicos meos ·: ·,
E t pdes oms qui tribulant animā
meam: qm ego seruus tuus sū ··,
DAUID ADUERSUS GOLIATH.
BENEDICTUS DNS DEUS
ms qui docet man' meas
ad proelium :
& digitos meos ad bellum ·: ·,
M isericordia mea & refugium meū ·-
susceptor meus & liberator meus ·:,
P rotector meus & in ipso speraui :-

A page from the tenth-century Ramsey Psalter. Note the similarity between the capital "N" in the word "BENEDICTUS" and the letter "N" which resembles a capital "H" in the inscription from King Arthur's leaden burial cross (photograph copyright of The British Library Board, Harley 2904, f.181).

In the tenth century, Abbot Dunstan ordered the old cemetery to the south of the Old Church to be enclosed by a wall and covered by a thick layer of dirt to forever seal and cover the ancient burials it contained. Some accounts tell of the ancient markers being removed and placed flat against the ground to guard the graves from future encroachment. A similar situation has been found in burials near Wells Cathedral, where grave slabs have also been marked by lead plaques.

Although a hoax cannot be definitively ruled out, there is ample evidence to suggest that the discovery of King Arthur's grave was not simply a fabrication. It is impossible to know for sure whether or not the bodies it contained were those of Arthur and Guinevere. However, both the inscription and the depth suggest a grave site last altered in the tenth century. It would seem most likely that the site was thought in the time of St. Dunstan to be that of the legendary king and his wife, or that there was some other indication to that effect on the original grave.

When the Great Church was consecrated in 1213, the abbey became an even more commanding presence on the landscape than it once was. It was greatest among all the monastic sites in England; some would say it was second only to Rome itself. Over the next 300 years, the site saw much addition, but only in a tangential sense. The most notable change took place late in the thirteenth century when the Lady Chapel was joined to the Great Church by the Galilee. Beyond this, the abbey grew outward with the addition of living quarters for the monks and a kitchen, almshouses, and side chapels such as the Loretto and Edgar chapels, and through rebuilding and remodeling.

One of the most interesting, and as fate would have it, unfortunate, renovations made to the abbey was the crypt that was built in the early sixteenth century below the Lady Chapel. Since this was the site of the original wattle church, allegedly constructed by Joseph and his followers, any archeological evidence that ever existed of the Old Church was forever destroyed during excavation for the crypt. Although we can assume the ashen remains of the wattle church were removed in preparation for building the Lady Chapel, any direct *in situ* evidence of its shape, size, or layout would have existed just below the floor of the twelfth-century reconstruction. It would seem odd that nothing of the Old Church was preserved or kept as a relic of Glastonbury's legendary past, but that would seem to indicate that it was the site itself and not the historical building that was deemed of greatest importance.

Although the reason for the crypt's creation is uncertain, it seems to have been a project of some importance. To embark on an undertaking such as creating an entirely new space below an existing building—and a building of such importance and veneration—was an act of spectacular daring, not to mention a feat of engineering. In so doing, a new site of pilgrimage was created. The floor of the Lady Chapel above was raised by several inches to accommodate a new vaulted ceiling for the crypt, and new access was created on the south and northwest sides. It is also traditionally held that the well just off the southern wall was rediscovered and once again cleaned out during the crypt's construction. Evidence remains that there was once a room of some kind, perhaps a chapel, built over the well, making it accessible from inside the Lady Chapel, from the crypt, and from outside in the ancient cemetery.

It has been theorized that the creation of the crypt was due to an upsurge in interest regarding the abbey's legendary founder, Joseph of Arimathea. The fifteenth century at Glastonbury saw the rise of what has been called the Cult of Joseph. Hence, the chapel inside the crypt has become known as St. Joseph's Chapel, and the well outside, St. Joseph's Well. It is said that the crypt area was built to accommodate increased numbers of pilgrims coming to take part in his veneration, although why is less certain. In following chapters, we will investigate the possibility that the discovery of Joseph's remains in that area could have been the nucleus for the growth in his popularity during this time period.

Rich as it was with sacred items of veneration, including the much-disputed body of St. Dunstan himself, the search for holiness was not the only reason for pilgrimage to Glastonbury Abbey. According to some accounts, the library was second to none in all of Christendom, housing many rare volumes that could be found only there. Indeed, no one can attest to this fact better than the account given by a man who has been called the first librarian — the Royal Antiquary to King Henry VIII, John Leland:

> I was a few years ago at Glastonbury in Somerset, where is the most ancient, and at the same time most famous, monastery in our whole island; intending, by the favour of Richard Whiting, abbot of that place, to refresh my mind, wearied with a long course of study, when a burning desire of reading and studying inflamed me afresh. This desire, too, came upon me more quickly than I thought it would. So I straightway betook myself to the library, which is not open to all, to diligently open out the relics of most sacred antiquity, of which there is so great a number as is not easily found in any other part of Britain. Scarcely had I crossed the threshold when the mere sight of the most ancient books took my mind with an awe or stupor of some kind, and for that reason I stayed my steps a little while. Then having paid my respects to the deity of the place, I examined all the bookcases for some days with the greatest interest [Hearn, p. 62].

John was given the task by King Henry of scouring the abbeys and monasteries of England for any such rare volumes that he could find, and returning them to his personal library. John serves as an important chronicler in Glastonbury's history, especially when dealing with the ancient texts once found in its library.

He had the opportunity to see the library both before and after the Dissolution of the Monasteries.

Whether for the worship of Joseph of Arimathea, the resting place of King Arthur, or simply as a site of great sanctity, Glastonbury was indeed a major site of pilgrimage. Its long-standing reputation as a center of worship and a place of unparalleled history made the abbey the most wealthy and powerful monastic establishment in England. Culminating in its golden age under abbots Richard Beere and Richard Whiting, the sprawling complex became the beating heart of a thriving medieval city that formed largely to accommodate the influx of pilgrims. While it is likely that the area surrounding the abbey was a beehive of activity from its earliest days, the town of Glastonbury was born only about 1,000 years ago.

Besides the abbey ruins themselves, the most noticeable feature in the Glastonbury township is the parish church of St. John's on the north side of High Street. Although the church building visible today dates from the late fourteenth century or later, excavations have discovered foundations of an earlier building dating from the early twelfth century or earlier. The earliest standing portion of the building can be seen in what was until recently called St. Katherine's Chapel — a small but significant alcove in the church's northernmost wall. Although St. John's is known for the impressive tower that rises from its western end, the church once had an equally notable central tower which collapsed in the mid-fifteenth century.

It was not uncommon for such smaller churches to spring up outside the boundaries of the larger, more impressive monastic complexes such as Glastonbury Abbey. Often these smaller local churches fared better than their grander relatives, surviving the fires of the Dissolution to service the spiritual needs of the community. Judging from post–Dissolution accounts of travelers and pilgrims alike, St. John's served the additional function of safe house for some of the abbey's more interesting relics.

One of the largest structures in the medieval township was the great market building that once took up much of what is now the meeting place of High and Magdalene streets. With a large market cross at its center, capped by a carved figure of John Stagg now kept in the Abbey Museum, this marketplace was once the town's center of commerce and traffic. Although this building was later demolished, the site is marked today by the famous Glastonbury Market Cross at the bottom of High Street. St. Benignus, the second local church in town, lies just to the west. Now called St. Benedict's, the church was built by Abbot Beere in the sixteenth century, although evidence suggests the chancel dates from roughly 300 years earlier.

The area known as the Beckery is a quite interesting piece of both Glastonbury's legendary history and its ecclesiastical development. It is at Wirral (or Weary-all) Hill that Joseph and his followers were said to have first arrived, looking down upon the even expanse between it and the tor where, according to legend, they would build their church of wattles. Early Anglo-Saxon structures uncovered on the Beckery would serve to link this landscape to another, later part of Glastonbury's legend.

It is said that in the late fifth century St. Bridget visited the Beckery, which later became a source of worship. It is also claimed that the legendary King Arthur was told in a dream to go to a chapel he would find there, dedicated to Mary Magdalene. Once there he allegedly had a vision of the infant Jesus and his mother Mary — a story outlined in the twelfth-century text *Perlesvaus* or *The High History of the Holy Grail*.

Next to St. John's, it would appear that the Abbey Barn, current location of the Glastonbury Rural Life Museum, is the oldest structure in town. Modern archeological work has found that the barn, incorrectly dated to the sixteenth century, likely dates to around 1300. The famous Chalice Well, which lies at the foot of the tor nearby, has become one of the most venerated locales in Glastonbury. However, this is largely due to a Victorian tradition that sprang up around it that Joseph of Arimathea deposited the Grail in its waters, turning them a deep red. Archeological evidence does not support this conclusion. Although some Roman and later debris was found, it would appear the well is a buried medieval well house dating from the twelfth century that was built to cover a natural spring that once flowed there.

This spring was the most likely source of water for the developing monastic settlement that grew atop the tor. Beginning with a small settlement in the fifth to sixth centuries, the remains of a small Anglo-Saxon church were discovered during excavations of the area around the tower that remains as the only structure on Glastonbury Tor today. Although some evidence has been unearthed indicating the presence of an earlier church built on the site as early as the twelfth century, the larger church of St. Michael's was built during the fourteenth century. After seeing its share of destruction at the hands of man and nature, the church was destroyed after the Dissolution of the Monasteries. In fact, the tower that stands at the 520-foot summit bore witness to the death of Glastonbury Abbey's last abbot, Richard Whiting, who was hanged there with two other monks.

The town of Glastonbury today is a busy but peaceful town full of shops, New Age centers, and lodgings that, like their medieval counterparts, owe their livelihood to the annual pilgrims who journey there to see the impressive abbey ruins, to seek peace at the Chalice Well Gardens, or to feel the power of the great tor. However, one cannot visit Glastonbury without making two stops, conveniently both found on High Street. The first is the fifteenth-century building called the Tribunal, which was thought to be a courthouse, but has more recently been thought to have been a wealthy merchant's home. Today it is the home for the Glastonbury Antiquarian Society, where artifacts excavated from the Lake Village are housed.

The second building surviving from the abbey's heyday is the famous George and Pilgrim Inn, built by Abbot Selwood in 1450. It is said this fine inn was built to serve as a retreat for the wealthy pilgrims who once visited the abbey. Apparently as a means for these well-to-do pilgrims to travel between the inn and the abbey without hazarding the environs of the common townsfolk, a tunnel was constructed to connect the two. Accounts exist from the early twentieth century in which visitors to the inn were invited to see the tunnel for themselves. One woman is quoted as saying that the small tunnel continued from one corner of the basement in the direction of the street some twenty feet before it was blocked by a modern water work.

Glastonbury's business as a center for worship, pilgrimage, and study came to an abrupt end in 1539. Following the Catholic Church's refusal to grant King Henry VIII his requested divorce from Queen Catherine of Aragon, the king formally declared himself head of the church in England by having Parliament pass the Act of Supremacy in 1534. In so doing, he forced all churches to declare him, and not the pope, the final authority on all church matters. Following this mandate, Henry sent out emissaries on a mission to visit all churches and monasteries in England, Wales, and Ireland. Ostensibly to instruct the organizations on the proper way of recognizing Henry as the first and only "Defender of the Faith," the emissaries' true purpose was to conduct an inventory of each one's wealth and holdings.

Further acts passed by Parliament stated that it was an act of treason not to declare the king the head of the church, or to act against any of his previous edicts. Those who refused to comply were met with the only punishment for treason: death. Some evidence exists to suggest that Glastonbury attempted to comply with the Acts of Supremacy by removing some icons and statues from their places of prominence around the church.

Accounts of the frail, aged Abbot Whiting marching proudly toward his fate atop the tor have led to an image of Whiting as Glastonbury's last protector, somewhat like a freedom fighter standing against the overpowering strength of the king's tyranny. However, this image does not hold with history. York University's James P. Carley, scholar of Glastonbury history, King Henry VIII, and Tudor England, describes Whiting more as a "country gentleman":

> As it turns out, nevertheless, Whiting's gentle Epicureanism may have helped his monastery limp along as long as it did. During the second half of the 1530's, especially, Whiting tried to satisfy the ever accelerating demands of those in power. Request after request was satisfied: [Sir Thomas] More's corrody went to Cromwell himself after the former's dis-

grace, the livings of churches were given to friends of the ecclesiastical commissioners, and on one occasion when a demand for a living could not be met because it had been assigned to a friend of a different royal protégé Cromwell had a simple solution; he suggested that a new sinecure be forthwith discovered. The old abbot submitted patiently, writing to Cromwell that "If you request it, I must grant it" [Carley, *Holy House*, p. 78].

Even King Henry's famed antiquarian, John Leland, who was reputedly indifferent toward the precincts he visited, had nothing but good words to say about Whiting. Although Leland later recanted, he wrote that the abbot was "a man truly upright and spotless of character and my sincere friend."

However, in the end his fate was the same as that of his abbey. Glastonbury's golden age officially met its end on November 15, 1539, when Abbot Whiting was hanged, drawn and quartered. Those who visit Glastonbury Abbey today should take a moment before passing through the great arch that forms the entry way, and consider the spectacle that would have met their eyes in the days following his death. As the venerable old buildings were being ransacked and torn apart, its holdings scattered throughout the kingdom, one could look up with sadness at the head of Richard Whiting, which was mounted over the gate — into the last eyes ever to see the abbey in its full glory.

When the great church was disbanded and the monks moved on, the grounds and township of Glastonbury fell on hard times. Once the ecclesiastical center of power in England, it lay on the landscape like a broken vase. The great buildings that stood on the holy ground were ruined, soon to be robbed of their stone for use in other buildings and boundary walls around the area. Just as Glastonbury had its second golden age, it had its second dark age as well. Among the holdings once belonging to the monastery, the fabled Sapphire Altar, the gift of St. David, is recorded among the items seized, and removed to the king's treasury. However, it would seem this was the altar only, the precious sapphire once mounted at its center having been removed. This one item of myth and fable is a notable exception. In fact, very little is known about what happened to the religious, historical, and intellectual treasures once housed there.

Sadly, the greatest treasure among all these, Glastonbury's library, met with an inauspicious fate. It is said that books from the over one-thousand-volume holdings met the same fate as many during this period — ripped pages cast to the wind, falling like leaves all around the town. In this time of upheaval when treasure was the objective, some books did survive, incredibly enough. Certain deeds and charters of importance were once found used as binding materials for another book that, from all available evidence, did not originate from Glastonbury. Stories have even been told of pages of old manuscripts being used to wrap tobacco leaves. In fact, it is only a partial joke passed around Glastonbury and the surrounding areas that one day, someone might be cleaning a cluttered attic and happen across an old box full of medieval vellum or a section of illuminated manuscript neatly pressed between the pages of a modern book.

The most famous book surviving the abbey's destruction is a rather large but short text known as the Magna Tabula. Abbot John Chinnock commissioned the great book in the fourteenth century as something of a pilgrim's guidebook, much like the Pitkin guidebook that can be purchased in the abbey gift shop today. This incredible book, measuring more than three and a half feet square, contains the stories that form the abbey's legendary past, beginning with Joseph's trip from Palestine to Glastonbury and followed by Melkin's prophecy regarding Joseph and the location of his tomb. The famous St. Patrick's Charter is recorded, as well as several other accounts regarding Glastonbury's history, including the discovery of King Arthur's burial site. Although this book cannot necessarily be used as proof of any of these claims, both the book's size and prominence of place demonstrate how seriously these stories were taken at the time.

After the tribulation subsided, peopled settled back into a day-to-day life in the town of Glastonbury. About twenty years after the monastery was dissolved, a colony of weavers was set up on the site. Some time later, the Market Cross served as a site of execution for captured members of the failed Monmouth Rebellion. With the few exceptions outlined earlier, the buildings in the medieval town slowly changed into those of a more or less typical eighteenth- and nineteenth-century English village. Although the town ceased to be a place of pilgrimage, it continued as a place of commerce by becoming a market town, having a farmer's market in the town square every Wednesday until a relatively short time ago, when it changed to Tuesday. However, besides the weekly market day, little of historical note happened from the time of the Dissolution until the Victorian Age.

As is the case with any ruined structure, the building was soon reduced to a carcass, its stones being harvested and reused in the ensuing centuries. It has been theorized that the stones from King Ine's original stone church can still be found today—first reused in the construction of the twelfth- to fifteenth-century structures, and later in houses, barns, and other buildings throughout the surrounding areas. In a strange way, the death of the once magnificent structure led to its modern life. A short time after the Dissolution, a sense of national historical pride took over, and people were once again intrigued by the abbey ruins.

Beginning about 100 years after its ruination, travelers and chroniclers began visiting Glastonbury, making mention of its state and recording in illustration. In the mid 1600s, an antiquarian named Sir William Dugale penned a text entitled *Monasticon Anglicanum* in which Glastonbury and its once great church are mentioned. The engravings made by Wenceslaus Hollar and Richard Newcourt were among the first to record the ruins and the views of the township after the Dissolution. In 1675, the next account was made by John Ogilby when he wrote an outline of the main roads and pathways throughout England. In this manuscript, the path from Bristol to Weymouth is beautifully illustrated in the form of a long, undulating scroll showing the path through Somersetshire, passing through Glastonbury and by its famed Glastonbury Tor.

The 1723 illustrations made by William Stukeley for his travelogue through Great Britain have become some of the most famous showing Glastonbury Abbey. Most notable of these are the depictions of the abbot's dwelling and apparently the only known depiction of the Chain Gate that once crossed Magdalene Street. Several other surveys and boundary assessments were made in the following years from 1799 to 1844 when the property changed hands or the crown wanted an updated inventory of its holdings. In 1831 the Abbey House was built to the east of the abbey, and its ruins became a fashionable feature in the house's gardens along with the fish pond and the newer pond on the grounds to the east. Finally in 1850, Edwin Dolby produced some of the finest engravings of Glastonbury Abbey for a booklet outlining the particulars of the grounds and ruins. The grounds and ruins became available for auction in 1850.

After a long and painful period of languor, what remained of the abbey was purchased in 1908 by the Bath and Wells Diocesan Trust after an intense fund-raising campaign aimed at saving the site. Although only slight archeological attention had been paid to the site since its destruction, learning its history and uncovering its secrets became priority one. Soon after the grounds were purchased, one Frederick Bligh Bond was given this seemingly herculean task.

> The appearance of the abbey today—well-cut lawns, paths and helpful notices—bears little relation to the ruins as Bligh would have known them in 1907. The ground was rough, trees and scrub grew unimpeded and sheep clambered over the crumbling masonry around the great arches, while the wind washed along the creeper-covered walls of the ruined church. These fragmentary remains were confined to a fairly small rectangular enclosure to the east of abbey house and beyond them lay the kitchen gardens and pastureland. The only building to remain intact was the Abbot's Kitchen, which lay someway to the south-west, cut off from the other ruins by fences and orchards. Although the prospect of excavating such a site might at first glance prove daunting—only a few upstanding remains to provide clues where to dig—things were not as puzzling as they might first appear.

> Not only were there descriptions of the abbey buildings available, written before the Dissolutions, but, like all medieval monasteries, Glastonbury Abbey was laid out according to the traditional monastic plan, with the church and domestic buildings surrounding a central cloister. Although this standard layout made the abbey easy to reconstruct theoretically, there were always irregularities caused by geography, finance and fashion. Because of the confused and fragmentary state of the site, Bligh knew roughly where to dig and what to expect, but not exactly what he would find [Hopkinson-Ball, p. 53].

Many familiar with Bond remember him more for his efforts to discover the history of the abbey through unorthodox means such as automatic writing, and the success he had in his efforts is seldom remembered. Arguably the most notable among these was the discovery of the Edgar Chapel to the east of the Great Church, began by Abbot Beere in the sixteenth century and completed by the last abbot of Glastonbury, Richard Whiting. Bond also discovered the remains of the Loretto Chapel, also built by Abbot Beere.

Several other aspects of modern Glastonbury can be owed to Frederick Bond in addition to his contributions to the outline of the abbey ruins. In front of St. John's Parish Church stands a memorial to the casualties of war. It is made of a modern base bearing the names of these honored dead, an upright decorated with a Celtic knotwork design, and at the top a wheel cross allegedly found during his excavations of the abbey grounds.

Frederick Bond is also responsible for another icon of modern Glastonbury. The familiar image of the Chalice Well wellhead was designed and created by Bond in 1919. The wellhead is decorated with the symbol of the Vesica Piscis — two circles crossing each other, symbolizing the intersection and comingling of heaven and earth, body and soul, joined together by a spear directly through the center of both. This symbol proves to be the best summation of the person that was Frederick Bligh Bond. As both a devout Christian and a devotee of radically New Age ideas, he, like his symbol, became a much loved and recognized part of Glastonbury.

Pilgrims who visit the abbey today are met with a vision where the very old and very new blend together in a way that makes it quite difficult to tell which is which. New Age ideas and modern rock concerts stand shoulder to shoulder with whispers of the Roman age. A chapel built as an echo of what is thought to be the oldest Christian church in England stands very near a place where a medieval well serves as a center for spiritualism and meditation. With the understanding that the oldest parts of the abbey date only to the late twelfth century, it is helpful to point out a few features of note around the ruins, as well as their dates of creation.

The Lady Chapel, the oldest part of the ruins, is the only part that can be seen above ground. The part in which people can walk around today is St. Joseph's Crypt, which was built in the fifteenth century. On the south wall of the Lady Chapel, the famous "IESVS/MARIA" carving can be found only a few feet from the south entrance. This stone has always been a place of great reverence, where boys were once taught to remove their hats. Although once thought to be the burial site of the Virgin Mary herself, its origins have been conjectured to be at the hands of an overzealous medieval pilgrim (which, given the quality and the time required to create this carving, seems a dubious idea at best).

Inside St. Joseph's Crypt can be found two points of interest whose age and place can be a bit deceiving. On the eastern wall of the crypt, one may find a carving of the crucified Jesus at just above head level. This carving is clearly old, and the patina on it and the surrounding stones in the wall suggest that it has been there as long as the crypt itself. However, this carving and a portion of the wall in which it is mounted was only set in place during a reconstruction effort in the 1930s. Although it is quite likely that this carving originally came from the abbey grounds, either as a larger carving or as a tomb lid, its place in the crypt is fairly recent.

While repairing a hole in the roof of the chapel in the 1960s, other renovations were made. The most notable alteration of this area was the creation of a new altar where a support beam once stood. Fully consecrated by five crosses, one at each corner and one in the center, this altar is used today during modern church rededications and other services conducted in the crypt. It is clear to anyone visiting the site today that this is the holiest location in the abbey. On any given day, one will find candles left burning on this altar as well as on the side tables and windows in the chapel.

The deep veneration of this site is palpable by anyone who comes to the Lady Chapel today. With ancient graveyards to the north and to the south, it was the place where the powerful and pious were buried. Built to resemble a reliquary for something of the greatest sanctity, one must wonder what was once there, long ago before it was just a small part of a great and powerful church. To understand what makes Glastonbury Abbey such a special place, we must investigate the original church — the Ealde Chirche. The wattle church built by Joseph of Arimathea in the first century is at the very heart of the traditions of Glastonbury and the Grail legend. Therefore let us look at how this small, wickerwork chapel might have looked, how it might have been constructed, and how it might have survived over the centuries.

Part II

Key Players

The Grail legend is possibly the most elaborated, convoluted, mystery-enshrouded, obfuscated, and generally interpreted-to-death myth in our culture. It has been reinvented by nearly every generation since the High Middle Ages. Anyone embarking on an expedition to find the truth behind it either is in it to sell their story, resulting in yet another topical treatment further muddying the waters, or does so with no idea of what they were getting themselves into. If the legend is to be believed, it began almost two thousand years ago and has been snowballing ever since.

This section seeks to separate popular opinion from historical evidence. Pointing out the main points in this investigation, we will begin to learn more about the evidence that supports the theory of the Grail as a historical object — Joseph of Arimathea, his wattle church, Melkin's prophecy, and a stone tomb sitting in St. John's Parish Church. In outlining these key players, we can begin to build an argument for the Holy Grail as an object of historical fact instead of fantasy.

Chapter 4

Joseph — Nobilis Decurio

> The Holy Grail ... Doctor Jones. The chalice used by Christ during the Last Supper, the cup that caught His blood at the Crucifixion, and was entrusted to Joseph of Arimathea. (*Indiana Jones and the Last Crusade*)

These are the words that launched my study of the Grail. There was a time when I was ashamed of admitting this, but then an interesting thought occurred to me. In years past, a young Howard Carter might have been inspired by reading Victorian stories of antiquarians cracking Egyptian tombs. Archeologists today may have been inspired by reading pop fictions like *The Hardy Boys and the Mummy's Curse*. The truth is that your inspiration is seldom found during university classes. If you haven't found inspiration by then, you likely won't.

I happen to be a child of motion pictures, and since watching *Raiders of the Lost Ark*, I knew I had found my hero; my inspiration. This was not when I fell in love with archeology, however. Now I eagerly admit that as a child the first book I chose for myself was *Modern Knowledge Library: Archeology*, published in 1976. I was five. I remember this so distinctly because I once lost this book in elementary school. I had actually left this school and during the following summer, I realized I no longer had the book. I was sure that there was no way I would ever find it again, but my mother thankfully thought to call the school and see if they had it. As I recall, she was told it had been in their lost and found for some time. Today, it holds a place of honor both in my library and in my heart.

Despite my life-long love for archeology, that is not my profession today. There are days that I feel a deep sense of regret for not having pursued my childhood passion. However, when I think of what life would have been like had I become the archeologist I so wanted to be, I actually feel better about the course I chose. I realize that I would not have been digging up lost civilizations, discovering Atlantis or the Ark of the Covenant. I would have been doing someone else's work, cleaning artifacts, and logging journal entries. While all noble pursuits, I am now quite thankful for my present course of study.

I found an interest to which I wanted to devote myself in 1992. While watching a documentary about the Ark of the Covenant, I discovered that someone had actually gone looking for the Ark in Jerusalem — not the source of the Ark legend, but the artifact itself. It was only then that I realized that these objects might not be just the pursuit of a fedora-wearing fiction. Soon thereafter, I began my own personal quest for the Holy Grail, and with my trusty bullwhip tucked neatly out of sight, have lived the life about which I had once only dreamed.

Early into my study I realized that to make people consider the Holy Grail a historical object, it had to be taken out of the realm of legend and placed into a historical context. Accomplishing that goal relies largely on one man — Joseph of Arimathea. Proving Joseph was indeed in Britain in the first century is key to presenting the Holy Grail as an historical object. It is toward this end that I devote the remainder of this book.

As mentioned early on, one must abandon a small amount of disbelief and accept a few points of contention to enter into this sort of study. One must accept that Jesus was an actual person, as was Joseph of Arimathea. Although no one possesses their birth certificates nor has their fingerprints on file, it can be accepted without much difficulty. Both were just men from first-century Jerusalem, one a holy man and the other a member of the Jewish upper class. Archeology dictates that such could have existed in the Roman-occupied Middle East, so if we again remove the mysticism surrounding both and reduce the question to a simple matter of possibilities, we can say with some assurance that both men could have very easily existed. With that having been said, we can proceed with an investigation of just who this man Joseph would have been, and how such legends could have been formulated around him.

The time during which Rome occupied Israel began in the first century B.C. and in a sense ended when Constantine adopted Christianity in the third century A.D. The time between was marked with leniency for some and harsh domination for others. Living conditions were typical of societies of the time. The ruling body, the aristocrats, held all wealth, and from what was left, a slim "upper middle class" arose consisting of Jewish spiritual leaders and some merchants. Everyone else lived a harsh life of subsistence. Most were tradesmen of some kind, such as carpenters, metal workers, potters, thatchers, and weavers as well as having small plots on which to grow their own food. Few managed to get by as what we would call farmers, most of these having orchards, vineyards, or olive groves.

These were the expendable people, those who didn't matter. For a Roman chariot to run down one of these people would be akin to a modern motorist hitting a squirrel on the road. Only a rare few in power saw them as anything more than subhuman. The only real difference between these common people and the merchant class came from what these merchants could do for the upper classes. If their wares or services pleased their patrons, they would prosper, potentially reaching a status near that of their aristocratic patrons. If they did not, or if they offended those from this upper class, their life could become worse than the commoner on the street.

It is to this "upper middle class" that, according to legend, the mysterious Joseph of Arimathea belonged. It has been said that Joseph was a metal merchant, not a craftsman but one who dealt with the purchase, import, and sale of metals used throughout the empire. While metals such as gold and silver were obviously precious and prized among the nobility eager to demonstrate their power and wealth, the true cash cows for the Roman metal merchant were the industrial metals such as iron, tin, and lead. Romans are most well known for their amazing constructions such as the Colosseum in Rome, however nowhere is their skill more clearly demonstrated than in their domination over water.

Few historians or archeologists will dispute the fact that the Romans loved their water. Aqueducts brought water from far-away mountains, lakes, or streams, and with precision amazing for the time, used nothing more than gravity to carry their prize to their city centers. The Trevi Fountain is still fed by the twenty-mile-long aqueduct called the Acqua Vergine, which was built in the year 19 B.C. to carry pure water from the Alban Hills into the heart of Rome. Whether these aqueducts fed fountains, palaces, or bath houses, this water wasn't carried in crudely carved, bare rock channels. Liners made of lead or a tin-lead alloy were used to maintain the purity and flow of the precious water over the many miles it ran from its source to its destination. Ironically, it is the lead the Romans used in all their plumbing that some scientists believe lead to their downfall; they theorize that the Romans eventually began to suffer from lead poisoning, resulting in disease and madness.

Those who dealt in metals were not only valued by the Romans. Many of the rich implements used in temples were made of metals, either ornamented by gold or made from bronze. Since the time of the Old Testament, metalworkers have shared much the same standing as possessors of nearly sacred knowledge as stonemasons. It must be remembered that one of the most important jobs for the fabrication of the Ark of the Covenant was for a metalworker to beat out the fine sheets of gold in which the sacred container would be clad.

During the time of Jesus, metalworkers played several important roles as well. With the Romans came the coin of the realm, and with it the need for coin production. One famous example is the Judaea Capta coins minted in bronze, silver, and gold to celebrate the conquest of Jerusalem. Some of these are known to have been struck in areas around Jerusalem such as in Caesarea. Certain ritual objects required metal for their creation as well. Ritual baths, for instance, were required before entry into the temple and on holy days. Therefore pitchers, cruets, small flasks and other objects were made to serve these purposes.

No matter the degree of interest one may have regarding life in Roman Judea and the inner workings of its society, one may wonder what the significance might be for our study to cement Joseph as a first century Israeli metal merchant. The answer to this question is quite simple, and serves to strengthen my previously stated intent in the earlier sections of this text. To make a historical connection between a Jew from the time of Jesus and his presence in far-off Britain, which was at the time merely an unremarkable Roman province, one must establish a scenario placing Joseph in Britain at the right time and explaining why he was there.

> During the Roman period lead became a commodity that was more actively sought and mined in its own right. Indeed, lead is sometimes referred to as a 'Roman metal' because of the increased intensity of its usage in this era. It began to be used in larger quantities and for more substantial application. Some writers have estimated that the quantity of lead mined during the period of the Roman Republic (from about 200 B.C. to A.D. 500) represented about one half of all the lead produced in the ancient world. The expansion of the Empire was driven by a demand for metals, and lead was an important one of these. Indeed it seems likely that the invasion of Britain in A.D. 43 was at least partly driven by the search for lead and other metals.
>
> There is evidence of lead mining in Britain prior to the Roman invasion but not on a large scale. The Romans believed there to be extensive mineral wealth in the country, and many have favoured Britain as a source of lead because galena ore was found close to the surface, in outcrops. This galena ore contained only small quantities of silver, and so was of value to the Romans primarily for its lead content. Pliny the Elder (died A.D. 79), describes in some detail early lead production techniques adopted by the Romans. After mining, ore was washed, screened and then smelted in round brick furnaces, or in furnaces which had been roughly excavated from hillsides. Lead mines were developed and worked throughout Britain over the three hundred years or so of the Roman presence. There is evidence of extensive mining activity in the North, in Wales and in the South East. The choice of York as the Romans' northern capital of Britain and the construction of Hadrian's Wall may both have been linked to the need to protect the rich lead mining areas of Yorkshire, Northumberland and Cumbria [Rich, pp. 5–6].

Considering this evidence, one could imagine that in the mind of a first-century metal merchant the newly acquired lands in Britain might have been seen as their version of the New World and its promise of "gold" in the form of lead ore just lying on the ground. It may well be that the introduction of this resource would create just another stop on his travels as a merchant to other Mediterranean ports such as Turkey, Egypt, Greece, and Italy. Vincent Rich goes on to discuss how lead was also taken as tribute to Rome from France and Spain. It is therefore quite possible that as a metal merchant, Joseph traveled extensively throughout the region, trading in the precious ore.

Of course Roman emissaries were not the first to travel abroad throughout the Mediterranean for trade with other countries. In fact, Romans would likely have used maritime pathways and knowledge set down long before them. Beginning several hundred years before Rome was founded, the Phoenicians traded a variety of commodities all across Western Europe — ranging from the shores of the Black Sea, throughout the classic civilizations of the Mediterranean, past the Straits of Gibraltar, and as far away as Britain. These Phoenician trade routes were as well known then as they are famous today, and surely became the time-honored paths taken by the traders of the Roman era. However, one can be certain that metal ore was not the only item of value that passed through Joseph's hands.

Traveling to so many different places throughout the Old World would expose him to many different cultures and traditions, as well as presenting him with the opportunity to acquire many things that would be unfamiliar and perhaps even wholly unavailable in his native land. These would include not only goods, but the written word and other knowledge as well. It would not be surprising if Joseph in his travels obtained many of the fineries that even the elite in his own country could not possess: fine linens from Egypt, perhaps taken in preparation for his own eventual death, or items of exquisite craftsmanship in stone or other precious materials, perhaps even balms and perfumes that would have made him the envy of his patrons among the Roman ruling class.

He may have been considered something of an ambassador as well, expected to forge new alliances or bring back knowledge of potential resources to those in power. The wisdom he encountered may even have made him appear somewhat scholarly among his peers. The potential for personal gain and acclaim was great for someone in such a position; however, one must consider the question, from whom would he gain? He was still in a precarious situation regarding his social standing. He was more than the average Judean to be sure, but not quite on an even footing with the Romans. He could never be part of the elite, although his ability to request the body of Jesus from Pilate indicates a certain amount of power and social standing.

4. Joseph — Nobilis Decurio

Considering the demand for metal by the Temple, religious devotees, the Roman aristocracy, and simple commerce, it seems clear that one who excelled in the metal trade had the potential to grow quite wealthy indeed, gaining access to some of the very extravagances only the rich and powerful could possess. A wealthy merchant such as this would be allowed certain other benefits that the average citizen was not. As today, wealth quite often carried with it power and respect. Although the Romans interacted with the wealthy among the Jewish population, most likely very little respect was exchanged. More likely, the acceptance that this wealth might bring would have come from the Jewish power elite, called the Sanhedrin.

The Sanhedrin was a council of elders or judges whose purpose it was to make sure their book of law, the Talmud, was obeyed and its rules and regulations followed to the letter. Called together by Old Testament law, this group of men served both as police and judges in matters of religion and Jewish social order until the third century A.D. Since the Jewish people were so devoted to following the laws and social mores set down by God, the Sanhedrin held the position of power that the Roman Catholic Church would hold during the Middle Ages. In other words, if you crossed them, it could spell disaster for you and those near you.

It is a well known fact that when the Romans invaded Judea, their approach was to allow the people to continue in their belief systems as they had before their arrival, so long as it did not supersede the Roman authority. In that regard, the Sanhedrin became something of a conduit between the Roman government and the people. The governors could persuade them to keep the peace so there would be no rebellion and the Sanhedrin could take their case before the Roman authorities when needed. Such was the case with the accusations they lodged against Jesus that began the process leading to His crucifixion.

When Jesus came upon the scene in Jerusalem proclaiming to be the Son of God Himself and leader of the Jewish people, that placed him in direct conflict with the Sanhedrin both in their doctrine and in regards to their hold on power. It was also a slap in the face of the Roman government because Jesus claimed to be the king of the Jews, although this was probably seen with little more than amusement by the powerful Roman Empire. It would seem more likely that the real threat He posed was to the Sanhedrin in questioning their authority on matters relating to God and His word.

The Bible speaks of the strife between them and the new prophet, Jesus:

> And they led Jesus away to the high priest: and with him were assembled all the chief priests and the elders and the scribes.
> And Peter followed him afar off, even into the palace of the high priest: and he sat with the servants, and warmed himself at the fire.

> And the chief priests and all the council sought for witness against Jesus to put him to death; and found none.
> For many bare false witness against him, but their witness agreed not together.
> And there arose certain, and bare false witness against him, saying,
> We heard him say, I will destroy this temple that is made with hands, and within three days I will build another made without hands.
> But neither so did their witness agree together.
> And the high priest stood up in the midst, and asked Jesus, saying, Answerest thou nothing? what is it which these witness against thee?
> But he held his peace, and answered nothing. Again the high priest asked him, and said unto him, Art thou the Christ, the Son of the Blessed?
> And Jesus said, I am: and ye shall see the Son of man sitting on the right hand of power, and coming in the clouds of heaven.
> Then the high priest rent his clothes, and saith, What need we any further witnesses?
> Ye have heard the blasphemy: what think ye? And they all condemned him to be guilty of death [*The Holy Bible*, KJV, Mark 14:53–64].

The book of John goes on to say that although the Sanhedrin wanted Jesus put to death, they had to rely on the Roman authorities to make the decision: "Then said Pilate unto them, Take ye him, and judge him according to your law. The Jews therefore said unto him, It is not lawful for us to put any man to death (*The Holy Bible*, KJV, John 18:31).

Despite modern theories to the contrary, it is also traditionally held that the Sanhedrin paid Judas Iscariot the infamous thirty pieces of silver to betray Jesus and turn Him over to be arrested. Although it was ultimately Pontius Pilate that gave the order approving the crucifixion of Jesus, it seems clear that the Roman power base cared little about the claims Jesus made to be king of the Jews, and that it was the Sanhedrin who felt truly threatened by this claim. The outcome of their plea to Pilate was in their favor, and as such demonstrates the kind of relationship this group of men had with their Roman leaders.

It would seem, however, that there were at least a few among the Sanhedrin that were sympathetic to Jesus and his teachings. Among these were Nicodemus and Joseph of Arimathea. Although the Bible tells us little of Nicodemus, it does tell us quite a bit about Joseph, albeit indirectly. However, let us first consider how and why Joseph might have been a part of the Sanhedrin, and how his later actions would put him and his position of influence in jeopardy.

If we agree with the theory that Joseph was a metal merchant dealing in the valued commodity of lead, traveling around the known world, possibly acquiring many items of value displaying his wealth, one can see that he may have been considered something of a mover and shaker in his time, allowing him to enter into the power elite among his people. Although some scholars debate that the specific wording used to describe his role is unclear as to whether he was an actual member of the Sanhedrin or was simply an advisor, it is agreed that he stood on equal footing with this powerful group. Further considering that Joseph was later assisted by Nicodemus, who according to the Book of John was also a member of the Sanhedrin and spoke during Jesus's trial, the likelihood that Joseph was among this powerful group of social and religious judges seems quite high.

Consider now the events that took place after the crucifixion. The Bible states that Joseph went "boldly" to Pilate requesting the body of Jesus to be turned over to him. Here we can determine two things of interest. First, that Joseph felt not only that he could approach the Roman governor with his request, but that he could stride up to him, feeling he could make a valid claim for the body. This demonstrates a certain social standing in the charged society of first-century, Roman-occupied Judea. This is not a scene of a lowly shepherd or fisherman crawling in on hands and knees, groveling for the favor of the powerful Roman leader, but one of a man of influence and some social power who felt he could converse with Pilate somewhat on his own level.

The second thing we can glean from this interaction is that it would appear Joseph had some legitimate claim to the body. Joseph, although a secret follower of Jesus, was a member of the Sanhedrin or at least one who could be otherwise considered of like mind. Since the Sanhedrin saw Jesus as a heretic, it is unlikely they would want His body. They would likely have preferred it to be thrown to the dogs or left out for the birds, as a warning to anyone else who might question their power. Joseph was not known to be a follower of Jesus, so there would have been no reason for him to ask Pilate for the body. In fact from Pilate's perspective, it would have seemed that here was a man who for reasons unknown wanted the body of a criminal.

It is tempting to think that Pilate assumed Joseph's desire for Jesus's body was to take it to defile before the people, but we must remember that to the Jewish people, a dead body was unclean and not to be touched unless absolutely necessary. To take a dead body and drag it through the streets, even as a demonstration of power, would have been met with horror and possibly violence. However, if Pilate thought that this was his intention, it would have served to make Joseph's case all the easier to win.

The question must then be asked, why did Joseph want to take possession of Jesus's body? After the crucifixion, he took the body to a tomb he had set aside for himself, used his own grave goods and those brought by another disciple, Mary Magdalene, to prepare His body for entombment. While it has always been accepted that this was simply an act of devotion, there is another tradition that suggests a different possibility. This theory states that Joseph of Arimathea was a member of Jesus's family.

Commonly known as the Traditions of Glastonbury, this theory ties together Joseph's actions at the crucifixion, his presence in Britain, and the "lost years" of Jesus's youth between His teaching at the Temple as a boy and his return to Israel to be baptized by John on the banks of the River Jordan. These traditions state that Joseph was none other than Mary's uncle, and great-uncle to Jesus. As astounding a claim as this may seem at first, there are several pieces of circumstantial evidence that lend credence to the theory.

Consider first Joseph's actions when requesting the body of Jesus from Pilate. According to Hebrew law, a member of the family was responsible for the care and burial of a person's body after their death. According to the commonly held version of Jesus's family tree, this claim should have been made by His mother, Mary, or if a male member of the family was required, His younger brother James. If a family member was not present to make the claim, it would seem logical that one among His followers would ask for the body. However, one should recall that they were all in hiding for fear of arrest and punishment themselves. Instead Joseph, who would at first seem to have no claim to it, made the request to Pilate.

Providing his own tomb for the body is also in keeping with Hebrew funerary traditions. If possible, and if the family was of sufficient wealth, a family tomb was commonly used instead of the individual burials with which we are familiar today. Being the son of a carpenter, Jesus did not appear to come from a family of great means, so it is unlikely that they could have achieved this by themselves. It then fell on another family member, one of some means, to provide the tomb for His burial.

Another facet, this time from the famous story of Jesus's birth, points toward Joseph being a member of the Holy Family. This little-considered feature of the story is commonly called the Exile in Egypt; in it Mary and Joseph are told by an angel that they must leave their home and travel to Egypt to protect the infant Jesus from the mad emperor Harod's edict to kill all children 2 years of age or younger, an event now known as the Slaughter of the Innocents. It has been said that Joseph of Arimathea could have played a vital role in this part of Jesus's life as well.

The times in which Jesus lived were quite different than our own. To pick up and move your family to another country was not then as simple as it is now, if that can even be said of doing so today. Mary, Joseph, and Jesus could not just hop a flight to Egypt, checking their meager belongings at the front counter. It was a major undertaking, not to mention a great risk, to commit to such an extended relocation. Many have wondered how they were able to successfully make this move without help.

While the most common theory on the matter has been that they simple found refuge among Jewish colonies in Egypt, this still does not provide a satisfactory picture of how they could have survived on their own. How would they have known of these settlements so far from their homeland? How could they have safely arrived in those foreign lands? How could they be assured that they would be welcomed there, much less provided for? It would seem more logical to assume that they had someone who could not only usher them to this new home, but also provide something of a connection to the community there. If Joseph was in fact a metal merchant, he would doubtlessly have ventured to Egypt and would have been familiar with this settlement, thus providing them a much easier time adjusting to their new situation.

While this serves as a logical if not verifiable theory, it only opens one possible door to peer into the life and role he played in the life of Jesus and His family. If Joseph was a member of Mary and Jesus's family, one must question to what extent he played a part in their lives. If he did in fact help the family reach Egypt, it is quite likely that he at least visited them regularly on his travels, and potentially lived with them for a time. It is this close family bond that formulates the last, most interesting aspect of the Traditions of Glastonbury, outlining his role in the life of the young boy who would later grow to be the central figure in a world religion.

Part of the legend surrounding Joseph and his presence in the British Isles is that he took a young Jesus there for some time after His father died. Having very likely traveled as a metal merchant to the lead-rich lands of Britain in the past, it is easily conceivable that after the death of His father, Joseph could have taken up the role of male role model or father figure in Jesus's life. It is possible that Joseph even attempted to train Jesus in a new life's trade in metals. Interwoven with the traditions of other saints and historical figures, this story of Joseph bringing Jesus to Britain as a youth is in fact much older than the eighteenth or possibly fifteenth century dates that scholars have accepted, and has nearly reached the status as accepted fact among people in southwestern England.

The Traditions of Glastonbury go on to explain how Joseph found himself and his small band of followers back on British shores after the crucifixion. This account begins with an apocryphal book of the Bible known as the Gospel of Nicodemus, or Acts of Pilate. This short but significant account details the happenings that occurred to Joseph of Arimathea and Nicodemus immediately following the discovery of the empty tomb in which Jesus's body had been lain.

Although the Acts of Pilate are commonly considered to be a medieval invention, the oldest portions of it have been dated to around A.D. 450–480, and other early church texts suggest a much older date, such as the *Apologies* written by early theologian Justin Martyr in the second century A.D., which references the Acts of Pilate. Although some say he simply assumed there would be some Roman account of the crucifixion, others maintain he knew of such a written record. In the Acts of Pilate, the reader witnesses the first interaction between Jesus and Joseph after the crucifixion. This passage follows Joseph's imprisonment, after he was accused of stealing and hiding the body of Jesus.

> Joseph said to them: In the evening of the Preparation, when you secured me in prison, I fell a-praying throughout the whole night, and throughout the whole day of the Sabbath. And at midnight I see the prison-house that four angels lifted it up, holding it by the four corners. And Jesus came in like lightning, and I fell to the ground from fear. Taking hold of me, therefore, by the hand, he raised me, saying, Fear not, Joseph. Thereafter, embracing me, he kissed me, and said, Turn thyself, and see who I am. Turning myself, therefore, and looking, I said, My lord, I know not who thou art. He says, I am Jesus, whom thou didst bury the day before yesterday. I say to him, Show me the tomb, and then I shall believe. He took me, therefore, by the hand, and led me away to the tomb, which had been opened. And seeing the linen and the napkin, and recognising him, I said, Blessed is he that cometh in the name of the Lord; and I adored him. Then taking me by the hand, and accompanied by the angels, he brought me to my house in Arimathea, and said to me, Sit here for forty days; for I go to my disciples, in order that I may enable them fully to proclaim my resurrection [*The Gospel of Nicodemus*, ch. 15].

While the Gospel of Nicodemus obviously says nothing about the Grail or how it may have come into the possession of Joseph, it does serve as a springboard of sorts for one of the earliest writers in the history of the Grail romances. Robert de Boron, author of *Joseph d'Arimathe*, elaborates on this apocryphal account of Joseph's imprisonment, and states that it is during his incarceration that the apparition of Jesus bequeaths the precious vessel to Joseph, and instructs him on the secrets of the Eucharist.

According to legend, Joseph was exiled from Israel along with a small group of followers, and placed aboard a ship with no sails, oars, or rudder — a theme one hears quite often in ancient stories of exile. As anyone familiar with sailing can attest, a boat set adrift with no means of propulsion or navigation would quite likely end up back on the shores from which it departed thanks to the prevailing tides. While some say currents could have taken the boat to foreign shores, it is much more likely that this is simply used as a device demonstrating that their lives and fates were left in God's hands, and as such, He delivered them to where they were intended to be. The theme of a boat or ship guided by either God or fate is repeated throughout Grail literature both as a literal and figurative vessel used to carry out God's will.

This ocean voyage may sound a little far-fetched, but in its most basic form, there is some historical evidence to support it. Rabanus Maurus, archbishop of Mainz, wrote of this group of travelers in his ninth-century *Life of Mary Magdalene*, outlining their path from what he calls Asia, through the Mediterranean, eventually arriving on the shores of Marseilles, France, where the company split up, some staying in France and some moving on to other venues in which to spread the word of God. If this path seems in any way familiar, it should.

In the earlier discussion of the trade routes set down by the Phoenicians, it was said that Joseph likely used these same routes during his travels in the metal trade. Therefore it was just such a path that he would have used to arrive in Britain. This account is further supported by another legendary tradition in southern France, which states that Mary Magdalene, her sister Martha, and their brother Lazarus arrived by boat (again with no means of propulsion or navigation) at the shores of Saintes-Maries-de-la-Mer, which is only a short distance up the coast to the west from Marseilles. This legend of their arrival in southern France can be traced back to nearly the time of its alleged occurrence and is celebrated by an annual festival.

It would seem that from the original company of some twenty people, Mary, Martha, Lazarus, and a handful of others remained there while Joseph and his followers continued north to Britain. Although some traditions state Joseph and his followers traveled through France and departed its northern coast for Britain, it is most reasonable to assume that he merely continued along the same ancient trade routes that continued out into the Atlantic, skirting the Portuguese coast, and found his way into one of the many small inlets that lead inland from the southern coast of Britain to the marshy stretches of Somerset. Finally landing on solid ground at the foot of Wearyal Hill, Joseph and his companions climbed to the top of this small hillock and looked down at the flat plain of tranquil dry land that continued for a short distance to the east, crowned by the towering mound now known as Glastonbury Tor.

As is the case with any biblical figure, there is very little historical evidence to substantiate any claim made about their life or their actions. However, the same cannot be said of others from the same time and just after. Due to their role in the development of the burgeoning Christian religion, much is known about the lives and deeds of several of the disciples and other early church fathers such as Saint Paul. In truth, it is only the combination of their role in the life of Jesus and our modern mistrust of such stories that brings their lives and actions into question.

It is nearly impossible to look at events surrounding such matters as the Holy Grail, Joseph of Arimathea, and the early church at Glastonbury in a historical light based solely on legends, questionably dated written material, and tradition. Gone are the days of taking such matters on faith or of trusting the accounts written by early church fathers. We today require proof. Should then the researcher of the Grail legends abandon the quest for a historical Grail as an endeavor which is ultimately impossible? Certainly not — especially when there actually exists proof, or more correctly, *evidence*, readily available to any who bother to look.

Chapter 5

Recreating Joseph's Wattle Church

Living in an age of reason does not lend itself to dragging a medieval legend into the realm of historical possibility. Our modern sensibilities do not easily abide legends, especially one derived from Christ's Passion. One might as easily try to revive the theory of a flat earth. However, science is something of a two-edged sword when it comes to such matters.

Proving that a vessel dates from the time of Christ is a simple matter of archeology. Calling it the Holy Grail is another matter entirely. The strange part is that the difference comes primarily from the name. A cup that is the Holy Grail is the subject of legend — a medieval romance fashioned to entertain. Cups from first-century Jerusalem, even ones found in burials, fill museums around the world. Sadly, the aspect that kills the credibility of this particular cup is not its alleged magical abilities, such as floating, dispensing food, or granting eternal life. What seems to relegate this object to the colorfully inked pages of fantasy is its owner.

The Holy Grail is a legend that originated with someone many see as a legendary figure. Therefore, to even suggest there might be some historical truth behind it all is to risk credibility, or to be labeled a zealot. To dissuade this belief, it becomes necessary to scientifically prove that the Holy Grail might well have existed. From that point, it becomes a different endeavor entirely to study the Grail in history.

Since the story of the Grail ostensibly begins in England, we must look to England for our evidence. We must find, in one place and in a fairly narrow window of time, a first-century container, Joseph of Arimathea, and some record of both. Additionally, having some connection with King Arthur would be a pleasant plus. The one place in England that meets with all these criteria can only be Glastonbury.

The key to placing the Grail and Joseph of Arimathea in a historical context is finding out more about the wattle church at Glastonbury allegedly built by Joseph and his followers.

What exactly was this wattle church, and what might it have looked like? Would there have been similar buildings in the area at the time? Most importantly, would it have been possible for such a building to survive for several centuries to become part of Ine's stone church complex? Wattle construction was certainly known in England at this time, but there is quite a difference between a chieftain's roundhouse and a public building of some size such as a church or chapel. Let us now investigate wattle construction and all of the external influences that might have contributed to Glastonbury's first church.

The term "wattle" refers to a building method, easily dating back 6,000 years, in which the form of a building was laid out using wooden stakes, or sometimes posts. Then thinner, bendable branches are woven in and out of the stakes. This wickerwork structure was then covered inside and out with a mud and straw daub resulting in a surface similar to stucco when dry. Some-

Pieces of burnt daub on display in the Glastonbury Abbey Museum of the type used in the wattle church. There is no way of knowing if this is daub from the Old Church or from another wattled structure on the site, but it does illustrate the endurance of wattle and baked daub construction (author photograph).

times the daub was burned slightly to make it into a harder surface akin to fired clay, and other times the daub was painted to prevent it from rotting in the damp climate.

Beginning a study of the wattle building tradition in England almost always means studying the classic Iron Age structure known as the roundhouse. Serving as the main dwelling for chieftain, farmer and farm animal alike, the roundhouse was a simple design that quite ingeniously solved the problems Iron Age man faced. A combination of tree trunks and large saplings were used to form the circular wall, the wattles woven around stakes between these posts. One large central post helped support the peak of the highly pitched thatched roof, framed with willow or elm branches, that descended beyond the outer wall to form an eave. Depending on the structure's use, the space would be filled by multiple generations of a family, the tools with which they sustained themselves, and occasionally livestock, although animals were typically kept in separate simpler structures nearby.

One of the largest examples of the roundhouse can be found at Milton Keynes in Buckinghamshire. Dating to roughly 700 B.C., in the late Bronze Age, this exceptionally large structure measures 60 feet in diameter, requiring additional support to hold up the massive roof structure. A roundhouse this large could have easily housed a large extended family or perhaps even a small village. Although the average roundhouse would have been only about 20 feet in diameter, there is another example of similar age and size that can be found in Taunton, not far from Glastonbury. This demonstrates that people living in this area were building truly magnificent examples of wattle and daub construction long before Joseph's legendary arrival.

British roundhouses may be the most recognizable form of wattle and daub building, but they are certainly not the only variety. This construction technique can be found around the globe. Although the earliest examples would have been simple pens and fences, archeologists have found Roman dwellings made of wattles, Viking longhouses, and many later medieval buildings. Even the famous Tudor half-timbered houses still seen throughout England used the wattle and daub technique to form the classic cream-colored walls between the wide timbers.

There is no question that building a structure formed of wickerwork and insulated with earth is a time-honored technique throughout Europe. The real debate begins when one starts trying to picture the wattle church at Glastonbury. The question has been asked for quite some time whether the Ealde Chirche would have been of the traditional round form or rectangular. Most historians suggest it would have been round since most of these structures of that time would have been roundhouses. This theory is given credence when one reads where William of Malmesbury states, "These holy men built a chapel of the form that had been shown them. The walls were of osiers wattled together."

This begs the question of what form might have been shown to Joseph and his band of exiles. The answer to this question seems fairly straightforward. Taking the Glastonbury Lake Village as an example, most assume it would have been the same style of roundhouse mentioned previously. One example of this classic design was recreated in 1992 at the Peat Moors Center in nearby Westhay. Although the center sadly closed in October of 2009, it provided its visitors not only a wonderful example of this traditional Celtic dwelling, but also reconstructions of the wooden trackways that once crisscrossed the area. It was this sort of scene that Joseph of Arimathea would have seen upon his arrival to the marshy lands of Somerset in the first century.

It is difficult to tell what other sorts of buildings might have been available from which he may have taken inspiration when planning his new church. During the Iron Age when this legendary band of refugees from the Holy Land reached the distant island that would become Britain, sacred sites were not marked by buildings. Instead places of great sanctity were places such as groves of trees, ponds, and great constructions of stone such as the famous Stonehenge on the Salisbury Plain. Although stone construction was an option for Joseph, it was mostly used for tombs, dolmens, and menhirs. Stone buildings were not common in Britain until after the Roman invasion.

It is actually the Roman conquest that helps to provide some bit of evidence that the traditional round wattle structures were not the only option available. With the Romans came a new European culture, as well as the technology and innovation that made Rome the most advanced civilization of its time. They did not typically adopt the philosophy of conquest through devastation to which some of the barbarian tribes subscribed. Theirs was conquest through assimilation, typically allowing indigenous cultures to continue as they had been, keeping the same traditions and worshiping the same gods, only now paying homage to Rome.

There are plenty of examples of Roman occupation throughout Britain to use as a guide; however, we must first determine the influence Rome had during the time in which Joseph and his company landed on Wirral Hill. From early writings of certain church fathers, it is generally accepted that if Joseph did indeed travel to England, he arrived some time between A.D. 30 and 70. Rome invaded Britain around the same time, roughly A.D. 40–50. Therefore, assuming Rome took some time gaining its hold over the native Britons, Joseph's actions were not entirely ruled by Roman influence. Depending on when exactly these events took place, Joseph either came into a world entirely devoid of Roman influence only to fall subject to it soon thereafter, or he came to a Britain beginning to be populated and changed by Roman culture.

5. Recreating Joseph's Wattle Church

This realization unfortunately does little to shed any light on our investigation of the wattle church. However, an investigation into Roman Britain, paying particular attention to its building styles, might yield greater success.

> Rome arrived in a Britain that was changing. Elite society, at least in the south and east of the country, was already experimenting with ideas influenced by contact with Gaul and Rome. In architectural terms this can be seen in the construction of rectangular houses in place of round ones [Perring, p. 30].

The rectangular buildings to which this quote refers were not made of stone or even wood; they were described as "rectangular timber buildings with wattle and daub walls" (p. 29). Perring states that these buildings were mostly found in southeastern England, but if nothing else, this does demonstrate that a form of wattle and daub building other than the roundhouse was present around the time of the Roman conquest.

Although the new European style of houses and the arrival of Roman influence in Britain is compelling evidence for a rectangular wattle church at Glastonbury, it is not conclusive. One must remember this was a church, not a house. It was a building which, albeit humble, had a higher purpose than simply keeping the head dry. Not quite the imposing stone structure later added by King Ine, this was to be a building of some importance. Therefore, we must wonder if it would have taken the simple form of a common dwelling or if it would have been made differently, to stand out among the round houses of the surrounding countryside. Perring also provides some insight into this question: "The first Roman-style buildings (c. A.D. 50–60) were built of timber and earth. Even the higher status houses of this period had wattle and daub walls, earth floors and thatch roofs" (Perring, p. 31).

Legend states that Joseph had been to England many times before as a metal merchant, meaning that he was well familiar with the traditional roundhouses. However, he himself came from a Roman-influenced world and would have been even more familiar and comfortable with the benefits of a rectangular building. One reading the Malmesbury passage above could take from it two meanings. It could mean either that those who built the wattle church were shown how to build a round house or that they were shown how to build a structure using wattle and daub.

Houses and other buildings in first-century Jerusalem were primarily built using mud brick, with the larger, more important buildings being made from stone blocks. In the absence of great stone quarries and in an environment where sun-dried mud bricks would be difficult if not impossible to produce, the builders of the first chapel at Glastonbury needed to rely on the building method with which the ancient Britons were most familiar even if they themselves were not. Therefore "the form that had been shown them" likely refers not to the roundhouse that many feel the wattle church would have been but rather the manner in which it was built.

Further evidence at Glastonbury suggests that the original wattle church was rectangular in shape. Historical accounts speak of a pillar that once stood on either the north or south side of the Lady Chapel in line with the east wall upon which a brass plaque was mounted detailing the layout and dimensions of the Old Church. Although the now-lost plaque and its inscription originated from around the turn of the fifteenth century, the historical account is valuable in that it translates not only the location of the original wattle church but also the idea that the Lady Chapel was built to mirror its outline:

> And lest the site or size of the earlier church should come to be forgotten because of such additions, he [St. David] erected this column on a line drawn southwards through the two eastern angles of the same church, and cutting it off from the aforesaid chancel. And its length was 60ft westward from that line, its breadth was truly 26ft; the distance from the centre of this pillar from the midpoint between the aforesaid angles, 48ft [Rahtz and Watts, pp. 43–44].

Signpost erected just north of the point where the Lady Chapel and Galilee meet. This is the location where the earlier pillar and sign stood, outlining the dimensions of the original wattle church (author photograph).

There is one additional feature found at Glastonbury to suggest that Joseph's wattle church was rectangular instead of round, albeit more in the form of supposition than evidence. If one looks at the abbey's floor plan, most especially in the area of the Lady Chapel and Galilee, it is easy to see that the Lady Chapel is not quite on the same east-west alignment as the rest of the building. It is on more of a slight east-northeast by west-southwest orientation. If the twelfth-century Lady Chapel was built merely to commemorate the spot of the original

5. *Recreating Jospeh's Wattle Church* 73

The meeting place of the Lady Chapel and Galilee. This image was taken with the signpost immediately behind the camera. According to the plaque that once stood mounted to a post at this spot, this transition point marked the end of the original wattle church (author photograph).

wattle church, round or square, it likely would have kept the same alignment as the Great Church built only a few years later. However, if the Lady Chapel was built as an echo of the wattle church, it would have been built to match, or more likely encompass, the footprint left by the older chapel, including the slightly incorrect alignment laid down centuries earlier. Although this sort of misalignment is not uncommon with small chapels attached to many great churches throughout England, the rule is almost always that those small, misaligned chapels are older than the larger building or have been built over the remains of an older chapel using the older foundations.

Ultimately there are some aspects of the Ealde Chirche that we can never know. There is either too much speculation or insufficient information to even postulate every aspect of a wooden building of this age. However, there is no doubt that the wattle church did exist. William of Malmesbury saw it himself, recording it in his histories, as did countless others who were witness to its reality for roughly a thousand years before it fell victim to fire. However, the fire of 1184 that claimed the Old Church was not the first time the history of Glastonbury's ancient past was put in danger.

There has been much dispute about what portion of William of Malmesbury's *De Antiquitate Glastonie Ecclesie* was original to William and what portion was added later by Glastonbury monks. In particular, the portions pertaining to the foundation of the church at Glastonbury by Joseph of Arimathea and his companions have been called into question. Although some use these segments of the text to damn the whole as completely unreliable, Malmesbury makes reference to some material he had seen that, while ancient and otherwise reliable, could not be verified and was thus omitted. A close reading of his manuscript, as well as his actions after writing it, demonstrates that he himself had to rethink his views on the antiquity of the abbey after his time spent researching the histories housed within its library.

One part of his *Antiquitate* alludes to another time in the church's history when things fell apart. As the story goes, after the wattle church was built, Joseph and his followers started dying off. It would seem that once they were all gone, there was either no one left to care for the wattle church or no one in a position to protect it. Once the original circle of holy adepts had departed, it was said that the once-holy place became a "lair of wild beasts." This can either mean that the building was no longer used, allowing animals such as snakes, mice, and similar creatures of opportunity to seek shelter within its remains, or that it became the place where "wild men" lived — meaning men no longer following the teachings of Christ. In fact, this term has been used throughout church history to refer to people who were not of the Christian faith.

One must remember that between that time of the wattle church's construction, which we can conservatively date around A.D. 60, and the time when Phagan and Deruvian visited those who remained at Glastonbury, some 100 years had passed. Although it is possible that during this time two or possibly three generations passed after the original followers of Joseph, it is doubtful that they would have devolved into a group of "wild creatures" and yet still be able to pass on their history to these two saints. It is therefore more likely that this passage simply transmits the message that over time, the original wattle structure began to collapse and became derelict.

If the wattle church built in the first century was in such a state in the second century, one may wonder how it was able to survive into the twelfth century. Further, if there were descendants of Joseph's followers in the area, available to talk to Phagan and Deruvian, where did they live? And did they still maintain a church even though the original church had fallen into disrepair? Although the earliest archeological evidence for another church in the area only goes back as far as the Anglo-Saxon age, remains of churches found both on the Tor and the Beckery suggest that a small, modest site was still being maintained in the vicinity. The Charter of St. Patrick mentions that the two saints were told of a small chapel on the peak of Glastonbury Tor in which they might find written record of their foundation by Joseph of Arimathea. It is possible that although the original wattle church began to crumble, those who came after Joseph's followers merely moved to more reliable and perhaps even more defensible ground atop Glastonbury Tor.

Regardless of one's views on the accuracy of St. Patrick's Charter, it is clear that the wattle church survived. Whether the original church fell into disuse and was repaired or was dutifully maintained for over 1,000 years by the group of devoted monks begun by Joseph of Arimathea, what began as a simple building became the beating heart of Glastonbury as a site of worship. Not only was it seen as the holiest place in England, it was known for being a holy house filled with numerous religious relics and ancient knowledge. This apparent dark period in Glastonbury's history does serve to illustrate one thing: A wattled construction cannot last forever unless it is maintained. Although some wattle-and-daub buildings can last several hundred years, they all eventually fall victim to decay. However, the tradition of the Ealde Chirche states that it stood until it was consumed in the fire of 1184. Whether by neglect or by a loss of faith, the original church built in Joseph's time began to fall apart by the second century, but survived as a sacred relic for much longer.

By modern standards, a building made in such a manner would seem quite flimsy indeed. The walls would have been less than a foot thick, finished in clay, and topped by a roof made of straw. Although little about this description would seem to indicate durability, wattle and daub was the reinforced concrete of its day. The posts needed to be quite sturdy to support the weight of the roof structure, and the branches used to weave between these uprights would not have been thin basketry materials. They would have been closer to small saplings, and were soaked in water to make them more pliable and easier to work without breaking.

The mud-and-straw mixture used to cover the walls likely would have been baked to a hard surface and painted with a whitewash to completely seal it. In addition, thatched roofs are more durable than they would seem. Although they require periodic replacement, modern thatchers boast that their roofs can last as long as ones covered in modern materials. In fact, individuals given the task of removing such structures today have found them to be quite difficult to tear down without the use of heavy machinery.

For the original wattle church to survive into the twelfth century, it would have required many renovations over the centuries — most likely around every 100 years. This would no doubt involve removing old material and patching it with new, replacing the panels of wattle that formed the walls, replacing the roof, and perhaps even performing minor modifications to the original structure. Although this would mean the chapel was not literally the same wattle and the same mud used by Joseph, the structure was the same. One must remember these were not times in which people commonly built with stone. With the Romans came new building techniques, but wattle-and-daub buildings were common throughout their time and even after. Therefore, there would have been no need to completely replace the original structure with one made of stone.

Joseph's church, preserved in largely the same form in which it was built, lived on for centuries. As the land around it changed, the Beckery and the Tor becoming sites of additional churches, the small wattle chapel stood in memory to its revered past. The Romans stayed in Britain a relatively short period of time, around 350 years. After they pulled away from this distant island frontier so far from home, other invaders swept through Britain, making it their land. First came the Jutes from the north in what is now Denmark, the Angles from further south on the Jutland peninsula, and finally the most dreaded invaders to come to Britain: the Saxons from a land east of Gaul, now northern Germany. When the Saxons arrived on Britain's eastern shore, a new legend arose that would also become inextricably intertwined with Glastonbury's already colorful history.

It is thought that the man who would become known as King Arthur was a Romano-Briton soldier and leader who finally picked up the shattered pieces of post–Roman Britain and formed a unified front against the invading Saxons. The victorious battle he waged against the Saxons at a site known as Mons Badonicus, or Badon Hill, halted their westward advance for approxi-

5. Recreating Jospeh's Wattle Church

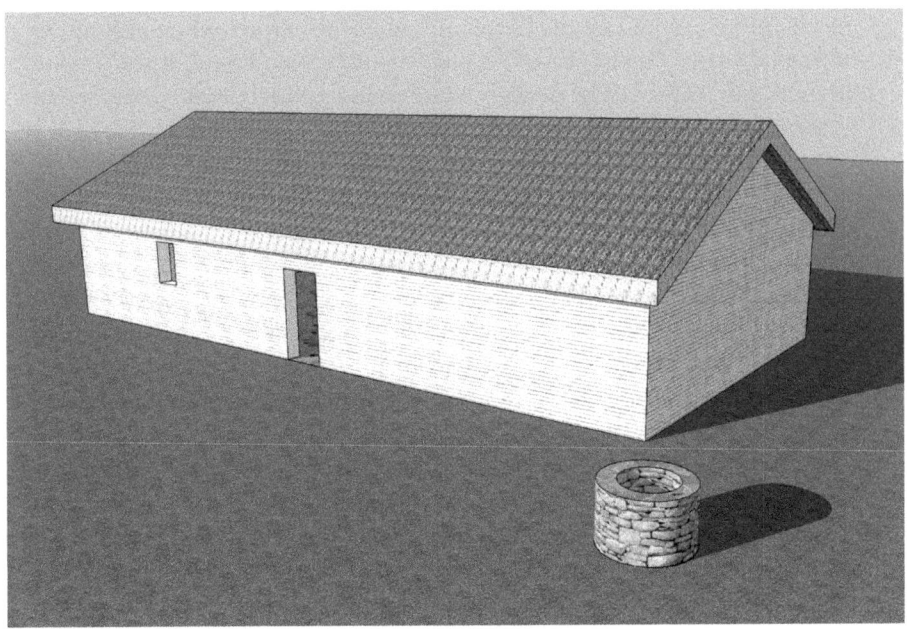

This is a 3D reconstruction of how the original wattle church might have appeared. Built by applying mud over a simple frame of sticks and reeds, this structure would have required frequent maintenance to survive into the twelfth century. Note the ancient wellhead for St. Joseph's Well just beyond the southeastern corner of the chapel (model created by author using Google SketchUp).

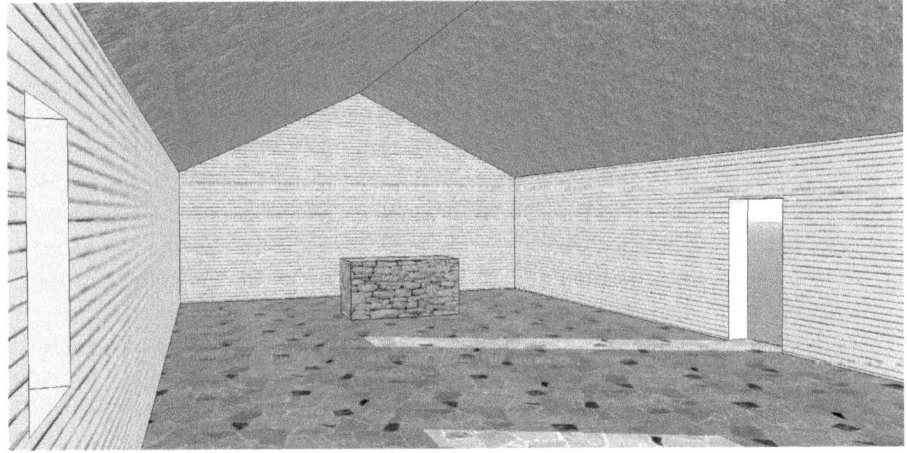

This image shows the interior of the wattle church computer model, giving some idea as to the proportions and inner space of Joseph's original first-century church (model created by author using Google SketchUp).

mately fifty years, leading the Germanic tribe to turn their eyes southward to France for a time. At the end of his reign as king, legend states that his death brought him to the Isle of Avalon, which many associate with Glastonbury. In addition, some say that the king's search for the Holy Grail led him to the area of Bride's Mound on the Beckery, adjacent to Glastonbury Abbey.

If King Arthur was taken to Glastonbury, the heart of the Isle of Avalon, what sight would have greeted his entourage upon their arrival? After journeying across the foggy marshland from the site of his last fateful battle at Camlann, where would they have taken his body? According to the tenth-century Welsh *Annales Cambriae*, this battle was fought in A.D. 537, although Geoffrey of Monmouth in the twelfth century dated Arthur's death to 542. Regardless of the exact date, this information allows us to envision Glastonbury as they would have seen it then.

The now well-known image of Arthur's death is as follows. The king's body was taken aboard a boat and accompanied to Avalon by a small party of women. Crossing the fog-shrouded waters dividing the sacred island from the mortal mainland would have been quite different than driving through the countryside today. It would have been surreal, with impenetrable mist on all sides and silence save the sound of the oars in the water and perhaps the call of the ravens. Once the party reached the island's shore, they would have been stepping into an otherworld of sorts — a place that was in a way set aside from the mortal world. It is most likely that his body would have been first brought into the church to be cleaned and properly prepared for burial. From there it would have been a relative short distance to his final resting place.

In the sixth century, the church at Glastonbury would have looked for the most part just as it looked when it was first built. No other buildings had yet been built around it. The construction of King Ine's stone church was still some 400 years in the future. King Arthur's party would have seen only the small thatched building with a well, standing out a stark white against the grey and green environment. Finally, Arthur's body was placed in a grave just to the south of the chapel in the old cemetery where many of the kings who came before him had been lain. It is reasonable, though unverifiable, to assume that the entryway into the Lady Chapel visible today was made to echo the doorway into the original church. Since the site of Arthur's grave is almost aligned with this door, it could be imagined that his marker once stood near the main walkway leading into the Ealde Chirche, so that his place in the region's history would never be forgotten.

As with any religious relic, there is the desire to protect it, to cover it and safeguard it for future generations. According to tradition, it was the same for Joseph's church of wattles. In the twelfth century, famous Glastonbury Abbey chronicler William of Malmesbury had the unique occasion to visit Glastonbury and see the Old Church before it was destroyed. It is thanks to his writings that we know as much about specific features of this original church as we do today. There are two particulars in his writing that bear closer examination.

The first feature has to do with his description of the Old Church. Malmesbury refers to it as a "wooden" church. Although this could still be in reference to its wickerwork design, it has been a question to scholars whether he meant this or that the church was actually "wooden"—specifically covered in wood, such as wooden planking. Although it is unlikely that the original church made by or for Joseph of Arimathea was made of wooden planking, it is entirely possible that later, when structures were being made with wooden walls, that planking was placed over the wattle structure for additional protection against the ages.

It is also possible that Malmesbury was referring to the work done in the seventh century to cover the Old Church for protection. In A.D. 633, Paulinus, the archbishop of York, came to the abbey and covered it with boards and either installed a lead roof or had the entire structure covered with lead. This was far enough in the past for the twelfth-century historian to think that the original church had been made of wood. However, regardless of Malmesbury's statement that the church was covered in wooden boards, it is clear that Joseph's original wattle church soon became an object of veneration at Glastonbury and was for the most part preserved as it was originally until the fire of 1184.

Now leaving the roof and walls, we come to the second curious aspect of Malmesbury's description of the Old Church. He makes a peculiar statement concerning the nature of the floor which suggests a more intriguing mystery:

> The very floor, inlaid with polished stone, and the sides of the altar, and even the altar itself above and beneath are laden with the [*sic*] multitude of relics. Moreover in the pavement may be remarked on every side stones designedly interlaid in triangles and squares, and figured with lead, under which if I believe some sacred enigma to be contained, I do no injustice to religion [Malmesbury, *Chronicles of the Kings of England*, book 1, ch. 2].

Many who have read this passage assume that the enigmatic design inlaid into the floor was some form of mosaic floor. Certainly the description of the square and triangular stones that formed this design would reinforce this notion. Most commonly, Roman mosaic floors were created using small square and triangular stones of different colors known as *tesserae*.

It has been well documented that Britain is rife with Roman ruins, many of which display evidence of once vibrant mosaic floors. Several examples of this elaborate artwork are on display at the well-known Roman town of Bath to the north of Glastonbury, then known as Aquae Sulis, at the exquisite Roman bath complex. A sign overlooking the green bubbling waters at this popular tourist site makes the statement that not only is Bath Abbey built on the site of an ancient Roman temple, but Roman remains spread out underground for miles in all directions. When one tries to picture Glastonbury's simple first-century chapel, an elaborately ornate mosaic floor seems somewhat out of place; however, there is one possibility that would provide an answer.

When Joseph returned to England, and thus to Glastonbury, he returned to a place he already knew. Having been a metal merchant, he would have traveled here regularly, trading Roman and other goods for the tin and lead ore that came from the surrounding areas. Therefore, one may wonder if the site he chose on which to build his church might have been a place he knew well, perhaps even a place where he once conducted business. It may well be that the simple Ealde Chirche was built on the foundation of a slightly earlier Roman building, perhaps including a tessellated mosaic floor.

If this were the case, one might wonder what sort of mosaic Malmesbury saw during his time at Glastonbury. What kind of "sacred enigma" did the tiny geometric stones laid into the floor create? Most often, Roman mosaic floors either were purely decorative panels with a contrasting border or depicted scenes from mythology. Although such an image would no doubt be beautiful and fascinating, it would not necessarily be described as enigmatic. One style of mosaic design popular among Romans might fit the bill in two ways.

Mithraism was one of the many mystery religions that came from Roman contact with other cultures. Mithras, recognized by his Phrygian cap, was the Roman god who was supposedly born from a rock and is commonly seen emerging from a cave, standing on a large stone, or slaying a bull. Mithraism has been described as a cult, its members often meeting in caves to go through the seven grades of initiation into its mysteries, and was popular in the Roman Empire from the first through the fourth centuries A.D. Examples of Mithraism in Britain can be found in the Mithraeum discovered in the heart of London as well as in small Mithraic temples found along Hadrian's Wall.

What is most interesting about the Mithraic connection to Malmesbury's quote is that a design often used in Roman mosaic floors was what is called the Mithraic zodiac. In this type of zodiac, Mithras is depicted at the center in an eye-shaped halo called a mandorla (the almond-like shape formed at the center of the Vesica Piscis symbol), with the customary symbols of the zodiac displayed in circles around this ellipse. Here we must recall the Melkin's prophecy in which he refers to "13 prophetic spheres." If there were such a Mithraic zodiac present in a mosaic tile floor in the Old Church, Melkin could have been referring to the twelve symbols of the zodiac depicted in spheres, and the image of Mithras in the center mandorla as the thirteenth.

The importance of the zodiac and astronomical alignments was not lost on the ancient inhabitants of southern England. Stonehenge, Avebury, and many other sites demonstrate that the people who created them were avid star watchers. Therefore having a zodiac at Glastonbury, even in a place of Christian worship, should not be surprising. In fact, some would argue there is another zodiac present in the Somerset area. John Dee made the assessment in the sixteenth century that several earthworks, rivers, and other landmarks created a giant zodiac on the Somerset landscape. It was not until 1923 that Katherine Maltwood reestablished this tradition. Although this is not the typical zodiac, some symbols being replaced by ones that most would find rather obscure, the theory is that each symbol is representative of the same constellations and are in the same order.

Although Mithraism was practiced in first century in Judea, it was not a growing movement until around A.D. 80, theoretically *after* Joseph arrived in Britain. Further, archeological data places the arrival of Mithraism in Britain in the second or third centuries. Therefore, it seems unlikely that the floor depicting these enigmatic designs did so in the form of a Mithraic zodiac. It is still possible that this was a mosaic floor, albeit not one based on Mithraism. It might well have been a floor from a Roman structure or was torn down to create the church. Although fragments of Britain's Roman past have been reused in just this manner, it is unfortunately quite unlikely in this case for the simple reason of practicality.

Mosaic floors are almost universally seen as a sign of high status in Roman culture. This would have meant a substantial building, most likely made from stone.

> Earth floors were standard, but higher status rooms were provided with something more impressive. In earlier periods mortar and *opus signinum* floors were generally more frequent than tessellated ones, whilst the reverse was the case after the middle of the second century. Stone-flagged floors are found in areas where suitable paving stone was readily available.... Tessellated pavements, usually executed in red, were widely used in similar contexts to the mortar and tile floors. Durable tessellated pavements were particularly popular in the corridors of later Romano-British villas, where simple mosaic designs were also sometimes used [Perring, p. 127].

From this it would seem that any Roman building Joseph might have encountered would have either been simple as the wattle church was, including a dirt floor, or, if it did have a mosaic floor, would have been a much more impressive building. In that case, the group most likely would have just taken over the use of the building, not torn it down to create a wattle structure over its mosaic floor. In addition, Joseph is said to have come to Britain around A.D. 63. The Romans came to Britain around A.D. 43, only 20 years before. Whatever Roman building might have been at Glastonbury, for which there is scant archeological evidence, still would have been in use when Joseph and his party arrived.

However, it takes less reasoning than this to disprove the idea of William's mystery simply being a mosaic floor. William of Malmesbury was a monk whose years of learning were mostly devoted to histories. It is likely that in his studies he happened across several descriptions of Roman mosaic floors, just as it is quite likely that he had seen Roman mosaic floors in person. In other words, had the floor at Glastonbury been a simple mosaic floor, he most likely would have stated that it was a mosaic floor, possibly commenting on how it might have come to be used there in that manner.

This does not preclude the possibility that someone other than the Romans created a mosaic tile floor inside the Old Church, including within it some secret message. Let us look again at the specific quote written by Malmesbury. He states two things of great importance. First, he describes the floor to be "inlaid with polished stone." This would seem to indicate not a tessellated mosaic floor but a floor made of smooth river rock, of which there must have been an abundance. Second, he states that "on all sides," meaning all around, there were "stones designedly interlaid in triangles and squares, and figured with lead." This is the truly interesting portion of this quote.

Stones designedly (purposely) interlaid in triangles and squares does not refer to designs made from triangular or square stones, as are tesserae, but rather to a design created in the shape of triangles and squares. In addition, these stones which were interlaid (which presumably means placed in between the other floor stones) were said to be "figured with lead." Although it is uncertain what this could mean, it seems to indicate that these special stones that formed the enigmatic design on the floor were made to stand out from the rest through the use of a lead coating or other embellishment.

It is ultimately impossible to know for certain what design William of Malmesbury saw on the floor of the Old Church, who made it, or when. Although one can theorize, all explanations fall short. It does seem fairly certain that it was no mosaic floor created in Roman times, or at another time afterward. However, there is one enigmatic design that comes the closest to fitting Malmesbury's description, although it too has its drawbacks.

If one searches for a symbol which combines lines forming squares and triangles, the spheres mentioned in Melkin's prophecy, and the suggestion of esoteric wisdom, there is one that readily fits the description. The Tree of Life, the dominant symbol in the discipline known as Kabbalah, is formed when ten or eleven spheres called *sephirot* are linked together by lines forming squares and triangles. This shape is said to outline the form of God Himself, or at least serves as an illustration for defining the divine in physical terms.

Although officially the study of Kabbalah can only be traced back to early medieval times, it is said that some form of its study dates back much further.

Several things are interesting with this interpretation. First, the term "sephirot" is similar to a term used in Melkin's prophecy where he says, "Abbadare, powerful in Saphat, most noble of pagans, took his sleep there with 104,000." If this theory is true, the sixth-century Welsh mystic might be referring to someone whose name is similar to "Abbadare" and who is well versed in the study of Kabbalah, or the study of the sephirot. With a little imagination, one is tempted to rotate the two b's into two d's, thus making the name Addadare — which in Welsh would be pronounced "Athadar" — very similar to "Arthur." Wild speculation at best, but it does serve to demonstrate the frustratingly obscure references found in the Prophecy of Melkin (the subject of the next chapter).

Second, the number of spheres mentioned in the prophecy was thirteen instead of ten or eleven. However, the number thirteen does come up in relation to the Tree of Life in Kabbalah. If you take thirteen circles and overlap them in the manner of the Vesica Pisces, you create a pattern with a six-armed star at its center which is known as the Flower of Life — a design that can be seen today in several carvings at Glastonbury. It also has been illustrated that a further elaboration of this design using more circles creates a design with the Tree of Life at the center.

All the teachings, meaning, and practice of Kabbalah aside, the Tree of Life does fit the description of the floor pattern as outlined above, although there are numerous facts which bring this conclusion into doubt. As stated earlier, it is impossible to know exactly what the design was on the floor of the Old Church, nor is it possible to glean from it any meaning. However, it would seem likely that the previous assumption that Malmesbury witnessed a tessellated mosaic floor is in error. At the very least, the matter requires further study.

Whatever else we might learn from Melkin's writing, he also alleges that he outlined Joseph's burial site. Although the wording is cryptic at best, it seems that Joseph's grave was located near the southern corner of the Old Church. Of course there are two southern corners of the structure, but for reasons I shall go into later, it is presumed to have been near the southeastern corner.

This presents a certain very specific set of circumstances. The well just off the southeast corner of the modern Lady Chapel was present during Joseph's time, so his burial needed to be well clear of that. This leaves the possibilities of his being buried inside the Old Church, just to the east of it, or further south of the well in the ancient cemetery.

The site to the south of the well would at first seem most likely, placing it in the ancient cemetery in which rest the honored dead of the area, both pagan and Christian. This location seems unlikely, however, simply because Melkin's description indicates a placement near the corner. Although a grave could be placed relatively close to the wattle church, the presence of the well would prevent it from being by the corner or indeed by the south wall at all. In this regard, such a location for Joseph's grave could be more easily described in a number of other ways. Therefore, a burial near the east end of the church would seem much more likely.

When investigating the east wall of the wattle church as the location for Joseph's burial, it comes down to a simple question of "inside or out." Looking first inside, one must consider that it was common for a person of high standing, such as a bishop or an abbot, to be buried within the church with which he was associated. In fact, when the crypt area of the Lady Chapel was cleared out over a century ago, several coffins containing the remains of what were presumed to be medieval monks were found. This assessment of Melkin's directions would seem most likely; however, it could be argued that since Joseph was raised as a traditional first-century Jew, he would not have wanted to defile the confines of the church with his own remains.

During the fifteenth century when the crypt became the site of St. Joseph's veneration, it was said that the elaborate tomb in which his relics were placed stood very near the location where the body first lay — just past the well in what had been an underground Norman chapel. This area of the crypt, now called St. Joseph's Chapel, is well outside what is claimed to be the eastern boundary of the Old Church. Therefore it is possible that the present site of the St. Joseph Chapel in the crypt is the very site where Joseph's body was originally buried. Though tantalizing, this description still doesn't make clear whether Joseph was buried inside or outside the wattle church.

For this investigation regarding the historical validity of the Joseph legend at Glastonbury, it becomes necessary to adopt a mindset akin to one used in a murder investigation. One must establish the key players. In our attempt to prove that this legend had at its heart a seed of truth, the two main points of interest are clear: Joseph of Arimathea and the wattle church. Prove those two exist at the same time in the same place, and one opens the door leading toward historical credibility. It has been established that a wattle church once existed at Glastonbury Abbey. It has been demonstrated that if created in the first century, it could have lasted until the twelfth century. However, this is not enough. If the legend of Joseph at Glastonbury is to be considered a historical possibility, we need to have some kind of physical proof. That would seem a tall order at first glance; however, it is possible. First we will delve deeper into the mysterious character of Melkin and see if he can be considered a credible source. With a better understanding of the man, we may then draw a link between his prophetic text and a damaged fifteenth-century stone coffin thought to have once contained the mortal remains of Joseph of Arimathea. When this all-important connection is established, it will finally be possible to bridge the gap between legend and history.

Chapter 6

The Prophecy of Melkin

In any investigation, there comes a time that can best be described as the Eureka moment — that time when you know you finally have an answer, or at least a big piece of the puzzle. At that moment, you feel you can stand proud knowing you are now where few others have been. It is that moment when you feel what it must have been like for Howard Carter to peer through the hole in the plaster door covering Tutankhamen's tomb and when asked if he could see anything, utter the words, "Yes, wonderful things!" Of course, the next step is to verify that you have actually made the caliber of discovery you think you have, allowing you to progress to even more incredible discoveries or realize it isn't what you thought. After my visit to Glastonbury, I came back home feeling I had many such answers. One of these answers came quite unexpectedly in St. John's Parish Church while taking pictures of the stone tomb traditionally held to be that of Joseph of Arimathea. Having but a short time to study this building and its treasures, I snapped several pictures of the tomb and shot several minutes of video tape, paying special attention to the size, condition, and carvings of this unique object. Running short on time, I wrapped up my studies and turned back toward the central aisle.

There I encountered two similar tombs with black marble covers with shallow indentations carved into them, each in the shape of a figure standing atop a rectangular base. It was not until we returned home that I remembered seeing several brass plaques in the Abbey Museum from which visitors could make rubbings as souvenirs. It occurred to me that these plaques, which were figures of knights and other importantly dressed characters, were nearly as thick as the indented carvings were deep. I called the abbey to inquire as to the nature of these plaques and was told that in fact they had come from St. John's some years prior, but little else was known about them. Eureka — I had made my discovery!

I began making associations among accounts of relics from Glastonbury Abbey such as King Arthur's lead cross ending up in the vestry at St. John's

6. The Prophecy of Melkin

for safekeeping, and the black marble tomb that once contained the remains of King Arthur and his queen, Guinevere. Considering the obvious pride of place near the altar and the fact that one carving was in the shape of a man wearing a short tunic and the other appeared to be a lady in a long gown covering her feet, I began to wonder if their remains had been secreted away to a hiding place right across the street. What else could it be? Fortunately for me, I waited to call the press conference until I had contacted several people in Glastonbury again regarding these tombs. It was then that I made an informative if disappointing discovery. These were simply the tombs of two fifteenth-century cloth merchants who had apparently left some property to the church upon their deaths, hence receiving elaborate burials and a place of honor in the church. In addition, the brass plaques in the museum were replicas that had been purchased by St. John's in years past for the same purpose as they served in the Abbey Museum.

Unfortunately, investigating the historical aspects of a legend such as the Holy Grail is rife with such dead ends. However, you are occasionally fortunate enough to happen across a truly valuable discovery. Such is the case with a few enigmatic lines purportedly written by a Welsh soothsayer some time back in the sixth century. Although there are many translations of the difficult Latin, the basic text of this prophesy always conveys the same message:

> Avalon's island with avidity, claiming the death of pagans, more than all the world beside, for the entombment of them all, honored by chanting spheres of prophecy; and for all time to come adorned shall it be by them that praise the Highest. Abbadare, mighty in Saphat, noblest of pagans, with countless thousands there hath fallen on sleep. Amid these Joseph in marble, of Arimathea by name, hath found perpetual sleep: and he lies on a two-forked line next the south corner of an oratory fashioned of wattles for the adoring of a mighty Virgin by the aforesaid sphere-betokened dwellers in that place, thirteen in all. For Joseph hath with him in his sarcophagus, two cruets, white and silver, filled with the blood and sweat of the Prophet Jesus. When his sarcophagus shall be found entire, intact in time to come, it shall be seen and shall be open unto all the world: thenceforth nor water nor the dew of heaven shall fail the dwellers in that ancient isle. For a long while before the day of judgement in Jehosaphat open shall these things be and declared to living men.

Although much of its meaning is difficult to ascertain, one portion of the prophecy stands out. Here for the first time, the description and location of Joseph of Arimathea's burial site are outlined in detail. This description by a Welsh bard named Melkin or Maelgwn was supposedly written and housed at Glastonbury Abbey and survived, at least in part, until the dissolution of the abbey in the sixteenth century.

Many attempts have been made to decipher this text's meaning, but the interpretation depends on how literally the translation is performed. Some of the most difficult-to-understand translations have come from trying to make meaning out of each word, while some of the more fluid translations seek to translate it as full sentences or thoughts. Some liberties have to be taken as well, particularly in parts where no clear meaning is apparent such as the passages dealing with the spheres of wisdom or prophecy. Imagine the difficulty someone unfamiliar with the English language might have fully and suitably translating the phrase "crystal ball." Much of the implied meaning would be lost if the object were described as a "circular stone thing you can see through."

The specific translation aside, some of the most basic aspects of its meaning can be interpreted as being a simple description of the area. If we are to take "Avalon" as being Glastonbury, the first part is simply describing the church's history as a place where the region's honored dead have been laid to rest. The Old Cemetery to the south of the Lady Chapel is well known as being a place where many truly ancient burials have been excavated. If you take the tone of the passage regarding "Abbadare, mighty in Saphat" as simply naming one particular "noble pagan" who has been buried with "countless thousands" of others, it is a simple continuation of this theme.

The meaning of the "chanting spheres of prophecy" has been debated for many years. One theory is that it refers to the stars, planets, or other heavenly bodies on which the early pagan inhabitants of the area put some special, sacred meaning. Another theory is that some sacred stones or maybe even something akin to crystal balls were used in some form of ritual honoring the pagan ancestors. I have even provided the theory that there is some link between the mysterious patterns William of Malmesbury found in the floor in the Ealde Cirche and the "spheres of prophecy" from the text, specifically in the form of a Kabbalist Tree of Life. Although it tends to shed light on the chanting spheres and the use of the phrase "powerful in Saphat," this theory does nothing to illuminate who Abbadare might be. For this reason, we will concentrate on the less contentious, slightly more straightforward second half of the text.

Albeit somewhat simpler to understand, the meaning can change dramatically depending on how you take the exact meaning of the phrases. Take for example the mere mention of Joseph of Arimathea. The writer has been talking about the thousands of pagan dead buried in the cemetery, and then he says, "Among these, Joseph of Arimathea has taken his sleep." Does this mean the writer sees Joseph as a pagan, or that he merely found his rest among pagans? Further, the Latin phrase *"linea bifurcata"* could mean several things. Most commonly it is taken to mean a forked, or bifurcated line, from which it is nearly impossible to take any real meaning. This could mean "on a split or forked line" or "where two lines cross," and has even been thought to refer to a split-fronted garment, much like a modern button-down shirt.

6. The Prophecy of Melkin

The promise of eternal moisture is another interesting insertion into this already curious text, stating that the inhabitants of this place shall never be lacking in water or the dew of heaven. Considering the rainy climate of the Somerset region, this may be considered by some more a curse than a blessing, akin to promising someone who lives in the desert a bright, sun-shiny day. It is made all the more curious when one considers that at the time of Melkin, the lands around Glastonbury were marshland, with dry land only a distant sight. It may tempt the modern reader to consider the possibility that Glastonbury's famously rainy climate is a result of this 1,500-year-old promise.

Finally, the description of Joseph's tomb and its contents are tantalizing. Several stone-lined burials have been excavated in Glastonbury's Old Cemetery, making it possible that Joseph's body was laid into a grave lined in rough marble. Although one might picture Joseph lying in a fine marble crypt, this sort of ornamented burial box would not have been at all common during this time. In fact the mention of Joseph being buried in a marble tomb only appears in a few versions, and is likely a mistranslation of "marmore." In fact if Joseph was indeed a lead and tin merchant, one would expect him to be buried in the sort of lead coffin that was common from Roman times through the Middle Ages.

Most edifying of all, however, must be the mention of the two cruets of blood and sweat belonging to the prophet Jesus. As much as the idea of a single grail cup might be to us today, any visitor to the area will be greeted by an image of Joseph holding two small containers in his hands, usually not much larger than salt and pepper shakers. What can be deduced from the description that these vessels were "white and silver"? While some depictions have been of just that, one white and one silver vial, it is also possible that they were white in color with silver ornamentation, demonstrating that these were vessels of the finest quality or the highest reverence.

The text is cryptic at best — chanting spheres of prophecy, Abbadare, Saphat, etc., but it seems fairly straightforward in conveying the idea that Joseph of Arimathea is buried somewhere near the wattle church (which is all that stood in the sixth century), and apparently with some kind of relics from the time of Jesus. If this odd little text is to be believed, here is also the first mention of the Holy Grail, though not in the traditional form to which we have become accustomed. One may ask, if this text is known to exist, and sheds such obvious light on the subject of Joseph and the Grail at Glastonbury, why is it all still a mystery?

The Prophesy of Melkin was incorporated into a mid-fourteenth-century book written by John of Glastonbury called *Chronicle of Glastonbury Abbey*. While this does not preclude the possibility that Melkin did in fact write about Joseph in the sixth century, the problem comes in the person of John of Glastonbury. Many scholars refuse to acknowledge John's *Chronicle* as anything but a historical fiction. It seems clear that John did enjoy intertwining aspects of the elaborate legends that had built up around the Grail, Joseph of Arimathea, and King Arthur at Glastonbury, but as his goal was to write a history, it must not be completely overlooked, nor should any reference from it be thrown out simply due to a scholarly distaste for its author. In fact these and additional writings associated with Melkin were mentioned by a more reliable writer named John Leland two centuries later.

Who was this mysterious bard who could in some ways be described as the first Grail romancer? Very little is known about Melkin, and since most scholars refuse to even entertain the notion that he is anything but pure fiction, little else has been found. The only lead we are given is that he was "before Merlin." Some have claimed that he was none other than the Welsh warlord-turned-monk Maglocunus. There is still another potential candidate known as Melkin of Avalon. Although it is unlikely the identity of Melkin will ever be completely proven, it is possible to shed a little light on the possibilities.

As this bard was allegedly writing from Glastonbury in the sixth century, let us first investigate the candidate known as Melkin of Avalon. As we have seen, Glastonbury has been identified with Avalon for centuries. In fact when one considers that Avalon has been called variously the Isle of Glass, the Isle of Apples, and has been described as a sacred island hidden by dark, misty waters, the once-island of Glastonbury would have fit the description quite well. Therefore, what more appropriate candidate for our Welsh mystery writer than Melkin of Avalon?

What little information can be found regarding Melkin of Avalon serves to prove that this is indeed our writer. Unfortunately, that's all it tells us. It would seem that this is simply another name given to the person who wrote the prophecy regarding Joseph being buried at Glastonbury. Some have said that the Melkin of Avalon was a different individual who lived earlier than the sixth century; however, this likely derives from the description that Melkin was "before Merlin."

If Arthur's time ended with his death in 537, as dictated by the *Annales*, many assume this would place Melkin in the previous century. While it is certainly possible, the Melkin responsible for this text is most often said to be contemporary with Arthur, even reaching his height after Arthur's death. Other sources have claimed that Melkin went on to write even more texts pertaining to the life and times of King Arthur, these being incorporated later into Arthurian literature. Melkin of Avalon has also been linked to an individual known as Melkin of Llandaff, supporting the tradition that he was from Wales. However, it would seem more likely that this name belongs to another of our candidates for Melkin the Bard of Avalon.

6. The Prophecy of Melkin

Maglocunus, whose formal name is Maelgwn ap Cadwallon, has been called several different names in historic texts, such as Maelgwn Hir (the Tall), Maelgwn Gwynedd or the Dragon of Anglesley (which was where the seat of his kingdom in Gwynedd was located), and Maelgwyn of Llandaaf (since Maglocunus was an early supporter of the Diocese of Llandaff). History records Maglocunus as a vicious warlord who killed his own wife and nephew so that he could take his nephew's wife for his own. According to a legend made famous by fairy tales, it would seem that this was not the only time Maelgwn experienced marital strife. Consider the legend of the fish and the ring.

As the story goes, Maelgwn was to be wed to a beautiful princess named Nesta from another kingdom. For this purpose, he gave the princess a ring that had been worn by all the past queens of Gwynedd. Soon after they were married, the queen was swimming in the River Elwy and somehow lost the ring. Knowing Maelgwn would be furious, she consulted the wise St. Asaph, bishop of Llanelwy. At a dinner hosted by the bishop, he explained to Maelgwn what had happened. In his true warrior style, he immediately became incensed, accusing the queen of giving the ring to a previous lover. Finally able to calm the situation, St. Asaph and the troubled couple sat down to their meal. Before they began, they together said a prayer that the ring might be found. When the king cut into his dinner, a fresh fish caught from the river Elwy, he discovered inside the very ring that was lost.

With all this in mind, it would seem fairly difficult to picture this Maelgwn as the writer of Melkin's prophesy. However, it is important to remember that what we know of such events and people of historical importance usually came from early church historians. Needless to say, this is not the sort of character these church writers would want to elevate in the minds of their readers. However, as it is war and war-makers who most often form the high points of any history lesson, it is possible this description does not provide the full picture. In his translation of John of Glastonbury's *Chronicles of Glastonbury Abbey*, James Carley makes the assertion that the sixth-century Welsh war chief Maglocunus would be the most likely historical person matching the description of John's prophetic writer Melkin:

> Both Bale and Pits thought that Melkin flourished in the mid-sixth century, that is, roughly at the end of the Arthurian period. There was another figure of considerable fame in the Middle Ages who also lived at this time: the Welsh king, Maelgwn of Gwynedd, who died in 547 according to the *Annales Cambriae*. Maelgwn was known as a powerful and tyrannical king but also as a bard and prophet. One very obvious corruption of his name would be Melkin, and this, I suggest, is possibly the ultimate origin of the name as it is found in the Glastonbury prophesy [Carley, *Chronicle*, p. lvi].

As is the case with any person of note from this time period, little is known regarding Maelgwn's birth, although it has been conjectured to have been as early as A.D. 480. However, the date of his death is confirmed as A.D. 547, when he fell victim to a "great mortality" that some have suggested was the Yellow Plague. Although there is no evidence his kingdom ever extended beyond that of his native Gwynedd, several historical accounts suggest he was seen as an authority figure and something of a leader throughout Wales.

The only clear description of Maelgwn is given by Gildas in his *De Excidio et Conquestu Britanniae*, in which any number of evils are ascribed to him, most of which could best be described as sins of lust or the desire for power. It would seem that at least some of his unfavorable deeds were committed in his youth. Gildas says that Maelgwn gave up his life of war and power to become a monk for a time but later went back to his previous ways.

Whatever the reason for Maelgwn's turning away from his life as a monk, it would seem it did have an impact on him. It is said that he was a keen supporter of Christianity throughout Wales, even outside of his own kingdom. While developing his religious life, he studied at Llantwit Major, a fifth-century monastery founded by St. Illtud, which has been called Europe's oldest university. Maelgwn's detractor Gildas studied there as well, purportedly surpassing all other students in piety. Although there is no direct evidence that Gildas met Maelgwn there, the time frames involved make this a distinct possibility.

The exact cause of Gildas's distaste for Maelgwn is unclear, but what can be taken from his writings regarding Maelgwn is that Gildas bore him and those near him no respect. Gildas likened Maelgwn and the other kings of the region to the beasts of the Apocalypse, with Maelgwn as the dragon at their head. Gildas also leveled charges of moral depravity and mental corruption against him, despite what would otherwise be indicated by his generosity toward developing churches throughout Wales. Some have gone so far as to call the degree of ire that Gildas obviously displayed for Maelgwn suspicious.

Something can be learned of these accusations, however, especially with relation to Maelgwn as a candidate for Melkin of Avalon. Gildas stated that Maelgwn was for a time a monk and studied Christian teaching and the history of the church fathers for some time while at Llanwit Major. Despite what Gildas suggests to be a split with his newly found faith, he continued to support the church and its growth in Wales. This presents a picture of a unique individual who may prove to be the perfect candidate for the mystery writer that we have been seeking. It is possible that, after his time learning about Christianity, he found that what he truly had no liking for was monastic life and the rigorous, structured doctrine put down by the established church.

Consider the fact that before he became a monk, he was a pagan warlord.

Then for some reason he adopted the quiet, contemplative life of a monk only to abandon this, according to Gildas, for his previous ways. Most have considered this to mean that he returned to what Gildas would have considered a life of sin — lust, greed, bloodthirsty warring, etc. However, it is possible that the previous ways to which Gildas referred simply meant to a previous religion, or otherwise a religion that did not meet with Gildas's approval. Perhaps Gildas did not turn away from Christianity as much as he turned away from the church.

With this in mind, let us return to Melkin's prophecy. Several aspects of the curious text stand out. It seems to venerate the pagan kings and dead of old, but makes special note of the burial of Joseph of Arimathea, who has been called Britain's first saint and Christian leader. It also uses a curious word to describe Jesus, calling Him a "prophet." Typically the term "prophet" is used to describe either a holy man from the Old Testament in the Bible or conversely a pagan soothsayer, almost in the same way Melkin himself is described.

From this we see an image of the writer as someone who perhaps does not feel completely comfortable with Christianity but has a great deal of respect for the faith as well as a familiarity with some of its early leaders. This description would be a perfect match for Maelgwn — a Celtic Christian, a poet and a bard, and a wealthy king who helped Christianity flourish throughout a region over which he held some degree of power. Even the strange wording that has stumped so many attempting to decipher the prophecy may have been the result of someone not entirely proficient with Latin and simply doing his best, knowing that histories were most often written in this, the language of the scholars.

Maglocunus was without question an intriguing historical figure, both in history and in our investigation of Joseph of Arimathea and the Holy Grail. However, taking into account the warlike past and tales of dreadful deeds committed by this man, it is difficult at best to see him as a Christian benefactor and historian. To feel better about finally calling him our Melkin the Bard, we will need something more than a short time as a monk and contrite retiring years. There needs to be some firm link between Maelgwn and Glastonbury leading from his indoctrination into the church to a familiarity with distant Somerset. Fortunately this very link can be found in an ancient monastery in southern Wales.

Llantwit Major is a town in Glamorganshire, sitting approximately twelve miles across the Bristol Channel from Somerset in Britain. Known as Llanilltud Fawr in its native Welsh, this peculiar sounding name is important in this course of research. Literally translated, "Llanilltud Fawr" means "The Great Church of Illtud." However, it is not the church that makes this place noteworthy, it is rather the school that was founded by its monastery. The Cor Tewdws, or College of Theodosius, was allegedly built prior to the fifth century and is called the "oldest college in the world." The history of the university at Llantwit Major reads like a "who's who" of post–Roman and medieval scholars.

Among its celebrated pupils are names such as Gildas the Wise, who is known for his texts about the early history of Britain, and St. Patrick who, after being captured by Irish pirates, escaped slavery to bring Christianity back with him to Ireland, becoming the country's patron saint. St. David also attended the school at Llantwit Major and later donated the famed sapphire altar to Glastonbury Abbey, the chief stone of which is now allegedly incorporated into the British Crown Jewels. Saints Simon of Dol and Paulinus Aurelianus, also attendees, were both born in Wales and later traveled to Brittany to become two of the region's founders. One of the more colorful individuals from British history who attended the ancient school was Pelagius, whose later doctrine ran him afoul of the orthodox Roman Catholic Church. This longstanding tradition of scholarship in Wales is largely due to Bishop Germanus and his crusade against Pelagius.

Llanilltud boasts one other student that has become a name of some interest: Maelgwn Gwynedd. According to the traditions that surround the ancient institution, the dreadful tyrant and bloodthirsty warlord of Welsh history had a more scholarly side as well. It has been stated that, for a time, he gave up his carnal life in favor of a more intellectual and spiritually enriching one later in life. It would seem that in this intriguing Welsh township we have found the place where Maelgwn, the most likely candidate for our historical Melkin the Bard, spent his all too brief years as a monk studying the Word of God and the history of the church.

The school was rebuilt in 508 following a fire in the middle of the previous century that completely destroyed the original structure. This fire was started during an attack by the very same Irish raiders that allegedly kidnapped the young Saint Patrick, carrying him away to Ireland where he would spend the next several years a slave. According to the accepted historical account, the monastery and school were founded by Bishop Germanus of Auxerre during his crusade to stamp out the Pelagian heresy in Britain. In so doing, he left the care of the resurrected facility to his follower and purported student, Illtud, who gave the church and school its name. In addition to Llantwit Major, Llanilltud Fawr, and Cor Tewdws, this site also seemed to have another name associated with it: Caer Worgorn.

In 1893, antiquarian and fellow of the Royal Historical Society Alfred C. Fryer published a very in-depth book regarding the history and legends of Llantwit Major, which remained a center for learning until it met with the same fate as Glastonbury in the sixteenth-century Dissolution. As with any ancient site, the most difficult and in many ways most intriguing questions surround its origins. Though firmly planted in history in the early sixth century, this place apparently had its birth some time before. The following is a particularly interesting passage from Fryer's book regarding this genesis story:

> Welsh chronicles, which are, doubtless, compilations of earlier traditions, tell us that long before the days of Illtyd a colony of Christians was settled at Caer Worgorn. In "Achan y Saint" we find the following: "It was the glory of the Emperor Theodosius, in conjunction with Cystennyn Llydau, surnamed the Blessed, to have first founded the College of Illtyd, which was regulated by Balerus, a man from Rome; and Padrig, the son of Mawon, was the first principal of it before he was carried away captive by the Irishmen." The emperor must have been Theodosius II, for neither Theodosius the Elder nor Theodosius the Great were contemporary with Cystennyn Llydaw. It is unfortunate that we cannot accept the tradition that St. Patrick was connected with Cor Tewdws, for his "Confession" states that he was only sixteen years old when he was made a captive, and so he was too young to be principal of a college [Fryer, pp. 14–15].

Although the traditional dating for Theodosius II does not match, the footnotes to this passage state that "Cystennyn Llydaw" was none other than the first Christian Roman emperor, Constantine, also called Constantine of Armorica, father of Flavius Constans, who was allegedly brother to Ambrosius Aurelianus and Uther Pendragon from Arthurian lore.

The above passage suggests not only that Llantwit Major was founded much earlier than 508 when Illtud was installed at its head, but also that there existed a colony of Christianized Britons at that location prior to the monastery's creation. Since this is an investigation of Joseph of Arimathea in Britain, this idea certainly should come as no surprise. However, according to Welsh tradition, someone with another name is given credit for bringing the Christian faith to these distant shores. A character of Celtic mythology named Bron is thought to be responsible for bring Christianity from Rome to Britain. The legend states that after being held captive in Rome for seven years with his son Caradawc, more commonly known as Caractacus, the pair returned to their native Wales to spread Christianity through this previously pagan land. Although this legend is far from conclusive and is seen as little more than a local fable, it does provide a link back to our study of Joseph of Arimathea.

In Fryer's book about the monastic school founded at Llantwit Major, he makes the following statement regarding its original foundation long before the time of St. Illtud in the sixth century:

> In the "Genealogy of Iestn ab Gwrgan" we read that Eurgain, daughter of Caradog (Caractacus), founded a school for twelve saints "near the place

now called Llantwit." St. Ilid at first ordered its policy, and its members went out into different parts of the country to extend the influence of the Church. In the "Genealogy of the Saints" Ilid is mentioned as a "man of Israel," and is said to have accompanied Bran on his return to his native land. Little is known of Ilid. The church of Llanilid is dedicated to him, and he is said to have returned to the Isle of Avallon, where he died and was buried (Fryer, pp. 15–16).

This passage provides a wealth of relevant information for our study. First, let us begin with a brief investigation of Caradog, or Caractacus. Mentioned previously in a discussion about Bron the Blessed, Caractacus was supposedly something of a Briton freedom-fighter during the Roman invasion. Leading his people to many victories in battle, he was eventually captured and sent to Rome for trial.

According to legend, he was sentenced to death, but an impassioned speech to Emperor Claudius (recorded by the Roman historian Tacitus) instead resulted in a period of imprisonment. He has already been linked to Christianized Britain through his father and fellow captive, Bron. However, there is some indication that he may have had some association with Glastonbury as well. Some evidence suggests that the historical Caractacus served as Geoffrey of Monmouth's inspiration for the more well-known character of Arviragus—the pagan British king who originally granted Joseph of Arimathea and his twelve companions their twelve hides of land upon which the church at Glastonbury was built. However, Caractacus is not the only link between the ancient university in Wales and Glastonbury's legendary past. In fact, he is not even the strongest link. It was said that his father Bron (Bran) had a mysterious traveling companion named Ilid who seems to be very closely tied to Glastonbury.

First let us differentiate between St. Illtud/Illtyd and St. Illid/Ilid. Llantwit Major is known for the monastic college governed over by St. Illtud, mentor to Gildas and Maelgwn, who was installed by Bishop Germanus in the early sixth century following the destructive fire approximately 50 years prior. St. Illid came some time before St. Illtud, apparently in the first century A.D. Accompanied by Bron and possibly by his son Caractacus, Illid would have been a visitor to Britain long before the establishment of the Roman Church to which Germanus, Illtud, and Gildas belonged. Who was this mysterious figure? The citation above provides plenty of answers.

The first important point is that "Eurgain, daughter of Caradog (Caractacus), founded a school for twelve saints 'near the place now called Llantwit'" (Fryer, p. 15). From this we can deduce that the granddaughter of Bron the Blessed, three generations removed, founded the school of Llantwit Major. Specifically, it is said that this school was founded for twelve saints, although the exact meaning of this is uncertain. The school either began in the honor of these twelve saints or was founded at their order. The next line would seem to indicate the latter: "St. Ilid at first ordered its policy, and its members went out into different parts of the country to extend the influence of the Church" (Fryer, pp. 15–16). Here St. Ilid seems to be something of an administrator, or otherwise one who in some way affects the administration of the school. It also sounds as if those who studied at this university were expected to take their knowledge and minister to the native people throughout Britain.

The most intriguing portion of this quote comes in the second half, taken from the "Genealogy of the Saints": "Ilid is mentioned as a 'man of Israel'" (p. 16). This alone is a very interesting statement. All of the other names mentioned in relation to Llantwit Major were native to Wales, or at least to Britain. Here we are told that St. Illid came from the distant land of Israel, a Roman province during the first century. Finally, we reach the most telling aspect of St. Illid's identity: "He is said to have returned to the Isle of Avallon, where he died and was buried" (p. 16). Now the identity of St. Illid seems quite clear. Illid was a man from first century Israel who had authority enough in the early British church to administer its policies, who returned to the Isle of Avalon (Glastonbury), where he died and was buried, and who was surely one of the twelve saints for whom Eurgain founded the monastic school at Llantwit Major. St. Illid was St. Joseph of Arimathea.

This is not a new association. It has been postulated that St. Illid and Joseph were one in the same by several scholars over the years. Of course this introduces the question of which came first, Glastonbury or Llantwit Major. Although there is certainly nothing that would prevent Joseph from founding a school in Wales before settling in Glastonbury, two factors make this less likely. It was said that Bron's granddaughter founded the school at Llantwit Major, making it many years after Joseph's alleged appearance on British soil. In addition, the citation above states, "he is said to have *returned* to the Isle of Avallon" (emphasis mine). This would indicate that Illid either went to the Isle of Avalon first or was living there shortly before he died and was buried there.

It could be argued that St. Illid might have been simply one of Joseph's companions instead of Joseph himself, but one specific aspect of these accounts indicates otherwise. Recall that "in the 'Genealogy of the Saints' Ilid is mentioned as a 'man of Israel,' and is said to have accompanied Bran on his return to his native land." Unfortunately, the second half of this statement is a poorly constructed sentence with its subject being vague. However, the application of a little deductive reasoning can tell us more. Since it would appear Joseph of Arimathea left Israel never to return, we must assume that it was Bron who was returning to his native land with Joseph playing the role of the passenger. Of course this assumes, possibly erroneously, that the voyage in question was between Israel, where Joseph originated, and Bron's native Wales.

Joseph and Bron have long been tied together in Arthurian and Grail literature. Robert de Boron stated that Bron was married to Joseph's daughter, Enygeus. Bron had a son named Alain — a name well known to anyone familiar with the story of the first Grail hero, Perceval. During Perceval's search for the Grail he learns of his lineage, beginning with his father Alain, leading back to Joseph of Arimathea, even including King Arthur himself as a distant relation. It has been assumed that Bron was one of the many who accompanied Joseph from Israel to Britain, although this may not have been the case. It is also possible that Bron indeed married Joseph's daughter, but only after they met in Britain.

Traditionally, Bron/Bran is seen as a Celtic deity — born a god, but later losing his immortality by becoming either purely mortal or trapped between life and death. He was considered to be a powerful protector of Britain despite his fallen state. According to tradition, his head was cut from his body upon his death and was buried under the White Tower in London, facing toward France to keep the French from attacking. Later his head was dug up by King Arthur and either turned away across the sea or removed entirely. Amid great uproar, Arthur stated that Britain would be defended by his might alone.

Bron's supernatural nature is reflected in Grail myth as well. The enigmatic character of the Fisher King, the wounded keeper of the Grail, lingering between life and death, is thought to be taken from the story of Bron. In the Celtic version of his tale, he possessed a cauldron of plenty by which the wounded could be healed. In addition, he was supposedly wounded in the foot by a poisoned spear, much like the lance wound in the thigh or leg from which the Fisher King traditionally suffered. One Grail text goes so far as to describe how Bron might have received the name of "Fisher King." In this story, Joseph tells his companion Bron to wade into the water and retrieve a fish for his company, later setting a table for Joseph and his followers from which the famed Round Table of King Arthur would be created.

In addition to the cauldron and spear wound, the story of the Grail has something more important in common with the Celtic version of Bron's story. In the story called *Peredur* as it is found in the Welsh *Mabinogion*, the Grail hero completes his quest not by finding a sacred chalice but by retrieving a severed head kept in a pool of blood in a golden platter. This head is the sacred talisman as described above intended to ward off invasion from France. The Holy Grail in *Peredur* is the sacred head of Bran the Blessed. The obvious similarities between *Peredur* and Chrétien de Troyes' *Conte del Graal* have led most scholars to conclude that the French poet simply learned of the story and altered it to suit the Christian, courtly audience for which he was writing in the twelfth century. However, as we have already seen, such conclusions are not always as certain as they claim to be.

There is another story relating to Bron that could actually corroborate the story of St. Illid and Joseph of Arimathea. First written in the early eighth century from older oral traditions, the Irish story known as the Voyage of Bron tells of a crew of twenty-seven men who set sail from Ireland and are coaxed to a magical island by a mystical woman holding a fruiting branch of an apple tree. When the boats near the island, called the Island of Women, the woman calls to the boats, beckoning them to come ashore. When she receives no response, she throws a ball of string to Bron. When he catches it, he finds it is stuck to his hand, and the woman simply pulls the boat in. The company find that the island is inhabited solely by beautiful young women who are more than happy to welcome the weary travelers.

Reminiscent of Homer's *Odyssey*, the crew remain on the island for what seems like one year, but over time they wish to return to their homes. The leader of the women warns Bron that the men will never be able to return to their native Ireland. She says they will be able to draw near to it and speak to the people on the shore, but they must never set foot there again. Bron promises to simply visit their home for a time and return. When the crew comes near to the Irish shore, one among them leaps from the ship and runs up the surf only to turn to dust. Bron yells out to his countrymen and tells them his name. A man on the strand tells him that the name of Bron features in some of their oldest stories. Realizing they have been gone for much longer than one year, Bron tells their story to the men gathered on the beach. Once his story has been passed on, they turn their ships back out to sea and are never seen again.

Called a classic tale of a voyage to the underworld, the Voyage of Bron is thought to be a derivative of the Welsh Bron tradition, told from the Irish perspective. If this is the case, let us reconsider the statement that St. Illid "accompanied Bran on his return to his native land." If we realize this story may be a fantasized version of a simpler story, it becomes possible that the Isle of Women, the island of the Underworld, may have been Glastonbury, which would have been an island amid misty marshes at that time.

This possibility is all the more reasonable when one remembers that it was a branch from an apple tree that the maiden used to signal the ships. As well as being called Ynis Witrin and Avalon, Glastonbury has also been called Apolonia, or the Isle of Apples, due to the plentiful apple groves growing around the base of Glastonbury Tor. Of course the early monastic community at Glastonbury certainly would not seem to match the "land of beautiful women" the story mentions, but we must remember that this is simply an image of an earthy paradise. In that sense, the island of the underworld may have simply been a sacred island seen as the underworld, or Annwn, by the Celtic Britons.

Therefore if we replace Ireland with Wales and the Isle of Women with Glastonbury, we can see a possible connection with the above quote. It is possible that the Voyage of Bron narrative simply harkens back to a trip taken to the sacred island of Glastonbury. The portion of the story in which the crew are held for hundreds of years and warned not to return to their homeland lest they fall to dust is clearly simple fiction, likely indicating their desire to remain on the plentiful island they call the Isle of Women. This could of course explain why they turned their ships back to sea, never to be seen again. If we agree that Bron could have been married to Joseph's daughter only after Joseph arrived on British soil, it could be that the island populated by nothing but beautiful women could have been changed over time, derived from the simple tradition that the Island of Avalon was where Bron found *one* beautiful young woman, causing him to return to Glastonbury.

There is also a similarity between Bron's extended lifespan on the otherworldly Isle of Women, turning to dust if he ever returns to the real world, and Bron the Fisher King's unnatural longevity, hanging between life and death. Although it is unlikely that a historical individual could live several lifetimes owing to either the Grail or as punishment for sin, the fact that a supernaturally prolonged life is associated with both figures is conspicuous. The Fisher King has been an obviously important character throughout the Grail saga, both blessed by a spiritual gift and cursed by immortality. The Grail initiate must search him out and ask him about the Grail in order to acquire it, setting the Fisher King free and releasing him to his eternal reward. If Bron refused to return to his home in Wales, instead sailing back to a fabled otherworldly island, this could have been enough to create the tradition that Bron was enchanted, blessed with a charmed life but cursed never to return to the mortal world.

Llantwit Major has proven to be a place of great interest regarding the arrival of Christianity to Britain as well as its spread throughout the land. However, we have been investigating Melkin the Bard and his time at Britain. Therefore, we may wonder why such interest has been paid to this spot in nearby Wales. The purpose of going into such detail about Llantwit was not only to shed further light on the character of Melkin, but also to demonstrate why he may have become so familiar with Glastonbury and its history. If Melkin the Bard was Maelgwn Gwynedd as it would seem, we must realize that his time spent under the tutelage of St. Illtud did more than introduce him to the idea of Christianity. It would seem that whatever time he spent as a monk made a profound change in him despite Gildas's harsh words about him after he left the church. The question must be asked, what happened to make Melkin leave the center of scholarship and piety at Llantwit Major and somehow migrate to Glastonbury?

The obvious ire aimed at Maelgwn by Gildas has been mentioned previously. As such it is possible that the pair had prior dealings while at the fifth-century university. Considering the praises heaped upon Gildas, it is possible that Gildas took issue with Maelgwn due to an attitude of superiority, causing Maelgwn to become disillusioned with life in the traditional church. Such a feeling of disenchantment with the structured life of the church may have been responsible for his departure as well. It is possible that Maelgwn found the transition from powerful master to humble servant more difficult than he could tolerate. The Middle Ages are well known as a time when the church used its power for its own benefit, and it is possible that Melkin saw too much of human pride and too little of the reason he became a monk.

When one looks at the larger picture that ties together Glastonbury and Joseph with Llantwit and Illid, it is likely that Melkin's years of ecclesiastical education were well-spent, and that he simply chose to go to Glastonbury in an effort to further his learning and satisfy an interest in the same legends that he must have encountered in Wales. If he had read the stories of the school's old patriarch who returned to Avalon, he may have wanted to learn more about the man he knew as Illid and find the place where the saint had been buried. If we are correct in thinking that Melkin and Maelgwn are one and the same, it would appear he accomplished his goal. It is very likely that as a Welsh youth, he heard the story known as the Voyage of Bron. Then with the same feeling of curiosity that has led to this investigation of the Grail, that feeling of wonder when you realize that the fantastic stories you've heard may have some basis in reality, he followed the history with the stories as his guide, and at last found himself at the ancient church of Glastonbury.

It was more than his change in lifestyle and new-found interest that made him such a formidable historian and writer. As a king and warrior, he would have been aware of, and possibly even participated in, many of the military campaigns that went on during the Dark Ages. Therefore, it is quite possible that he was responsible for several of the oldest histories that John Leland claimed were housed in the great library at Glastonbury Abbey, some of which involved the deeds of King Arthur, who was Maelgwn's contemporary. One may wonder what else Melkin might have written that could benefit us on our search for the Glastonbury legends' historical roots.

Although Melkin's prophecy allegedly dates from the sixth century A.D. and could potentially provide a great deal of information both regarding the Joseph of Arimathea legend and the Grail legend, one fact remains. The account first appeared in John of Glastonbury's fourteenth-century *Chronicle of Glastonbury Abbey*, which most scholars suggest is utterly useless in presenting any real truth about the abbey's history. Many would claim that anyone attempting to find prior evidence of Melkin's writing will find nothing but later accounts that could have been derived from John's *Chronicle*. However, there is one body of medieval histories, also called unreliable for historical research, which almost certainly disproves this assertion.

Known as the *Chronicon*, this series of texts written by Helinand of Froidmont during the last ten years of his life attempts to outline history from the time of creation to roughly 1204. Completed around 1223, these works are said to be a general historical compilation interspersed with Helinand's own comments and passages from the Bible that he deemed relevant. Many consider these treatises too scattered to be trusted; however, even a work not specifically intended as a pure history can bear the fingerprint of an actual historical event. Written around the year 1220, one entry dated 720 might provide a reference to Melkin that predates John's debated prophecy.

> At this time in Britain, there was shown a hermit, through the help of an angel, a miraculous vision of Joseph (of Arimathea), the decurion who took the Lord's body from the cross, and concerning the vessel in which the Lord ate from with his disciples, [and from this vision] the hermit proceeded to write a history called "Of the Grail." The Grail, called "gradalis" or "gradale" in French, is a wide and deep saucer, in which precious mater [food] is ceremoniously presented, one piece at a time, richly provided in the various courses. This is called in the vernacular "greal," as it gratifies and is welcomed at such a meal, is made of silver or some similar precious metal, and so because of its content, an overwhelming succession of expensive delicacies. This history I have not found in Latin, but so far only written in French in the possession of certain chieftains, and not even then in a complete form.

This mention of a "hermit in Britain" having a vision of Joseph and a vessel which would be called the Grail is highly reminiscent of Melkin's prophecy, so much so that it can scarcely mean anything else. Melkin, who was described as being "before Merlin," was called a Welsh bard and was in essence the first to write about Joseph and the Grail. The hermit mentioned here proceeds to write a history called "de Gradale" or "Of the Grail." In fact, several historical works dealing with this time period, including the subject of King Arthur, have been credited to Melkin.

It is worth noting that the particular syntax used in Helinand's *Chronicon* is nearly identical to that used to describe the discovery of King Arthur's burial site in 1190. The account given by Gerald of Wales states that King Henry II was told by a certain soothsayer or bard in Britain about the exact whereabouts of Arthur's grave, leading to the now notorious discovery of his remains in the ancient cemetery at Glastonbury Abbey. While this discovery is considered a hoax, and John's "Prophecy of Melkin" simply a derivation of this story, the fact remains that its description of the British hermit mentioned by Helinand is so close to that presented by Melkin that it almost certainly references the same individual, or at least his writings.

One might conjecture that John based his Melkin on the account given by Helinand, were it not for John Leland's account of seeing the fragmentary remains of Melkin's writing upon his visit in the sixteenth century. It was not said that he saw a copy of Helinand's *Chronicon*, which would have been a mere few hundred years old at the time of his visit and certainly recognizable to him. John said he saw ancient fragmentary writings written by the same Melkin mentioned by John of Glastonbury. It would now seem quite unlikely that John of Glastonbury created the character of Melkin out of his own fanciful elaboration. The Chronicles of Helinand seem to provide evidence that Melkin's writings were known long before John wrote his *Chronicles of Glastonbury Abbey* in the fourteenth century.

However, this is not the only source to corroborate the existence of Melkin as a credited history writer. He was used as an accepted source for historical treatments dealing with Glastonbury and King Arthur for many years after John's history was written. Melkin's prophecy likely served as inspiration to the man who first journeyed to Glastonbury in search of Joseph of Arimathea's grave some years before John wrote his *Cronica*. Indeed, it would seem likely that John was merely the earliest to mention this Welsh bard and soothsayer by name. For the most complete treatment of Melkin, his prophecy, and his presence in Arthurian and Grail literature, I would refer the reader to the introduction to Professor James P. Carley's translation of *Chronicle of Glastonbury Abbey*. However, for the purpose of further illustration, I have picked out several pertinent passages:

> The first surviving reference to Melkin in a context apart from Glastonbury and John's *Cronica* comes in John Hardyng's rhymed chronicle of English history which was written in the mid-fifteenth century, probably in Kyme, Lincolnshire.
>
> His chronicle is significant because it stands as a witness to a national knowledge of Glastonbury traditions in the fifteenth century and because it supplies a reference to Melkin's name outside the context of Glastonbury.
>
> The next citation of Melkin appears in Capgrave's *Nova Legenda Angliae*, where there is a life of Joseph of Armithea taken verbatim from John's *Chronica* with one significant abbreviation [p. liii].
>
> The most important pre–Dissolution witness to the tradition of Melkin is John Leland. Leland reported that he found in Glastonbury's library an ancient fragment of Melkin's *Historia* and that he took notes from it.
>
> John Bale discusses Melkin in his *Illustrium Majoris Britanniae Scriptorum Summarium*, and cites Capgrave, Hardyng, and Leland as his main

sources. Bale's discussion of Melkin also contains interesting additions to the material found in these sources [p. liv].

Finally and most interesting, Carley outlines other works said to have been authored by Melkin beyond his prophecy mentioned by John of Glastonbury.

> The chapter on Melkin in John Pit's *Relationum historicarum de rebus anglicis tomus primus quatuor partes complectens* is basically a synopsis of Bale's discussion, but Pits does make several significant elaborations. Like Bale he credits Melkin with three books, although the titles vary slightly:
>
> | | |
> |---|---|
> | De antiquitatibus Britannicis, | Librum vnum |
> | De gestis Britannorum, | Librum vnum |
> | De Regis Arthurii mensa rotunda, | Librum vnum [p. lv]. |

Here for the first time we see other works allegedly written by Melkin that might have existed in Glastonbury Abbey's library. If Melkin did exist and wrote several histories in the sixth century, it is quite likely that some of these works were damaged or destroyed in the great fire of 1184. However, it would seem that some fragments did survive to become part of the traditions embedded in the Arthurian and Grail legends. John Leland, who inventoried the literary holdings at Glastonbury Abbey, later wrote a text dealing with the history of King Arthur in Britain called *Assertio Arturii*, the origin of which he attributes to fragmentary remains of ancient texts written by Melkin that he found at Glastonbury.

John's *Chronicles of Glastonbury Abbey* has been a point of contention among scholars and historians for decades. Not seen as a true history, this work has been almost completely thrown out as a source of information regarding Glastonbury Abbey or as a means by which legends might be verified. Sadly, writers during the medieval era didn't always put posterity above prosperity, writing to suit whoever commissioned their work. However, the mere presence of Melkin's prophecy in this work gives us something of great importance.

The fragmentary writings of Melkin, witnessed by John Leland and referenced by John of Glastonbury, have been relegated to the unfortunately large pile of "untrustworthy" documents that abound in a historical investigation of Glastonbury Abbey. Worse than its label as a fabrication, its importance has been completely overlooked. In fact, this one sixth-century writer has provided the very thing that detractors of the Joseph traditions at Glastonbury have demanded. These writings constitute proof, or the nearest thing to it: solid evidence. These texts were not conjured up by John of Glastonbury. They truly existed. It is not important if their exact translation remains elusive. The gist of their meaning was deciphered some time ago. More importantly, there is no reason to disbelieve the references they make to Joseph of Arimathea, his burial, and the vials this tomb once contained.

It also matters little who exactly the historical Melkin was. Although it seems apparent that Maelgwn Gwynedd was the person from that region's history who most clearly fits the role, his true identity will never be known for sure, nor does it have to be. If there actually were documents written by Melkin, there must have actually been a Melkin. Similarly, it doesn't matter if you agree with the theory that St. Illid, the enigmatic patriarch of Llantwit Major, was the same "man from Israel" known as Joseph of Arimathea in Britain. It may seem an unlikely myth all too common to the legendary early history of Britain, but it is curious that these two places feature a character so closely related to another called Bron or Bran, who originated in Israel, who was a power in the early British Church, who retired to "Avallon," where he died and was buried, and who is associated with twelve individuals who would later be called saints.

What is truly important about the Prophecy of Melkin is that it existed. This one fact provides the proof not only that there was a tradition of Joseph in England long before the medieval interest that spawned his cult at Glastonbury, but also that there was once definite knowledge of where this saint and disciple of Jesus was laid to rest. These documents show that the legends of Joseph and the Grail can't be simply thrown aside and labeled simple fantasy. What is truly important about this reference made by John Leland and others is the glimpse they provide of documents that would have otherwise met with an inglorious fate — documents that now appear to be exactly what they claim to be. Melkin reaches forward to us from the sixth century to hand us exactly what we needed. Not only do we have evidence of Joseph of Arimathea at Glastonbury, we have evidence of the Grail at Glastonbury as well. However, evidence contained in documents that no longer exist provides a hollow victory. We still need some physical evidence, still in existence today, that can help corroborate Melkin's story.

The Prophecy of Melkin provides one of two points in a line that points toward a historically factual basis for the Joseph tradition at Glastonbury. A second point in the line would serve to provide direction — the means with which to chart a course. A historical reference, especially when dealing with mythical matters such as the Holy Grail, no matter how potent, requires corroboration. In this case, John Leland provides that corroboration. In making a case for a real Melkin writing about a real Joseph of Arimathea at Glastonbury, the texts written by Melkin are the evidence, and John Leland has testified to that evidence.

Critics of John of Glastonbury's history have a point in saying that it's not a true history. It is a history of its time in which fact is nestled comfortably inside an artistic elaboration. But as a painter needs a subject, a writer must obtain the basis for his stories from somewhere — a setting for his artwork.

How much could be learned about the woman who modeled for the *Mona Lisa* if we could find the area whose landscape is painted just outside the window? Therefore, if John's *Cronica* is an artistic illustration of the truth, let us now take a closer look at what might be the most telling piece of the stage dressing.

Chapter 7

The Mystery Tomb of "J.A."

Anyone studying Arthurian literature will learn something very quickly. There are many things that happen and you're not sure exactly why. For example, one of Arthur's brave, honorable knights might be riding through the forest one day and find a woman tied to a tree being guarded by a great and evil-looking knight. One knight engages in battle with the other in order to free the damsel in distress. There is a great deal of swordplay and displays of both knights' skill and fortitude until both combatants are knee-deep in their own blood. In the end, Arthur's brave knight defeats the evil knight, usually by cleaving some body part asunder. After the damsel is freed, she curses him for being a churlish knight and vows revenge, taking the body of the defeated knight away into the forest. This encounter usually sets the stage for another battle or war between Arthur's knight and another at some point further into the text.

There are many strange things such as this to be found in Arthurian texts, and when the Holy Grail is introduced they easily double. Then come visions, signs, and great mysteries to be witnessed by the brave knights who go in search of the Grail. Why for example does the Grail hero of the twelfth-century romances, having proven himself a great and powerful knight, fail to ask the needed question in order to achieve the Grail, and only again finds the Grail Castle and wins the relic when he is broken and admits his own failing? When confronted with such a willfully created oxymoron, one must question its purpose. What is this paradox meant to teach us? What idea did the writer want to convey by this curious turn of events?

One such event can be found in a mysterious Grail story entitled *The High History of the Holy Grail*, which is also known by the name *Perlesvaus*. In this story, the classical retelling of the Grail story is presented, but with a little twist. Perceval, who lives in the Welsh countryside, is kept ignorant of his lineage of great knights. He one day sees a band of knights from Camelot riding through the forest and is mesmerized by their radiance. Seeking to become a knight himself, he leaves his mother and journeys to the court of King Arthur. There he finds he must fight the Red Knight and gain his armor in order to win his place at Arthur's Round Table.

After accomplishing his goal, he embarks on further adventures to prove his worth until one day he happens upon an old man fishing in a boat in the waters surrounding a great castle. He is given shelter in the castle and there witnesses a spectacle he can scarcely believe. He sees a holy procession which includes certain implements of such sacred beauty that he cannot speak. When the procession leaves the room, all others with whom he has been dining, including the infirm king, depart and leave him alone in the castle. The next morning, he can find no one and leaves the castle. Once outside, he is jeered at and taunted, being told that because he failed to ask the question, the king is forced to remain in languor, and the kingdom must remain in misery.

As is customary at this point in the story, the focus then switches to the actions of other knights who also ride out on the quest to find the Holy Grail. Since only one of them is worthy enough to find the Grail, each encounters a different form of defeat, either because he is too worldly, or carrying some hidden sin. Their failure typically is not known until they find they have been to the Grail Castle and that the holy relic did not appear before them. However, in this tale, every knight but Perceval receives a much more immediate verdict.

When they approach the castle, which does not always present itself as it did to Perceval, they see before them a shrine that contains a tomb of exceedingly great age. When they approach it, either nothing happens or a great roar is heard, making it clear that this knight is not the one to unlock its secrets. It is explained to them that Joseph of Arimathea, described as a holy knight, rests in that tomb, and that it will not open until the best knight in the world draws near to it. It is not until Perceval finds his way to the castle again and draws near to the tomb that it opens to reveal the bones of Joseph and the relics that are held within.

This may seem an odd literary device, to use the bones of a Biblical character to determine who will achieve the Grail. In other medieval romances this task is accomplished by a test of arms under the eyes of God, or by means of the Seige Perilous, the seat that will swallow up any but he who is destined to find the Grail. However, in *Perlesvaus*, Joseph's lineage proves to be quite important. King Arthur himself is a descendant of Joseph, as is the Fisher King, the wounded king of this castle. Perceval finds that he is also of Joseph's bloodline, and next to be the Grail's protector. The old Grail King is then allowed to die, and the Grail and its new king disappear to be seen no more.

Strange as it may seem to us now, this mysterious tomb can guide us in our own quest for the Grail. Stranger still, we as modern-day questing knights

7. The Mystery Tomb of "J.A."

can walk right up to this tomb and see if it wails or offers us answers. We don't have to go through trials in the forest, or in fact even look very far in order to find this relic's hiding spot. It's very near the place where Joseph was supposedly laid to rest at Glastonbury. The truth is, it's just across the street.

St. John's parish church stands just off High Street in Glastonbury, its great four-spired tower a local icon. Visitors to St John's today can walk through the doors, drop a donation in the box just inside, and stroll around the modest little church admiring the architecture, recalling its history, which potentially dates to before the twelfth century. Though most of what is visible today dates from the thirteenth to fifteenth centuries, the oldest part still standing can be found in the North Trancept, formerly known as St. Katherine's Chapel. It is here that you will find the tomb allegedly belonging to Joseph of Arimathea.

Dating from the twelfth century, this chapel also contains the now famous eighteenth-century stained glass windows by A. J. Davies depicting in vivid colors and incredible artistry — a rendition of the Joseph legend. In the larger panels stand the figures of Joseph of Arimathea, St. Aristobulus, disciple of Christ who was martyred in Britain, St. Simon of Zelotes, known as the

St. Joseph's tomb in St. Katherine's Chapel, North Transept of St. John's Parish Church, c. 1930. The glass case that now contains Richard Whiting's medieval cope is not present, revealing the roughly square carved indentation in the lid. The shield containing the caduceus symbol and letters "J A" can be seen on this end (courtesy Glastonbury Antiquarian Society).

"Bishop of Britain," and finally King Arviragus who gave Joseph the original 12 Hides of land. Below these are scenes depicting Joseph protesting the condemnation of Jesus, Joseph present at Jesus's entombment, Joseph bringing the two cruets to Glastonbury, and finally Joseph planting his staff atop Wearyal Hill.

Sitting in a very inauspicious location below the stained glass windows sits a stone crypt or tomb. Its condition is good but damaged, missing several pieces of its corners and edges. It has several quatrefoils carved into its sides containing either shields or diamonds and is topped by a glass case holding the cope once belonging to Abbot Richard Whiting. This case makes it impossible to see many features of the lid, but from historical accounts and photographs, we know it has a shallow indented space carved into it for some missing item such as a box. Accounts from the past also state that around the top are the remains of some kind of iron fittings. It has been suggested that they once formed an iron grille to which pilgrims could affix tokens or other offerings in honor of the person it contained. It is said that the tomb had been moved, and in a rather hasty and indelicate manner, breaking much of the metal joinery that helped hold the stone box together.

Those who have reported seeing the tomb in its original condition say that inside the hollow, they saw a raised plinth or platform on which something else once rested. Some have suggested that this could have been an ornamented silver casket into which the saint's bones were once placed. Others have suggested that a mechanism once existed that allowed the remains to be raised and lowered for viewing. However, the most curious feature of this stone tomb is not found on the inside but carved on one end.

Inscribed in a shield on the right side of the tomb are the initials "J. A.," with each letter resting on either side of a symbol called the caduceus—a staff with wings near

Illustration of shield with inscribed caduceus symbol and letters "J A." This shield is carved on the "eastern" end of the tomb thought to be that of Joseph of Arimathea, now found in St. John the Baptist Parish Church on High Street in Glastonbury. It is agreed that this tomb was once part of a shrine devoted to Joseph that stood in Glastonbury Abbey, but its exact meaning and function are still under debate (author photograph).

7. The Mystery Tomb of "J.A."

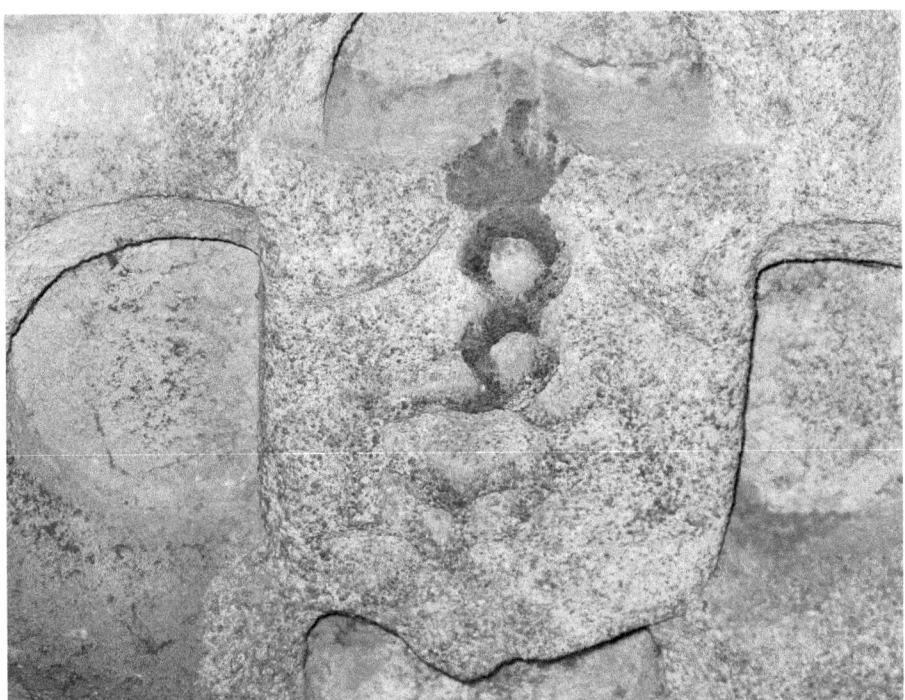

The shield carving showing the "J A" inscription as it appears today. The wings and lower portion of the caduceus symbol are clearly visible; however, the initials on either side of the symbol are more difficult to see — the shadowing alone makes the letters visible (author photograph).

the top encircled by two loosely coiled snakes. Although this is recognized today as the symbol of medicine, this association only dates back to the eighteenth or nineteenth century. Before that, the symbol for medicine was a version of the Rod of Asclepius, which is a gnarled branch or staff with a single snake twisted around it. Originally, the caduceus was the symbol for Hermes who was, appropriately enough, the messenger of God.

This tomb is thought to be that of Joseph but what evidence is there to support this claim? The carvings on the sides indicate that this tomb was made some time in the fourteenth or fifteenth century, clearly not the time of Joseph and his church. The tomb's history can further illustrate its significance. To start at the beginning, we will need to revisit the only known account of his burial — the Prophecy of Melkin.

This enigmatic text gives a fairly clear description of Joseph's final resting place considering the rest of its incongruous Latin: "Amid these Joseph in marble, of Arimathea by name, hath found perpetual sleep: and he lies on a two-forked line next to the south corner of an oratory fashioned of wattles for the adoring of a mighty Virgin." First, let us consider the first and largest of the reference points we are given. This passage says that the grave lies next to the south corner of an oratory fashioned of wattles. This is clearly a reference to the original wattle church. Although there were other oratories built on the grounds that were made of wattled construction, none were dedicated to the Virgin Mary as was the Old Church.

For further guidance, we must consider the first and somewhat more problematic portion of the directions. Melkin says that he is buried on a two-forked, or bifurcated line. As stated previously, this has been interpreted in several different ways ranging from some kind of broken or crossed line to a description of the type of shirt in which Joseph was buried. Since the rest of the description has to do with giving specific directions to the gravesite, there seems little reason for the writer to interject that Joseph was buried in a "split-front garment." Therefore, this passage could mean that the burial site is either on a line that intersects another line, or that it lies on a line that is broken, such as by a door or a separation between two walls.

It is tempting to think of the Glastonbury patriarch Joseph being buried right in the doorway into the chapel (a broken line in the wall of his chapel), but it is quite unlikely. The only other way there could be a "broken line" in the church wall is if there were another wall in the same line, such as another building. At the time of Joseph's death and burial, there is no indication that any other structures existed besides the wattle church. There was likely a well-head just off the southeast corner of the building, but it was also unlikely that they would have had a burial there since it was so near their water supply. If there was not a clear broken line on which the burial could have taken place, that leaves only the second option.

This portion of the original Latin in which Melkin's prophecy was written has been translated as "bifurcated," which means "two-forked." Using this description to find the burial site, we should be looking for a forked line near one of the south corners. The corner itself could be called a forked line, specifically a squared corner, but if Melkin had meant the corner, why be redundant and say "a two-forked corner." Much later in the Middle Ages, many churches used buttresses that made a corner that was not squared, but rather X-shaped. The treasure hunter in all of us loves an "X marks the spot" scenario, but this is again unlikely. If we are talking about the wattle building that formed the first church, there was no need for buttresses, nor would typical wattle construction ever use a situation where horizontal members overlap to form a "forked corner." While it is possible there was something on one of the southern corners to make such a fork, there is no evidence.

If the forked line in the prophecy is not the corner of the building, what other forked line might it describe? Considering scenes like that in the motion picture *National Treasure*, one might picture a cross placed on one end of the rooftop with the sun forming a shadowy cross, a forked line, on the ground where Joseph was buried. It is similarly possible, yet entirely conjectural, that there was a cross in the church yard somewhere that formed the required forked line. This is also unlikely since these were first-century Jews and Britons, not Templars or Masons. It has also been suggested that there were once two pyramids on either side of the church yard that formed one of the two lines, and the other line was simply that of the church. Although there are references to these pyramids in accounts of Glastonbury Abbey's early history, they have more to do with the discovery of King Arthur's grave, and seem to refer to Anglo-Saxons who are buried there rather than burials from Joseph's time. So if none of these explanations are suitable, what else might have formed the forked line we seek?

From Melkin's prophecy, only two sound options emerge. Joseph could have been buried in one of the southern corners of the wattle church along a line drawn from opposite corners (in effect draw an "X" through the center of the building), thus forming a line with two forks. The second option is that it simply refers to one line crossed by two others, specifically by walls. This could be where the southern wall is crossed by the eastern and western

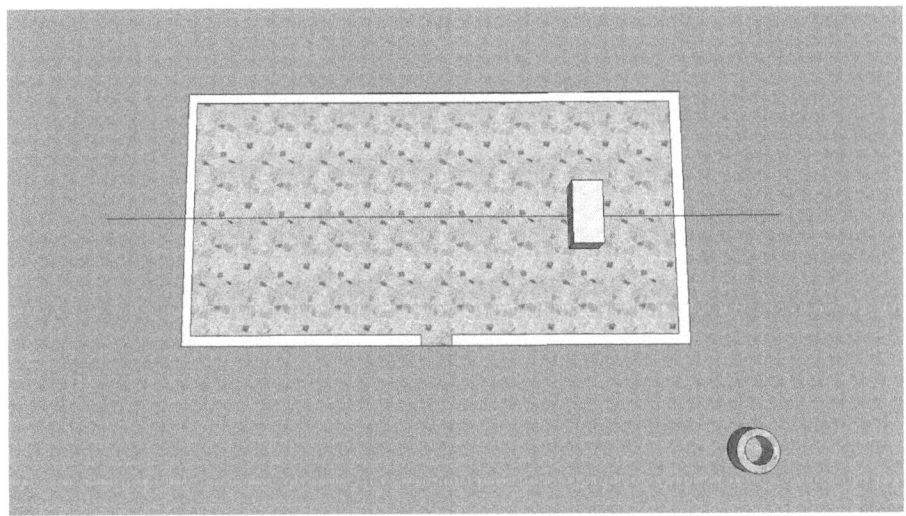

In this floor plan of the wattle church, the centerline has been marked to indicate the first possible meaning for the "bifurcated line" mentioned in the Prophecy of Melkin. In this scenario, Joseph of Arimathea would have been buried just outside the church to the east on the southern side of the midline (model created by author using Google SketchUp).

walls, or perhaps where these walls cross the center line of the chapel. Either explanation would fit the description given by Melkin, but which one would make the most sense?

Let us first examine the option that the "bifurcated line" of Melkin's prophecy simply referred to a line broken by the eastern and western walls of the wattle church, such as the centerline or the southern wall. In either case it is a line, the church's longest dimension, that is broken by two others, namely the end walls, making it a twice broken, forked, or divided line. This means Joseph was buried near a southern corner formed in the section these divided lines made. In the case of the divided centerline, Joseph would be buried along the centerline of the church near a southern corner. But if the burial was along the centerline of the church, why did Melkin say it was by the southern corner instead of something more like "the southern side"?

It makes sense to think of the broken line formed by the intersections of walls to be that formed by the south wall. In this case, there are clear corners formed on the south side of the wattle church. However, a new problem then presents itself. To which of these two southern corners was Melkin referring when he stipulated that Joseph was buried "near *the* southern corner"? It seems clear he had only one corner in mind.

It seems most likely that the eastern end of the chapel was of the greatest

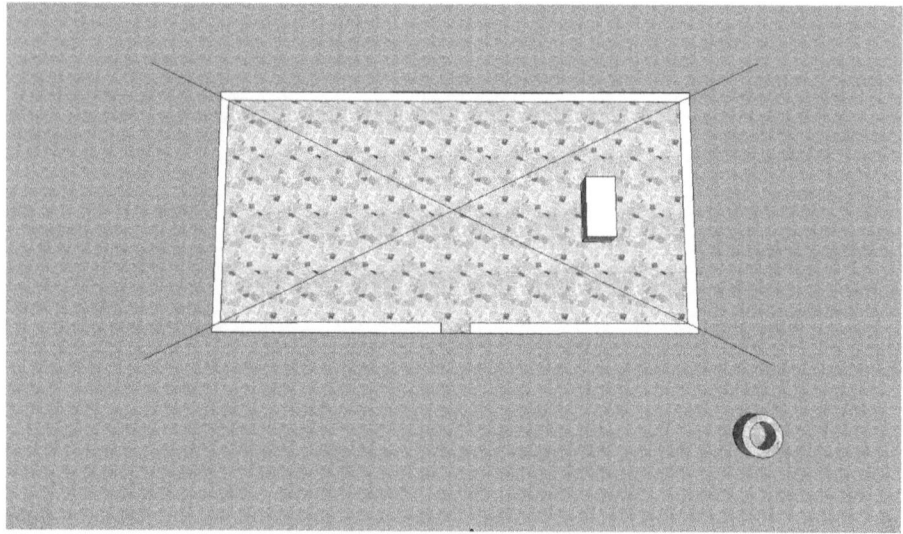

In this floor plan of the wattle church, the more likely the meaning of the "bifurcated line" mentioned by Melkin is that Joseph of Arimathea was buried near the southeastern corner of the wattle church along a northwest–southeast diagonal (model created by author using Google SketchUp).

importance to Joseph and his followers. Most of the earliest Christian churches around the world exhibit an east-west alignment, typically with the sanctuary placed at the eastern end of the structure. Allegedly built to mirror the footprint of the Old Church, the Lady Chapel displays the same alignment. Although it is not perfectly east-west with respect to the center line of the later Great Church, the alignment of the Old Church was clearly intentional. This variation demonstrates that the Lady Chapel was built to the pre-existing specifications of a much older building whose alignment could not be determined as exactly as in the later centuries. Therefore, it would seem most reasonable to assume that the specific southern corner mentioned by Melkin was the southeastern wall of the wattle church, meaning the corner nearest the well now known as St. Joseph's Well.

Let us now examine the second option: two crossed lines drawn from corner to corner, forming an "X" in the interior of the building. This two-forked line also provides a clearly defined corner if we again assume that a greater importance was given to the eastern end of the chapel. This would

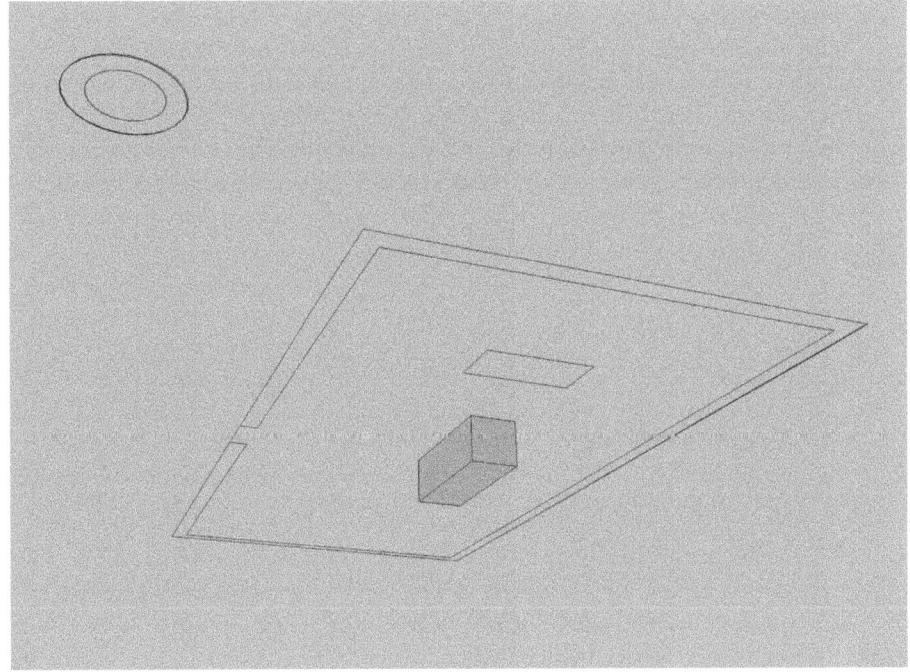

In this view from below of the wattle church model, Joseph's most likely burial site can be seen. Just inside the bounds of the church, near the southeastern corner, the lead coffin appropriate to a metal merchant was placed in an east–west alignment (model created by author using Google SketchUp).

mean that Joseph's grave was placed inside the confines of the wattle church. But this presents a problem. Most have placed Joseph's burial out in the ancient cemetery to the south of the chapel, and this is likely the location where any medieval attempt to find his grave would have started.

It is unlikely that Joseph, having known an entire life under Hebrew funerary laws, would have chosen to be buried inside a building, much less a holy building, for the simple reason that a dead body was seen as ritually unclean. In his eyes, it would have been nothing less than a desecration of the church. However it is possible that Joseph did not choose his own burial site, leaving the decision to his followers who may not have been familiar with, or as strictly against, the notion of burial within a building. We must consider that this was very much a church built on a distant frontier, and dedicated to the teaching of one who was not Himself one to hold completely with established tradition.

Just as our leaders and founders are today buried in a place of highest honor, it is quite possible that Joseph's followers chose his gravesite within the church he founded, the place of *their* highest honor. This sort of burial, called a "nuclear burial," can also be found in the later Anglo-Saxon churches founded on Glastonbury Tor and the Beckery. In this situation, the founder would be buried with pride of place within the church, with all other contemporary burials placed outside. Later in the medieval period, burials of other holy or especially important individuals would again be placed inside the church building. Indeed, this is an idea that will become important when we later examine the fourteenth and fifteenth-century attempts to discover the whereabouts of Joseph's grave.

Although the exact meaning of Melkin's "bifurcated line" may never be known, there is one additional piece of information that helps support this theory of where the grave was placed, although from a time long after Joseph.

> One of the early printed books was *De Sancto Joseph ab Armathia*, printed by Richard Pynson, A.D. 1516. He narrates various miracles alleged to have been performed in the year 1502 before the shrine, including the healing of Mrs. Lyte of Lytes Carey, a notable of the neighborhood, and the Vicar of Wells. This shrine of St. Joseph was at the east end of the crypt under St. Mary's Chapel, and caused the whole chapel constantly to be called St. Joseph's Chapel. Apparently a Norman underground chapel was converted into his shrine. Can this have been the site before the fire of 1184 of the wonderful underground chapel which William of Malmesbury (cap. XL) tells us that King Ina caused to be built (about A.D. 700) "below the greater Church," a chapel laden with silver and gold? The chapel was originally approached by a stair-case past the ancient Norman well of St. Joseph, close to where he was first buried [Lewis, pp. 151–152].

While excavations at Glastonbury Abbey have uncovered an Anglo-Saxon burial vault, called an hypogeum, allegedly built by King Ine around 720, this structure was further east from the wattle church, past the nave, and under the transept before entering the choir. Since Joseph's burial place was described as "approached by a stair-case past the ancient Norman well of St. Joseph, close to where he was first buried," this would indicate that the original site of his burial was close to the eastern wall of the wattle church, just as we have surmised.

Because Melkin's writings are highly contested among medieval scholars, most claiming that his histories were pseudo-historical inventions of John of Glastonbury, what we really need is mention of Melkin and his account of Joseph's burial that predates John of Glastonbury.

In an article about the tradition of Melkin and his writings, Aelred Watkin writes:

> The whole of this is couched in terms which defy exact translation and any interpretation of it abounds with difficulties of every kind. Dr. Margaret Murray has made an ingenious plea for its Coptic origin; others hold that it stems from Arabian astro-mythology, while Armitage Robinson seems to imply that it was a fourteenth-century forgery. Certainly it could be of oriental origin and ancient in date. It could be ancient but have been interpolated by the hand of a fourteenth-century discoverer — perhaps the John Blome who in 1345 secured permission to search for the body of St Joseph at Glastonbury "because it is said in certain ancient writings that the body was there buried" [Carley, *Arthurian Tradition*, p. 26].

From this quote, it seems quite clear that Blome was already aware of Melkin's prophecy describing the grave's whereabouts, providing evidence of Melkin that predates John of Glastonbury. Written in 1350, John's *Chronica* would not have been known to John Blome in 1345 when he made his request of King Edward III to excavate at Glastonbury.

Blome's was the first attempt to find archeological evidence supporting the Joseph tradition at Glastonbury. His petition was to search for Joseph's grave anywhere that would not disturb the monks and would not damage the buildings. The monks at the abbey granted him permission to dig, presumably in the cemetery in which the oldest burials might be found. Although it was never officially recorded whether or not Blome achieved his goal, several years later a separate account reported that the bodies of St. Joseph of Arimathea and his companions were found.

From this account, it would seem that the disputed body of Glastonbury's legendary founder had finally been rediscovered thanks to Melkin's ancient guidance, once and for all establishing the story as historical fact. Sadly, this is not the case. Many scholars believe this citation recording the momentous discovery was a mere error of assumption or misunderstanding. One may also wonder why it took so long for news of Blome's success to be recorded or why the only notice comes from so far away. To answer these questions, we must further investigate the monk who made this statement in conjunction with Blome's investigation.

A Benedictine monk named R. de Boston wrote in 1367 that the bodies of Joseph and his followers had been found. Based in Lincolnshire, a district on the other side of England, this account written twenty-two years after Blome's excavations is thought to be in error. Many say it is more likely that he read the account of John Blome's dig at the abbey and simply assumed the bodies had been, or else interpreted his search as a discovery. However, it seems likely that this assertion is based on little more than the legendary nature of the subject matter.

To judge whether this is a valid source of information, we must learn more about the chronicler of the alleged discovery, R. de Boston. Very little is known of him, but through the work of early Glastonbury Abbey researchers, it is possible to at least learn who he was, and the location where he committed this reference to writing:

> The belief that Joseph of Arimathea was really buried in the cemetery appears in the fourteenth century; when in 1345 J. Blome obtained a royal license "to seek within the boundary of the monastery of Glastonia for the body of Joseph of Arimathea," in consequence, as he asserts, of a divine injunction and revelation made to him. The license, dated June 10, 1345, permits him to dig within the precinct of the monastery for this purpose, provided that it be done without endangering the church and buildings, and also with consent of the abbot and convent.[2] This is the only record left of the project, but the chronicle of R. de Boston (p. 137), under the year 1367, states that the bodies of Joseph of Arimathea and his companions were *found* in this year at Glaston[3]; a probable mistake for *sought* [Willis, p. 15].

Following the footnote regarding R. de Boston in the above quotation, specifically "Sparke, *Script*," a work written in the eighteenth century provided the necessary historical reference. The 1723 *Historiae Anglicanae Scriptores Varii, e Codicibus Manuscriptis* stated that R. de Boston of Lincolnshire was actually Robertus de Boston, also known as John of Boston or John of Peterborough, who was a monk at Spalding Priory, a branch of Croyland Abbey founded in 1052 in Spalding, Lincolnshire.

Croyland Abbey is a Benedictine abbey founded in the eighth century, famous for its valuable histories. Although it met the same fate in the end as did Glastonbury Abbey, it stands as a source of scholarship and reliable historical information dating back centuries. For this reason, it is likely that the

1367 account was part of a compilation of important events in church history up to that day. It is possible that Robert did learn of John Blome's search for Joseph's gravesite, only to record it twenty-two years later. However, it is equally likely that, given Croyland Abbey's tradition of writing histories, the 1367 account records an actual historical event — either one that occurred at the same time as Blome's search, or several years afterwards.

Unfortunately, we cannot be completely sure whether John Blome succeeded in finding Joseph's burial, or if he searched in the Old Cemetery and ultimately found nothing. All we know is that a written record exists, from a place known for recording historical events, stating that Joseph's body had been found. Even if we assume this dig was successful, little information is provided about the discovery. Because of this, we can't compare it to the Melkin text to see if Joseph's remains were in fact where the ancient Welsh bard claimed they were. It does seem that John Blome was aware of Melkin's description, and therefore likely started his search somewhere very close to the southeast corner of the Lady Chapel where once stood the original wattle church.

Some fifty years later, there was allegedly a second discovery. This time, there is a written account fully detailing the event. Upon discovering that the monks at Glastonbury had conducted their own excavations, both in the Old Cemetery and inside the confines of the abbey buildings, King Edward III wrote a letter to Abbot Nicholas Frome inquiring about their findings. The abbot then wrote a reply to the King citing, among other things, St. Patrick's charter and Melkin's prophecy. He then goes on to describe in tantalizing detail the discoveries they encountered during their excavations. The following is the relevant portion of Abbot Frome's letter:

> Also, most illustrious prince, concerning the remains discovered at Glastonbury in the seventh year of your most glorious rule and power. In the south side of the cemetery of the Old Church were discovered three ancient coffins in the earth at a depth of about fourteen feet. The coffin which lay in the northern part contained the bones of a decayed and perished man, the bones arranged according to the manner or death. Near the bones of the head there was an abundance in grains of green and sweet-scented herbs with their seeds. In the coffin which lay in the middle there were contained the bones of twelve corpses, which were so ingeniously and so finely arranged within the casket that after their extraction, indeed, nobody there knew how to arrange them again in the aforesaid casket. In the third coffin which lay to the south were the bones of a decayed and perished individual lying in the manner of nature and away from the middle of the aforesaid corpse towards the head a great abundance of fluid, which appeared as fresh blood to those present in that place both by its color and substance. All these coffins were found outside the chapel. Within the chapel, however, under the southern corner of the altar another coffin was

> found with the bones of a decayed man. This coffin was adorned most excellently beyond the others, with linen cloth inside all over. And because it excelled all the other in delicacy of scent and eminence of place it was enclosed in another large coffin until clearer notice of it will be able to be had in the future [Carley, *Arthurian Tradition*, pp. 301–302].

Because this account mentions St. Patrick's charter and Melkin's prophecy, the historical veracity of the correspondence has been called into question. However, one aspect of Abbot Frome's letter helps seat his account in verifiable history. In an earlier part of the abbot's letter, he mentions that other coffins were found buried under the Lady Chapel. He states quite clearly that wooden rods were interred with the bodies — one the length of the body, and the other across under the feet. Similar burials with wooden rods were discovered in the nineteenth century when mud and debris were cleaned out of the crypt area under the Lady Chapel. Below is a description of the archeological find.

> An especially interesting group was found in 1825. Steps which led down to the crypt of the Lady Chapel were being repaired, and lengthened into a passage extending to the north (as seen today). Eighteen coffins were found, one 2.5 m (8ft) long internally; they were made of oak 7.5 cm (3in) thick, preserved in the damp ground. Under the head and shoulders of each skeleton was a bundle of wood shavings, perhaps stuffing of pillows. Beneath and to the right side of each skeleton was also a rod of thorn or hazel, of the same length as the coffin. Such rods or wands have been found in several sites in Britain and Scandinavia with medieval ecclesiastics, but their function or symbolism is unknown [Rahtz and Watts, p. 113].

These coffins were present in the crypt after the Dissolution. Therefore, this letter demonstrates that these were earlier burials which were discovered while the crypt was being built (around A.D. 1500) and were replaced in their earlier resting places once the crypt was completed.

It is noteworthy that the first three burials mentioned by Abbot Frome were located in the Old Cemetery, presumably where John Blome conducted his excavation, but the final burial of such fine quality was found inside the area once covered by the wattle church, specifically under the southeast corner of the altar in the Lady Chapel. The location mentioned in Abbot Frome's letter is almost identical to the account provided in Melkin's prophecy. It also provides corroborating evidence for the theory that the "bifurcated line" could mean that Joseph was buried along one of the crossed lines drawn between opposing corners of the Old Church.

This discovery outlined in Abbot Frome's letter has been called everything from an archeologist's dream to a devious plan orchestrated by the king himself to attract pilgrimage revenue. This is the sort of detailed evidence some scholars say they need, yet Glastonbury's reputation as a hoax factory instantly makes any such account appear dubious. The unique set of descriptors such as the staffs included in the other coffins and the specific descriptions of the remains uncovered certainly lend themselves to the story's credibility. In addition, Frome makes no claim to their identity, never openly stating that the remains found were those of Joseph and his followers. What are we to make of this letter and the story of the alleged remains discovered in the fifteenth century?

If the story was merely a ploy to separate the faithful from their money, it can justly be said that it was a brilliant yet fruitless one. The descriptions given of the bodies and items found interred with them were accurate according to monastic burials. The mention of how the bodies were found sounds like a valid description of what someone actually saw instead of the elaborate sort of medieval holy fable that often came with the discovery of a saint's body, such as having "supple skin still pink and warm to the touch." Even the depth of burial and description of the coffins themselves sound convincing.

First let us consider the manner in which the coffins were found. Abbot Frome's letter stated that these coffins were not simply old, but ancient. Also it was said that they were found at a depth of seventeen feet, a similar depth to that at which the much debated bodies of King Arthur and Guinevere were found. Ancient burials found at this depth could be considered graves that were "twice buried"—once when the individual died and again in the tenth century, when Abbot Dunstan raised the level of the cemetery outside the Old Church. It is possible that this is when Arthur's famous leaden cross, discovered at the depth of about seven feet, found its way into the burial.

We can similarly make some inferences about the coffins themselves, since they were said to be "ancient." The monks of Glastonbury were surely familiar with traditional burials of their own as well as the type of burials used for all those who came before them. To call a coffin "ancient" was to say something quite specific. The oldest burials at Glastonbury were cist burials in which pseudo-coffins were created by lining earthen graves with flat stone slabs. However, to say an ancient coffin had been uncovered could not have meant a cist burial. It would more likely refer to a lead coffin of the sort used during the Roman and Anglo-Saxon ages. This could help explain the story of Joseph of Arimathea's remains being kept in a silver coffin that was raised and lowered from a larger stone tomb. It is possible that this silver coffin was merely silver in color, and was in fact made of lead. Under the right conditions, remains buried in a lead coffin can survive remarkably well for centuries. Such was the case in 1981 when archeologists discovered medieval remains that came to be known as "St. Bees Man." In this case, the body was discovered to be largely undecomposed, neatly wrapped in linen, displaying the appearance of an individual, "not long dead." Another example is that of a 1700-year-old burial near Rome encased in a lead "burrito" where initial investigation suggests the body inside could be extraordinarily well preserved. While it is possible that such a coffin could have been ornamented in silver, most likely after rather than before it was rediscovered, it would have been incredibly expensive to create an entire coffin made of pure silver.

Since Frome's letter states that "three ancient coffins were found," this would indicate that all three coffins were found very near each other, as if they were a burial grouping. Since they were found at the same level, it would suggest that all three were buried around the same time, specifically some time before Abbot Dunstan added to the cemetery's ground level. Although it is impossible to tell exactly how old these remains are given the evidence stated in this account, we can assume that all three coffins were of exceedingly great age, and appear to be redeposited burials.

The burials were clearly ancient, but what else can be learned from them? The only other description given was regarding the remains they contained. It was stated that two coffins contained bones arranged "in the manner of death," which we can assume means the bones were laid out as complete bodies. What makes this curious is that the coffin containing the disarticulated bones of twelve separate individuals, carefully interred together, was placed between the other two. This would either mean that the coffin of the twelve was so carefully buried between two other burials as to appear to belong together, or that these burials were intended to be a contemporaneous grouping of coffins with the bones of the twelve flanked by two other individuals.

If we look at the two individual burials, we see signs that these two people were found in the same coffins in which they were buried. This is demonstrated by the items found inside the coffin, such as herbs and bundles of twigs. It has been theorized that the twigs were once at the center of a pillow placed under the head of the deceased. The herbs found interred with the bodies were likely grave goods placed alongside the body. In addition, the account of blood-like fluids visible in the coffin suggest it was the same in which the body originally decomposed.

While it is tempting to call these two coffins *in situ* burials, there is the troubling matter of the coffin buried between them. The coffin containing the combined bones of 12 individuals is obviously a reburial, not an ancient undisturbed burial. Whoever these bones belonged to, they very likely did not die at the same instant, resulting in one shared coffin. They were not twelve bodies buried together, but the removed, redeposited bones of previous burials. Since these were remains that were moved, we should assume they were reburied at around the same time as the two individual burials. As previously stated, the description presents the image of three coffins buried close together, which suggests they were purposefully grouped together.

The number of bodies to which these bones belonged is also highly evocative. The remains of twelve bodies immediately bring to mind the twelve original followers of Joseph. While it is not specifically stated in Abbot Frome's letter, this would have been the first thought in his fourteenth century mind as well. One may wonder why the bones of Joseph's followers from the first century would end up in one coffin, presumably made of lead as were the other two. It is possible that these individuals were originally placed in a simpler grave such as a cist burial or simply buried in an earthen grave, only to be reinterred later in a single coffin.

These bones were arranged so carefully in this coffin that once removed, it was difficult if not impossible to put them back as they once were. Given their location in strata below the layer of fill added to the cemetery by Abbot Dunstan in the tenth century, it is necessary to confine our examination of this burial within the time period ending in Dunstan's abbacy. However, we cannot make the mistake of assuming these coffins were made at this time. The mere fact that these burials included mass-redeposited, or "charnal" burials, means we must assume that these three closely buried coffins were all redeposited from earlier burials, dating from before Dunstan. This pushes the dating for these coffins back into the time of the Anglo-Saxon church.

Ancient burials of their time have been found with ritually arranged disarticulated bones thought to indicate ancestor worship. However, within a Christian context, it is possible that early converts who became part of the monastic scene at Glastonbury brought with them their traditions of bone reburial. In many early Anglo-Saxon monasteries, archeological evidence has been found demonstrating reverence for bone relics of saints and other important local spiritual leaders. Outside the eastern end of the chapel, there would often be a free standing stone altar, usually topped by a wheel cross. This sort of outdoor altar, or *loculus* as it is now called, would serve as a reliquary or shrine, containing a few pieces of bone collected from some person of importance within the monastic community or surrounding region. Therefore, when a group of church patriarchs were found buried in simple graves, it would have been fairly easy to take their bones, and rebury them in a place of prominence.

Although the identity of the individuals buried in these three coffins in the old cemetery cannot be established with any certainty, we can easily assume who they were thought to be. The bones of the twelve were surely assumed to be those belonging to the twelve founders of Glastonbury's famed wattle church. Since the Charter of St. Patrick was mentioned earlier in Abbot Frome's letter, it is possible that the two bodies buried in their own coffins were thought to be those of Sts. Fagan and Deruvian, sent as missionaries to Britain in the second century. The only other "founding fathers" of note to visit Glastonbury before Dunstan became abbot in the tenth century were St. Patrick and his two lay brothers, Arnulf and Ogmar. Although it is possible that one of these two burials belonged to St. Patrick, this is unlikely since it is debated whether Patrick truly died there, or in fact ever came to Glastonbury at all. In addition, Arnulf and Ogmar were both thought to be buried atop Glastonbury Tor near the chapel where they were monks for the remainder of their lives. This is of course only one of many possibilities that can never be proven. All we can say for certain is that the coffins containing the two individuals were buried, or most likely re-buried, prior to Dunstan's addition of one to two meters of fill dirt to the ancient cemetery, intended to forever seal and preserve the bones of Glastonbury's revered dead.

If these burials were easily identifiable by the fourteenth-century mind, the burial found under the Lady Chapel was surely thought to be that of Joseph of Arimathea. The coffin is described as being much higher in quality, decoration, and status than those found in the cemetery. If these were the remains of the fabled founder of Glastonbury Abbey, Joseph of Arimathea, his burial would have been the previously mentioned "nuclear burial" around which all other burials were centered in the early church. Furthermore, this burial so perfectly fit the description given in Melkin's prophecy that there would have been little doubt that this was the coffin belonging to Joseph himself. In fact the discovery of this grave matched the details presented in Melkin's fragments so perfectly, it has been claimed that this was an obvious hoax and in no way should be taken as an actual historical account. If this was a hoax, the end result was so dismally poor that even the most hardened skeptic must wonder why an abbey with such a rich history of hucksterism was so very bad at it. Compared to the illustrious discovery of King Arthur's tomb, this find remained relatively unknown until the creation of the crypt nearly eighty years later.

Lastly, when we recall the final line of Frome's account, we are told that the coffin found inside the confines of the Lady Chapel was placed into another, larger stone box (a tomb), until it could be further examined. This account matches perfectly with the medieval tradition that Joseph's remains were kept in a silver casket which could be raised and lowered from the larger stone tomb that once sat at the eastern end of the crypt at Glastonbury Abbey. Considering the location which was consistent with Melkin's prophecy, the richness of the coffin, and the raiment in which the body was buried, it seems very likely that this was the body of Joseph himself. It has been suggested that this discovery was simply part of a plan engineered by King Edward to attract more pilgrims to Glastonbury that was later derailed by the king's death.

Although this sort of conspiracy theory is common to Glastonbury Abbey, there seems to be no valid reason to assume this since there was no real use of Joseph's remains as a source of pilgrimage until almost 100 years later, when the crypt was built.

Abbot Frome's account might suggest, if not state outright, that the remains of Joseph and his followers were discovered due to an excavation that took place in the Lady Chapel and in the old cemetery. If we are to take this account at face value (which I believe we can, given the wealth of corroborating evidence surrounding it), we must wonder how these coffins remained undiscovered until the early fifteenth century. If these are the remains of the original members of the wattle church, why were they not found during John Blome's search in 1345? If we consider only one aspect of this account, the depth at which the coffins were buried, one possible answer can be found in a long-vanished chapel that once stood at the southern boundary of the old cemetery.

Let us first consider the three coffins found outside the Lady Chapel. If they were buried at a normal depth of six to seven feet, and were later covered by an additional three to six feet of earth during the time of Abbot Dunstan, this would mean the coffins were buried at this location prior to the second half of the tenth century. Since the three coffins found outside the Lady Chapel appear to be reburials, we must try to ascertain at what point in the church's history something happened to warrant the moving of ancient, venerated burials from their original site to their final resting place in the cemetery. The only alteration to the site during this time period took place to the east of the original wattle church, so we must look there for the source of the original burials.

Although it is possible that Dunstan was responsible for exhuming these remains, it is unlikely. By the time Dunstan came to Glastonbury, there had already been extensive building beyond the wattle church. In A.D. 720, Saxon king Ine of Wessex commissioned the building of his stone church some distance east, and forty years later enlarged it further, joining it to the Old Church with an atrium — an enclosed area outside the main entrance to a church where people could pray and wash their hands in fountains or wells. It is interesting to note that the well now known as St. Joseph's Well stood only a few feet away from the southeastern corner of the wattle church, and would have either stood just outside of, or possibly even built into the southwestern corner of Ine's atrium.

When one looks at the location of Ine's stone church and later atrium, its distance from the Old Church becomes immediately noticeable. According to archeological evidence unearthed in the early to mid-twentieth century, the atrium was nearly square in dimension. It was wider than Ine's original stone church, and was not quite as wide as the later enlargement. The space between Ine's stone church and the Old Church was intentional, either to ensure the atrium encompassed the well or to include a space that was deemed important for another reason.

Can we learn anything relating to the burials discovered in 1419 from this atrium and the space contained within? To find one possible answer, let us refer back to the thirteenth-century texts called the *Chronicon*, specifically a citation entered under the year A.D. 720.

> At this time a certain marvellous vision was revealed by an angel to a certain hermit in Britain concerning S. Joseph, the decurion who deposed from the cross the Body of Our Lord, as well as concerning the paten or dish in the which Our Lord supped with His disciples, whereof the history was written out by the said hermit and is called "Of the Graal" (de Gradali). Now, a platter, broad and somewhat deep, is called in French "gradalis" or "gradale," wherein costly meats with their sauce are wont to be set before rich folk by degrees ("gradatim") one morsel after another in divers orders, and in the vulgar speech it is called "graalz," for that it is grateful and acceptable to him that eateth therein, as well for that which containeth the victual, for that haply it is of silver or other precious material, as for the contents thereof, to wit, the manifold courses of costly meats. I have not been able to find this history written in Latin, but it is in the possession of certain noblemen written in French only, nor, as they say, can it easily be found complete. This, however, I have not hitherto been able to obtain from any person so as to read it with attention. As soon as I can do so, I will translate into Latin such passages as are more useful and more likely to be true [Evans, *The High History of the Holy Grail*, pp. 293–294].

This first sentence in the citation almost certainly refers to the prophecy of Melkin. Although Melkin's writing is dated to the middle of the sixth century, this reference is listed around the year 720, almost 200 years later. Referring back to the history of Glastonbury Abbey, we can find a possible connection.

Around the same time of this citation in Helinand's *Chronicon*, King Ine had built his first stone church at Glastonbury, alongside the wattle church, by now clad in boards and covered with lead. Considering Melkin's prophecy was written in the sixth century, one can presume it was available for King Ine to read. If Melkin's description of Joseph's burial and the relics it contained are mentioned in Helinand's chronicle under the year 720, the same year the stone church was built, it is reasonable to think that Melkin's text resurfaced, (most likely brought there from safekeeping in other area Anglo-Saxon churches, such as that atop the Tor), and was later used in the discovery of the ancient burials at the east end of the wattle church.

The main reason Melkin's prophecy has become so widely known today is that it details the location of Joseph of Arimathea's grave. It is likely that the text was first used in an attempt to locate the grave, both for religious reasons, and to simply make sure the remains were not destroyed during future building. This could explain why the atrium was later added to Ine's original stone church when it was enlarged in 760. If these were thought to be the original twelve inhabitants of Glastonbury's wattle church, whoever discovered their remains using Melkin's direction may well have thought the bones belonging to Joseph himself were among them. Joseph has been varyingly considered one of the twelve original members while others see him as the leader of twelve followers. For this reason, it is possible that whoever found the burials thought they had found Joseph's remains among the twelve potentially unmarked graves, resulting in the mass reburial in a single lead coffin later discovered in the south cemetery in the fifteenth century.

This theory is further justified when one considers the massive remodel Ine completed on his own monastery a mere forty years after his first stone church. The 720 church was a simple Anglo-Saxon form, consisting of a main rectangular building with an apse and two side chapels, but with a crypt or *hypogeum* beyond the east end. However, the larger church completed by Ine in 760 was of a much grander design. It had several rooms or chapels, the previously mentioned atrium adjoining it to the wattle church, and curiously,

This is a 3D reconstruction of King Ine's first stone church built around 720 A.D. This was the first building on the site of Glastonbury Abbey constructed after the Wattle church. It was a simple Anglo-Saxon design of a single long church and tower with north and south wings and an apse at the eastern end. Beyond the apse is the *hypogeum*, or slightly above ground crypt. This sort of free-standing outdoor center of worship, called a *loculus* or *confessio,* was common in Anglo-Saxon churches of the period, and always stood outside the eastern end of the church just beyond the altar (model created by author using Google SketchUp).

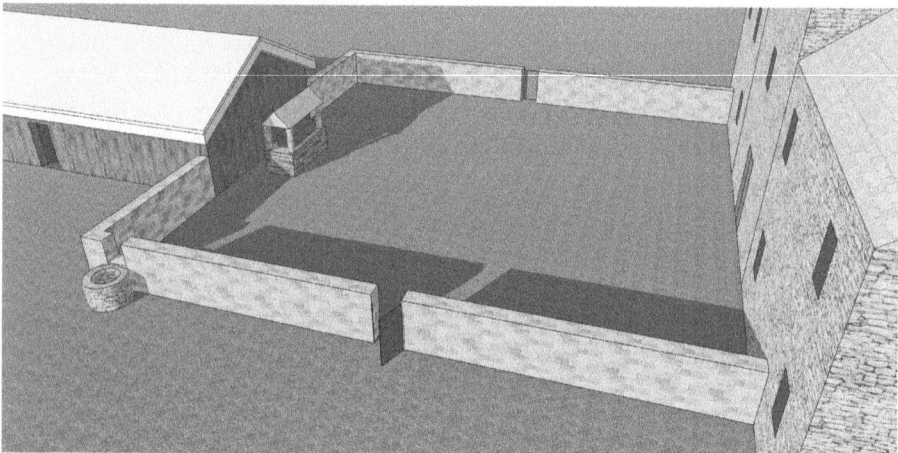

Top: This is a 3D reconstruction of King Ine's stone church built in the mid eighth century. This would be the "second phase" of construction, adding to the smaller Anglo-Saxon church built earlier, and including an atrium connecting it to the Wattle Church, which had been covered in boards and lead by Paulinus in the seventh century. Note here how the *hypogeum* has been enclosed by the eastern chapel, removed from its status as the church's *loculus* in favor of the outdoor atrium chapel just outside the eastern end of the Wattle Church. *Bottom*: King Ine's larger stone church completed around 760. The small outdoor chapel in the atrium is centered around the coffin containing the bones of the twelve individuals who were discovered just past the eastern wall of the Wattle Church. St. Joseph's Well is just outside the bounds of the atrium enclosure, but likely would have been integrated into its use, here portrayed as accessible through a small shelfed opening in the south wall (models created by author using Google SketchUp).

the hypogeum was then enclosed in its own chapel, in essence removing it from its role as the church's *loculus*. It is possible that when the graves of the twelve individuals were found using Melkin's prophecy, the bones were exhumed, redeposited in a single lead coffin, and displayed in the atrium created for this very purpose, causing the focus of relic veneration at the church to be switched from the hypogeum at the eastern end to the coffin displayed in the atrium.

While this would explain the coffin containing the remains of twelve individuals, it does not shed any light on the two coffins containing remains that were apparently reinterred in their own original coffins. If our assumption is correct that these three coffins were reburied at the same time, thus making a burial grouping, we must find a time when the coffin containing the twelve people were removed from the atrium, and buried in the old cemetery, along with the two individual coffins, before Dunstan added one to two meters of fill dirt. Granted that the time between Ine's atrium and Dunstan's changes on both practice and building at Glastonbury spans a relatively brief period of roughly 200 years, a great deal can happen in that amount of time. Fortunately, the very thing against which these remains were safeguarded serves to provide the best dating evidence available to pin down the exact sequence of events.

When Dunstan became abbot of Glastonbury, he introduced a number of changes. One of his first acts was to institute Benedictine monasticism in an effort to reform life at the abbey, focusing on learning and expansion of Christianity throughout Britain. He is widely known for the story in which the Devil appeared to him to tempt the pious man only to have Dunstan take up his red-hot blacksmithing pincers and take the Devil by his nose, causing him to emit a scream that could be heard for miles around. However, at Glastonbury, he is known more for his expansion to the already large church and grounds. In addition to expanding Ine's great stone church, he also bounded the ancient cemetery by a revetment wall, containing the great volume of soil he used to raise the ground level.

Earlier, Dunstan's impact on the landscape in the cemetery was examined in relation to the alleged discovery of King Arthur's burial place and the famous leaden cross on which his name was scribed. Here the unusual depth of the burial was explained as being the usual deep burial the people of the sixth century might give to a great man such as a king, with the additional one to two meters of fill added to give the fifteen to seventeen foot depth described by various accounts, (not accounting for the usual slight changes to ground level over the centuries). This would seem further demonstrated by my assessment that the much debated cross found at the seven foot level was created during the tenth century or slightly earlier to mark this as the site of Arthur's grave. If this were the case, the cross would have been laid flat, possibly covered by a stone, and Dunstan's addition would have placed the cross neatly in between. But Arthur's grave was not the only one to be found at this unusual depth. The three mysterious coffins found outside the Lady Chapel in the cemetery in 1419 were also found at a similar depth.

As Dunstan's intention upon creating this new layer was both to preserve the ancient burials in the older southern part of the cemetery, as well as building a new layer in which to place new burials, we find an instant in time in which the reburials of the communal, "charnal" coffin, and the two individual coffins might have been buried together in the southern cemetery. If it was Dunstan's wish to protect the ancient forefathers at Glastonbury, any remains he might have seen as threatened would have been reinterred, and covered by his layer of fill. Therefore, if the coffin that sat in the atrium, by now in place for around 200 years, was seen as being in any danger of compromise, Dunstan would have likely taken this opportunity to put the remains in their rightful place in the cemetery among their honored companions.

I make the assertion that the coffin in the atrium was at this time removed to the cemetery and reburied along with the two other coffins containing the remains of some other unknown individuals, also seen as having honored standing in the monastery's history. It is possible that these other two indi-

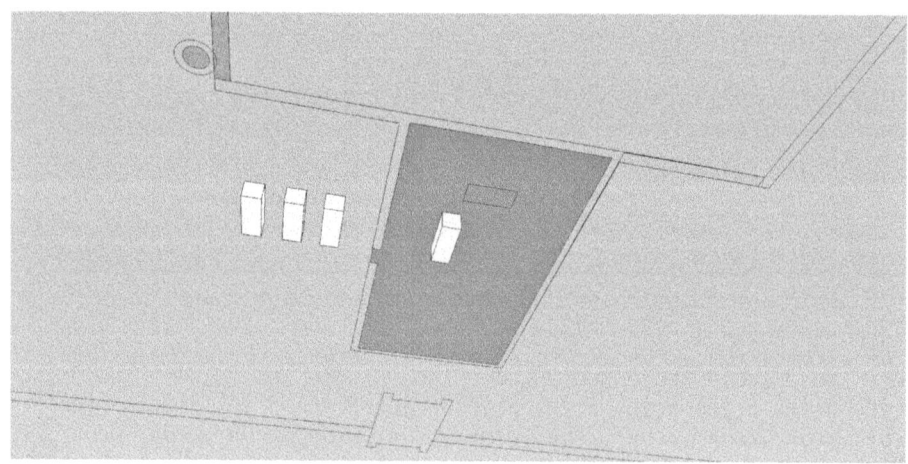

This below ground view of Dunstan's church shows the burial I theorize to be that of Joseph of Arimathea (single lead coffin inside and under Wattle Church), and three additional lead coffins — a group reburial in one coffin (likely Joseph's followers discovered by King Ine in 720), flanked by the coffins of two unknown others. This depicts the layout of discoveries made during the 1419 excavation under the Lady Chapel and in the Old Cemetery (model created by author using Google SketchUp).

7. The Mystery Tomb of "J.A." 131

viduals were being kept in similar above-ground places of honor, or that they were merely other burials of antiquity that would have otherwise been left outside Dunstan's newly enclosed cemetery, leaving them at risk of future disturbance. However, the value of having such ancient, revered remains on display was surely not entirely lost on Dunstan. If this coffin had been on display in the atrium for the past several centuries, it would have brought pilgrims from some distance. In fact, further evidence of this can be found a short distance away from where the wattle church stood in Dunstan's time, just on the southern boundary of the old cemetery enclosure.

At one time, a book of great proportions was on display in Glastonbury Abbey. Called the Magna Tabula, it was made from several wooden plaques on which illuminated manuscript pages were pasted. The great book drew from several available sources outlining the abbey's legendary beginnings. Although few consider this book as anything but an early version of the modern tourist guide, it does contain one bit of information that will prove to be quite useful.

> Apart from excerpted historical materials, the *Magna Tabula* contains two small pieces not found elsewhere among Glastonbury documents: one list of the indulgences and the other a short chapter "De capella sanctorum Michaelis et Ioseph et sanctorum in cimiterio requiescentium." According to this latter text there was an ancient and ruinous chapel in the cemetery, under whose altar numerous relics had been stored. In 1382 Chinnock had it rebuilt and rededicated to the memory of St. Michael and of the saints resting in the cemetery and the chapel, the chief of whom was Joseph of Arimathea. The *Magna Tabula* account, like others already noted, asserts that Joseph's remains had been buried in the cemetery, but also makes clear that his precise burial place remained a mystery. Joseph is simply the chief among the saints whose "reliquias incognitatas" make Glastonbury's cemetery one of the holiest places in the kingdom [Carley, *Arthurian Tradition*, p. 288].

It is important to note that this citation mentions the chapel called "St. Michael in the Cemetery" where no other known source records such a chapel. In fact, this chapel has been found in the archeological record at Glastonbury. Excavations have uncovered the foundation for a small chapel on the south side of the cemetery in an area that would now be between the eastern end of the Galilee (where the western end of the stone church once stood), and the abbot's garden that was once behind the monk's kitchen. The archeological evidence seems to indicate that this small chapel was in fact incorporated into the south wall of Dunstan's cemetery enclosure.

When Abbot Chinnock rebuilt and rededicated this small chapel, he did so in honor of all the honored dead in the cemetery, Joseph of Arimathea being chief among them. While it is certainly possible that Chinnock simply

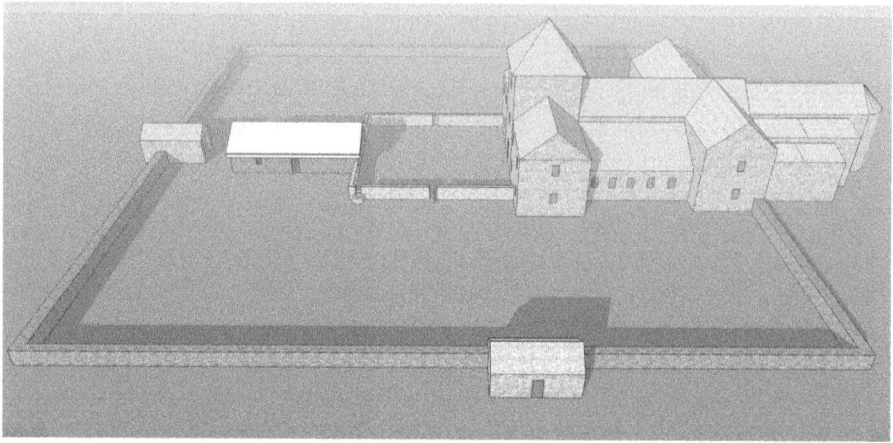

This 3D reconstruction depicts Dunstan's church as it stood around the end of the 10th century. Ine's original stone church can still be seen at the heart of the developing complex, but has roughly tripled in size. The Wattle Church stood for nearly 200 years before it was consumed in the fire of 1184. The atrium chapel has been removed, resulting in the reinterment of the coffin containing the bones of twelve individuals as well as the two others found in the 1419 excavations. In addition, the site has been enclosed by Dunstan's revetment wall, enabling him to raise the ground level in the cemetery by as much as 2 meters (model created by author using Google SketchUp).

made this assertion based on the growing popularity of the Joseph of Arimathea cult slowly developing on the site, there was already ample interest in Joseph's resting place long before this medieval interest began. Therefore, it is more likely that this tradition existed surrounding this small out-chapel before its rededication. If this chapel was built by Dunstan when he put the revetment wall around the cemetery, it is likely that he took this opportunity to remove some of the bones from the coffin in which it was thought the twelve followers of Joseph (including Joseph himself) were contained, and placed these sacred bones into his chapel, so that future visitors could still visit the holy relics. This theory is further supported by the thirteenth century Grail Romance, *The High History of the Holy Grail*, in which there is a reference to a curious monument containing the remains of Joseph of Arimathea (see Chapter 9).

The chapel was described as "ancient and ruinous" in Chinnock's time in the fourteenth century. It is worth noting that the two "pyramids" that once stood in the old cemetery between which King Arthur's grave was allegedly situated were also called ancient and were in a gravely eroded and "ruinous" state at the time of William of Malmesbury. These pyramids have been estimated to originate from between the late seventh and ninth centuries, and were present during the abbacy of Saint Dunstan. Therefore, one must

In this view of Dunstan's church, one gets a clear view of the old cemetery to the south of the Wattle Church where lay Glastonbury's honored dead. To the west of the Wattle Church is the small "gateway" chapel known as Dunstan's Chapel. The atrium still stands, but no longer serves as a center for veneration. In one regard, that role has been translated into the chapel of "St. Michael in the Cemetery," restored and rededicated by Abbot Chinnock in the late fourteenth century — dedicated to all of the unnamed saints that lie in the cemetery, chief among which was Joseph of Arimathea (model created by author using Google SketchUp).

wonder if this chapel could have dated from the time of King Ine 200 years prior. It has been stated that this chapel could have had its foundation at an earlier date, such as with a previous, possibly wooden structure, but the archeological remains seem to place it around the time of Dunstan.

Although archeological excavation of the site in the early twentieth century seemed to indicate that all remains found in relation to this chapel date from no earlier than the fourteenth century, it is clear that this chapel existed prior to this time, and as such, likely contained earlier remains. If it was "ancient and ruinous" in the fourteenth century, this gives some dating evidence to support our theory. If this chapel had been constructed by Dunstan, as it would seem, the chapel would have been standing for nearly 450 years when it was remodeled in 1382 by Abbot Chinnock — plenty enough time to become "ancient and ruinous," especially considering it would have survived the catastrophic fire of 1184.

The presence of this chapel during the fourteenth century may also shed some light on the uncertain outcome of John Blome's 1345 excavation. If the coffin found under the Lady Chapel in 1419 was actually Joseph's, it would explain why Blome did not return from his expedition claiming success. It would also explain why R. of Boston would write that his remains and those of his followers had been found in 1367. It is likely that when John Blome went to Glastonbury Abbey in search of Joseph's mortal remains, he dug in the cemetery without success and was then shown the relics contained in the chapel as somewhat of a consolation. In that regard, Blome both failed and succeeded in finding the bones of Joseph of Arimathea. He was simply told whatever remains there were of Joseph were kept above ground in the chapel. However in the eyes of R. de Boston in distant Lincolnshire, the remains had indeed been found.

In Abbot Frome's letter to the king, we potentially see the discovery of Joseph's original burial in a lead coffin under the Lady Chapel. In truth, it tells us more than that. This fourteenth-century account also establishes the stone tomb now in St. John's Church as that once seen as Joseph's tomb — the "larger stone box" in which his original coffin was placed. This stone tomb's path can now be traced from a chapel at the east end of the crypt through the Dissolution and eventually to St. John's Church, where it stands today. To further illustrate this, let us now examine what is known of the area known as St. Joseph's Chapel.

Referring to the previous quote regarding the location of St. Joseph's Chapel as cited by Lionell Lewis, the original chapel was described as being "at the east end of the crypt under St. Mary's Chapel." He adds that "a Norman underground chapel was converted into his shrine." Lewis goes on to say, "Later, in the fifteenth century, a piece of great vandalism was carried out. The crypt to the west of it was dug out, disturbing saintly dead" (p. 152). This tells us a great deal about the original chapel of St. Joseph. First, it tells us that it was a much smaller space than the crypt is now; second, that the crypt came later than the original chapel; and third, that the "saintly dead" mentioned by Lewis were likely the burials in wooden coffins containing wooden rods to which Abbot Frome refers in his letter to King Edward III.

From this, we can piece together what the original chapel might have been like. It was a small, underground room located to the east of the current "basement" level of the Lady Chapel, known as the crypt. It most likely would have been lit only by candlelight and accessed by one door only. Lewis also states that it was originally accessed via a staircase just past the Norman well now called St. Joseph's Well, the wellhead of which once stood just off the southeast corner of the wattle church.

We could assume this staircase to be the one that once led from inside the Lady Chapel down into the crypt past the well. This well is now covered by a Norman arch which was once a window frame in the eastern wall of the Lady Chapel, demolished in the thirteenth century when the Galilee joined the chapel to the Great Church. However, if we are to assume that the crypt

7. The Mystery Tomb of "J.A." 135

Top: The stairway leading from the interior of the Lady Chapel down to the crypt, now covered by a steel grate. The misalignment of the steps is not due to age. They were apparently built in this fashion, possibly to indicate one path down, and another up. These were not the first set of stairs leading to an underground chapel used to venerate St. Joseph of Arimathea, but the second. The crypt, built around 1500, was later added to an existing chapel for St. Joseph's remains. *Bottom*: The spiral staircase at the bottom of the uneven stairs leading from the Lady Chapel, down past the well and into the sixteenth-century crypt (author photographs).

St. Joseph's Well. The arch is composed of 2 window frames previously placed in the now-demolished eastern wall of the Lady Chapel. Old photographs of this archway show brickwork behind the well very similar to the sixteenth-century brickwork seen elsewhere in the stairwell, crypt, and St. Joseph's Chapel (author photograph).

was built after the original St. Joseph's Chapel, the staircase in question could not have been used to gain access to the crypt, because if it were the original way down into the chapel, this stairway would have led to nowhere. The crypt was not created until around 1500. We must remember that the crypt was only added on to, or expanded from, the original, smaller St. Joseph's Chapel.

There is another explanation for this mysterious staircase that once provided access to the chapel containing the mortal remains of St. Joseph. Visitors to Glastonbury Abbey today can see a curious feature in the Galilee chapel. In the southern wall, there is a Gothic door reconstructed in the early twentieth century under the supervision of Frederick Bligh Bond from what had been nothing more than a great hole. This opening showed signs that it had indeed once been a door before the finished stonework was robbed out following the Dissolution, effectively turning the once great abbey into an above ground stone quarry. It is not the presence of this door that is curious; rather that it

The south wall of the Lady Chapel. From this perspective, King Arthur's alleged grave site is just off camera to the right. The mysterious "IESVS/MARIA" stone is about eye level between the ornate door on the left and the small doorway on the right. The slight scar of the roof covering the room or chapel built over the stairway down into the crypt is still visible above the doorway (author photograph).

is now covered by a wall, specifically a wall with windows in the bottom, providing light to shine down into the crypt.

In the abbey museum, there is an exquisite model of Glastonbury Abbey as it existed in the early 1500s before the Dissolution. On the southern side, the modeler created two small rooms on the outside of the Lady and Galilee chapels — one providing a cover for pilgrims walking down the stairs from the Lady Chapel into the crypt (the scar of its roofline still visible on the Lady Chapel's south wall), and a slightly larger adjoining room. This larger chapel was built in the same general area as the "mystery door" mentioned earlier, presumably allowing access from the Galilee down to the well and crypt. The modeler presumed both rooms or chapels existed at the same time, but a closer inspection brings this assumption into question.

One may assume that the wall now covering the door was simply the back wall of the larger room leading to the crypt, but this wall includes a window at the bottom that allows sunlight to illuminate the crypt. If there was a room or small chapel built where the model suggests, this window would have been covered, blocking any light the window might have otherwise provided. In any configuration one might imagine to explain this discrepancy, we are left with either a door with no room, or a wall that makes the door

Opposite: The "mystery door," now covered by a southern exterior wall, as it is found inside the Galilee just to the east of the Lady Chapel. The arched doorframe is fifteenth century (reconstructed in the early twentieth century), as is the brow arch below it. It likely replaced a smaller door into the earlier Chapel of St. Joseph before the crypt was built around 1500. *At right*: In this image of the "mystery door," the original step can be seen (from a time before the floor level of the Galilee and Lady Chapels were raised to accommodate the creation of the Crypt below). In addition, the exterior window arch can be seen just at the bottom of the wall covering the doorway. It is clear in this image that this doorway was built later than the Galilee, as it cuts through earlier decorative stonework (photographs courtesy Sophie Morse).

140   II: Key Players

obsolete. The only configuration of this area that makes sense is that the two exterior chapels did not exist simultaneously, but instead that the wall wasn't built when the larger of the two rooms was removed, and the smaller room was built, most likely when the second, present set of stairs to the well and crypt were constructed around 1500.

Recalling Lewis's description of the original St. Joseph's Chapel as "originally approached by a stair-case past the ancient Norman well of St. Joseph, close to where he was at first buried," we see that the original chapel was small

Opposite: Here the exterior wall that now covers the "mystery door" in the south wall of the Galilee prominently displays the window that allows sunlight to reach the underground crypt and Chapel of St. Joseph. There would have been no need for these windows if another room once adjoined this wall. Therefore, the wall and the window would have been built only after the doorway was no longer needed, specifically when access to St. Joseph's Chapel was moved, leading to the larger, grander crypt (built around 1500) to accommodate the mass of pilgrims (photograph courtesy Sophie Morse). *Above*: Model of Glastonbury Abbey at its height on display at the Glastonbury Abbey Museum. This is the southern exposure of the Lady Chapel, Galilee, and cemetery. Please note the traditional concept of two small attached rooms or chapels on the southern wall covering interior access to the crypt and well below (author photograph).

and was accessed by a staircase on the south side. This would suggest there was no room for windows to allow external light to illuminate this area. Therefore, it would seem likely that the existing windows in the east end of the crypt, including the one in the wall covering the "mystery door," were created in the sixteenth century when the windows in the bottom of the Lady Chapel were built as part of the crypt. This would indeed be very near where the elaborately decorated coffin was unearthed under the Lady Chapel in 1419 — the coffin that was later placed inside the larger stone tomb that now sits in St. John's Parish Church.

We now have two dates that help narrow down the time frame in which the original chapel of St. Joseph was created. The fact that the "mystery door" apparently cuts through original ornamental stonework suggests this door was not originally part of the Galilee Chapel's plan. Since the letter from Abbot Frome to King Edward III was not written until 1420, the original Joseph chapel dedicated to St. Joseph must have been built sometime between this date and 1500, when the crypt was dug out. If we assume that this smaller chapel replaced the larger one that once existed a few feet further east, the stairway to the crypt that exists today must have been created around the 1500 date that the Crypt was built. For approximately eighty years, this "mystery doorway" may well have been the portal through which pilgrims descended to the original St. Joseph's Chapel. It is likely that only after this chapel was demolished was the well truncated and the Norman arch that once graced the east end of the Lady Chapel placed over it as a structural member.

When Lewis described Abbot Richard Beere's creation of the Crypt as "a great act of vandalism," the description was quite appropriate, especially from an archeological standpoint. Not only did it destroy any remaining evidence of the wattle church, it dramatically altered the architecture visible at this critical time in the 1400s when Abbot Frome's excavations took place. In

Opposite top: Based on the model found in the Glastonbury Abbey Museum, this computer-generated image shows a "reconstructed" chapel or room over a now-demolished stairway that once led down to the original, smaller St. Joseph's Chapel, before the crypt was built around a.d. 1500. Note that there are no windows in the foundation of the Lady Chapel and Galilee and the Great Door leading into the Galilee is not bricked over. *Bottom*: Based on the model found in the Glastonbury Abbey Museum, this computer-generated image shows the traditionally held notion of the chapel or room built over the stairs leading down into the crypt. Note that the earlier room and stairwell are gone, the doorway from the Galilee into this room is covered by an exterior wall, there are windows in the foundation of the Lady Chapel and Galilee, the Great Door leading into the Galilee is bricked over, and a window has been incorporated at the bottom (author photographs).

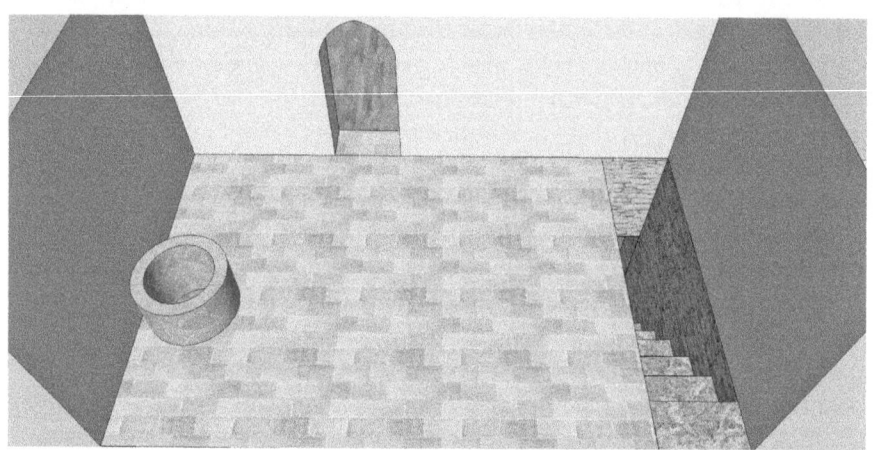

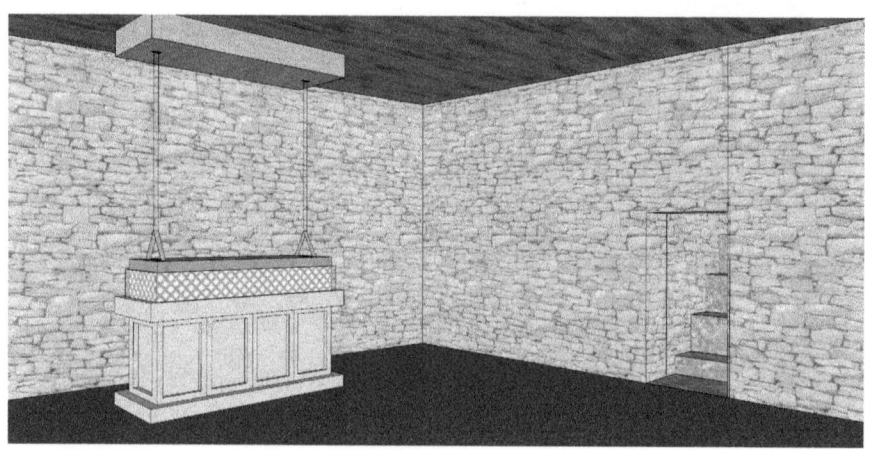

addition to the staircase and enclosure in the south wall, another stair and doorway to the crypt was created in the northwest corner of the Lady Chapel. The floor level of the Lady Chapel was also raised slightly to allow more headroom in the space below, making stone benches that once lined the walls of the chapel above simply part of the new floor.

The new underground chapel was surely a place of great reverence, teeming with people who had come to have their souls enriched by drawing near to not only a saint, but one who had once walked with Jesus Himself. This area was so important in fact that the elaborately ornamented doors leading into the Galilee from the north and south were bricked in so that more windows could be made for the Crypt. According to fifteenth-century pilgrims' accounts, it was also here that the mechanism by which the silver casket held within the stone tomb could be raised and lowered for the benefit of spectators. If one recalls the stone tomb currently housed in the church of St. John the Baptist on High Street, it is also possible that the indentation on the lid was the cavity in which the bones were laid out for display, with lead box (or perhaps an actual elaborately ornamented silver box or other covering) lifted to uncover the sacred bones, protected by the iron grate that once surrounded this indentation. This bit of showmanship, as well as the presence of the stone tomb, has been corroborated by people who kept diaries of their pilgrimages to the abbey just before and for some time after its dissolution.

Antiquarian John Leland, the last to see the Glastonbury library in its

Opposite top: This is a computer reconstruction of the Galilee at Glastonbury Abbey in the early fifteenth century. This view looks roughly southwest, incorporating a view into the Lady Chapel to the right, and a glimpse through the "mystery door" now visible in the south wall of the Galilee, covered by an exterior wall. This model indicates that the well was not truncated into a dark underground room of its own at this point, but was part of a processional path out of the Lady Chapel, built to echo Joseph's own wattle church, into the short-lived room just off the Galilee, past the well and down the stairwell into the original, smaller St. Joseph's Chapel. *Middle*: This is a reconstruction of the original, early-fifteenth-century St. Joseph's Chapel, before the crypt was created around A.D. 1500. Tradition states that Joseph's remains could be raised and lowered before the eyes of the faithful from their tomb. I would suggest that the remains instead remained in the shallow carved indentation in the lid of the stone tomb now found in St. John's Parish Church, and the lead casket that once contained them, now used as a cover, was instead raised and lowered to reveal the remains. *Bottom*: This view of the early fifteenth-century room (roof and south wall removed) depicts the relation between the "mystery door" that once led into the Galilee, St. Joseph's Well (before it was truncated approximately eighty years later during the construction of the crypt), and the stairway leading down to St. Joseph's Chapel and the tomb displaying his remains (models created by author using Google SketchUp).

entirety, surely went down to the crypt to see Joseph's tomb on one of his visits. However, due to King Henry VIII's order to terminate any type of saint worship, it is possible that Joseph's bones were carried off, destroyed, or otherwise lost to history. One may wonder what happened to the stone tomb. Did the alleged relics inside, the original Holy Grail, survive? Unfortunately, the present location of Joseph's cruets remains a mystery. The same cannot be said of his tomb.

Lionell Lewis makes reference to two men, Raphael Holinshed and John Ray, who came to Glastonbury after the Dissolution. Both reported seeing Joseph's stone tomb in the crypt below the Lady Chapel. Holinshed stated that the sepulcher was still at the abbey in 1577. Ray later claimed he saw Joseph's tomb in the east end of the ruined chapel of St. Mary on June 22, 1662. Later that same year, the tomb was moved from the ruins of Glastonbury Abbey to St. John's Parish Church just outside the east end of St. Mary's Chapel.

St. Joseph's Chapel at the eastern end of the crypt, under the Galilee. The altar here was built in the 1960s, possibly to reflect both the dimensions and tradition of St. Joseph's tomb, now found in St. John's Parish Church nearby. It is customary for pilgrims to leave a lit candle to honor Joseph's tradition (author photograph).

7. The Mystery Tomb of "J.A."

Although little today is known about this tomb, most agree that it came from Glastonbury Abbey and was once part of an altar to Joseph of Arimathea. This is surely the same tomb that Holinshed and Ray saw in the crypt of Glastonbury Abbey. Therefore we can say with reasonable certainty, due to both these written accounts and the time period to which this tomb has been dated, that this is the stone coffin seen by countless pilgrims who came to Glastonbury Abbey to see the relics of Joseph of Arimathea. This tomb sat in the original, smaller Joseph's Chapel before the crypt was made, and it is likely that this is the larger tomb into which the monks excavating within the Lady Chapel transferred the finely made coffin discovered in 1419.

In the early twentieth century, this stone coffin was moved from the churchyard into the church to the very spot where it now sits. Old photographs show the coffin in the churchyard, complete with its lid, where it remained for about 250 years. For many years, the tomb was said to belong to a fellow named John Allen, as witnessed by the "J. A." carved on a shield at one end. However this did not explain the caduceus symbol carved between the letters. It was common for symbols and initials to be carved on tombs, but not the caduceus. Although it is easy to assume this is just another person's tomb and that perhaps Victorian romanticism has turned it into a source of Arthurian hysteria, it is hard to reconcile the notion of this being a simple tomb when

St. Joseph's tomb in the cemetery of St. John's Parish Church, c. 1920. It was moved here following the Dissolution and the subsequent destruction of Glastonbury Abbey (courtesy Glastonbury Antiquarian Society).

one considers all of the "out of place" features found on this stone tomb such as the symbols, the metal grille, and the indentation carved into the lid. Because it is known to have come from an altar to Joseph that once sat inside Glastonbury Abbey, and because written accounts of its presence at Glastonbury exist right up to the time when it was moved to St. John's, it seems nearly beyond question that this is indeed Joseph's stone tomb.

Here in this one object, we see the culmination of the Joseph of Arimathea tradition at Glastonbury. The enigmatic writing of a sixth-century Welsh bard named Melkin, detailing the exact location of Joseph's burial place, once existed among Glastonbury Abbey's vast historical works. John Leland saw it, and later used it as a resource for his own writing. Several other writers who followed Leland also cited Melkin as a reliable historical source from Dark Age Glastonbury. Clearly familiar with Melkin's writing, John Blome requested and was granted permission to search for Joseph's grave in 1345. Although the ultimate success or failure of his efforts is unknown, a monk from Spalding Priory recorded that the grave was found, albeit several years later in 1367. Then in 1419, monks digging under the Lady Chapel allegedly found one ancient burial that obviously stood out from the rest which they later moved into another coffin for later study.

An existing subterranean chapel at the east end of the Lady Chapel was repurposed, creating a place where Joseph's remains were held as relics. A short time later, a larger space was created to accommodate the flood of pilgrims. It is from this point in time that we can directly trace a relic from this chapel. Although not the bones of Joseph himself, the stone coffin in which they were once housed has a clear history dating back to before the Dissolution, and has been recorded by several chroniclers who visited Glastonbury when the coffin was still in the crypt. Today, this coffin can still be seen sitting peacefully in a somewhat forgotten corner of St. John's parish church on High Street.

Here is the proof we need to bring the legend of Joseph of Arimathea and the Holy Grail into the realm of history. Melkin's prophecy is the earliest, most important mention of Joseph and of the cruets that would later become the seeds of the Holy Grail legend. Although this text is ridiculed as the pure fantasy of John of Glastonbury, it appears that several individuals were aware of it prior to John's *Chronica*. Joseph of Arimathea is the key to our investigation of the Holy Grail as a historical object, and in this stone tomb, we can see historical evidence of Joseph's presence at Glastonbury.

Now that we have evidence that Joseph of Arimathea might have actually been present at Glastonbury in the first century as legends claim, we might wonder what else these fragmentary writings of Melkin tell us about King Arthur, the Grail, and the other traditions of Glastonbury? If Melkin was writing historical accounts at Glastonbury in the sixth century, what incredible things did he see? What mythical characters did he actually meet? It has already been said that Melkin was "before Merlin." Could he have known King Arthur himself? To learn more about Melkin and his times, we must look to his unintentional chronicler — the man who last read his writings. We must search out other mentions of Melkin in the famous, infamous, and contentious works of the first librarian and Royal Antiquarian, John Leland.

PART III

The Written Record

All that remains of the Holy Grail today is what has been written about it. We do not have a relic to test for authenticity as with the Shroud of Turin. Nor do we have an ancient treasure map with enigmatic clues to follow. Although there is a majestic ruin at Glastonbury to see, there is sadly little physical evidence to examine in our search.

However, as the archeologist finds answers by digging through layers of earth, we can find the answers we seek by digging through the mountain of words that have been heaped onto this one subject. Sometimes the answers will be given, sometimes they will have to be extracted — a needle in time's haystack. By analyzing these written accounts, it is possible to see not only how the Grail legend began, but also that the Grail is more than just legend. Reading the words written by John Leland, King Henry VIII's Royal Antiquarian and librarian; a Grail romance written by someone at Glastonbury itself, Chrétien's famous *Conte del Graal*; and the German Grail romances; we can finally bridge the gap between legend and history.

Chapter 8

John Leland — The King's Antiquarian

History is replete with examples of how good things can come out of bad. The Roman Empire overran countless smaller countries in its bid for world domination, but brought with it new technology, new art and literature, and exposure to world trade. The British conquered so much of the world that it was said, "The sun never sets on the British Empire," in the process tilling under native cultures and practices. However, they also brought literacy, commerce, and industrialization to many underdeveloped parts of the world. So it was with the Christian church.

Christians today find themselves answering for offenses they did not commit, most attributable to the Catholic Church, specifically the medieval Roman Catholic Church. However, it is thanks to their power and dominance in the Western world that so much of our early history has been preserved. While the world burned during the Dark Ages, monks in remote monasteries copied Greek masterworks so that they could be read by future generations. In truth, it would likely astound the modern archeologist, historian, theologian, and fiction writer what is truly kept inside the Vatican archives.

It is also sometimes good for the church to turn on itself, not only as a means of course correction, but as a way to ensure that turbulent periods in history do not go unrecorded. Nothing "makes ink" like a power shift in the church. Such was the case with King Henry VIII's break with the Roman Catholic Church and the Dissolution of the Monasteries in England during the sixteenth century. Although this action was undertaken for the most self-serving reasons since David and Uriah, it also provided an inventory of all relics, wealth, and holdings of knowledge in the possession of English churches and monasteries at that time. While this inventory was simply to see what could be plundered, it serves as an invaluable tool in the study of church history in England.

8. John Leland — The King's Antiquarian

During the Dissolution, the final destruction of all church infrastructure was carried out by the English military, but the job of taking inventory fell to one man. This royal accountant and the first to hold the title of antiquarian was none other than John Leland. Although Leland was partly responsible for the removal of the local wealth, power, and independence that the large monastic structure provided, he is viewed today throughout England as something of a hero. Today visitors to Glastonbury can pick up brochures prompting one to "Hike the Leland Trail." A strange combination of travel writer, historian, librarian, and archeologist, he traveled throughout the British Isles not only commenting on the churches he visited, but also on the landscape, nature, and general atmosphere of each area.

Because Glastonbury was second in wealth and power only to the cathedral in Wells, much time was spent making certain of what the abbey had to offer. Leland visited Glastonbury twice, once before the Dissolution and once after, making careful notes of what he found on each visit. Before we examine his discoveries, let us take a closer look at the man himself, so that we can make sure we learn all that we can from him.

John Leland was born in London on September 13, most likely in 1503, and had an older brother, also named John. Being orphaned at an early age, he was sent off to St. Paul's School under the supervision of their first headmaster, William Lily. He then progressed to Christ's College in Cambridge where he received a degree in the arts. After achieving his first degree, he went on to attend Oxford, becoming a fellow at All Souls College. He soon found its style of learning too confining and began looking elsewhere.

Although he displayed a keen interest in learning, particularly in literature, he did not fully come into his own until he traveled to Paris in 1526 to continue his studies. There he studied under François Dubois, and he developed a passion for antiquity, most especially ancient documents. Having received a classical education, studying Greek and Latin as well as many examples of classical literature, he quickly set himself to learning all he could from the past. Finally in 1530, he found work as a librarian in one of King Henry's many libraries.

He is most famous for his *Itinerary*, a treatment of his work as Royal Antiquarian, but in fact he was quite a prolific writer. In 1533, he wrote a series of poems commemorating the coronation of Queen Anne Boleyn. Soon thereafter, Leland was commissioned as Royal Antiquary and given the task to "search after England's Antiquities, and peruse the Libraries of all Cathedrals, Abbies, Priories, Colleges and also all places where Records, Writings and secrets of Antiquity were reposed." Although Leland surely saw this as a unique opportunity, this was simply a first step in the king's grand plan to overthrow the Roman Catholic Church in England.

John spent the better part of a decade traveling the hills and valleys of the English and Welsh countryside, recording most everything that he saw — not only the holdings of the local religious establishments, as he was commissioned, but every monument, every bridge, and much of the general landscape and scenery. Some have said that he made these records as reminders to himself for when he ventured that way again, perhaps to complete a more ambitious work. In fact he had planned on making several new works once his *Itinerary* was completed, including a list of all major British writers, a traveler's guide of sorts to include a map and some commentary on the areas he had visited, a history, and an outline of British royalty.

Upon completing his gargantuan task at the end of his travels in 1543, he published his findings and presented them to the king. Of course by this time, the heinous act of seizing all the wealth, literature, and holdings belonging to the churches and monasteries throughout England had already taken place. It is uncertain to what extend Leland was aware of his role in the Dissolution, but from what can be learned of his character, it is more likely that he undertook his work either as a pure learning experience, at least initially unaware of its consequence, or as an attempt to catalog what would have been completely lost otherwise. It would seem that in his study, he felt it important not only to describe and inventory, but also to learn what he could from local customs, legends, and traditions. It is for this reason that we find so much of the Arthurian and Joseph legends interlaced with his writings regarding the Somerset and Cornwall regions.

Of Leland's most valuable work, Carley has the following to say:

> In its present form, the *Itinerary* consists of rough travel notes. Unfortunately the autograph manuscript is badly damaged, leaves have been lost or bound with other manuscripts, and the text has not been accurately edited. Nevertheless, we can deduce that Leland made a number of trips throughout the kingdom, taking measurements of buildings, noting inscriptions, calculating distances, and discussing such miscellaneous details as crops and local customs. The notes' arrangement comes from the context of the journeys themselves. Leland's motivation for his travels is a combination of antiquarianism and patriotism: "I trust that thys your [*i.e.*, Henry VIII's] realme shall so wele be knowne, ones paynted with hys natyue colours, that the renoume thereof shal geue place to the glory of no other region." The *Itinerary*, as does much of the poetry, displays an intellectual curiosity combined with a love of landscape and desire for topographical accuracy. The clue to the past, Leland suggests, lies in an analysis of surviving monuments of all sorts, local legends as well as architecture. Leland wants to see all the kingdom, in all its details [Carley, "Manuscript Remains," p. 113].

It seems clear that John Leland put value on every aspect of a region's individuality and flavor. He did not filter what he encountered through a vanity of intellect, nor did he discount any piece of information as unnecessary or unscholarly. Were he alive today, Leland would most likely be called a investigative reporter and photo journalist, recording every piece of information he could, amassing hundreds of hours of interviews, historical footage, and commentary. Ultimately, Carley sums up Leland's work thus:

> John Leland's collections — poetry and prose — provide a great store of information about Leland's own contemporary scene and about the medieval world of monastic libraries, of which he was often the last witness. Leland was an accomplished poet, a man sensitive to his surroundings, an avid bibliophile, and an accurate observer and recorder of detail [p. 118].

Thankfully the same can be said of those who became the keepers of his work. For the most part, these texts were maintained, safeguarded, and when transcribed, kept as close to Leland's original sentiment as possible. Although we may not have his complete and fully fleshed-out vision to call upon, what we have is as complete and close to the original source as we may hope to have these four and a half centuries later.

To fully appreciate the complete life's work Leland made of his *Itinerary*, the reader would have to sit down with the full five-volume set that is obtainable in many libraries around the country, and spend the time it takes just looking at the maps, poring over the lists of counties and shires through which he traveled, and begin reading about any region to appreciate the amount of care and detail he put into his observations. However, since this would require a depth of study far in excess of our current investigation, a simple description of his path will provide a good summation.

Starting from London, he traveled through nearly every county in central England, including Northampton, Cambridge, Bedford, Hertford, and Leicester. He then went further north, into Nottingham and Lincoln, pushing into Yorkshire and Durham as far north as Gateshead, only a short distance from the Scottish border. Returning to London, he then ventured westward through Middlesex, Berks, Oxford, Gloucester, and Wilts, south through Bath and Wells, and finally through Glastonbury. Continuing west, he went through the remainder of Somerset, Devon, and Cornwall, eventually reversing direction at Land's End. Going back through Cornwall, he went along the southern coast through Plymouth, Torquay, and Exeter and on through Dorset and Hampshire.

Venturing out toward Wales, he went through Warwick, Stafford, and just into Wales at Shropshire, returning through Hereford, Worcester, Oxford, and back to London. His further investigation of Wales took him throughout the country, north through Denbigh, Carnarvon, and Merioneth, south through Radnor, Brecknock, Monmouth, Glamorgan, Carmarthen, and Pembroke, and finally along the coast through Cardigan and into Montgomery. From Wales, he turned again north through England, only this time along its western coast, going from Shropshire through Cheshire, Lancashire, Cumberland, and Northumberland.

Returning to London, he journeyed eastward toward the place of pilgrimage, Canterbury, through which he passed after each circuit around the different regions of Kent. In the last three parts of his great work, Leland returned to areas previously investigated, first to the north to Cumberland and Northumberland, then back southwest through Glastonbury and Somerset, again through Yorkshire, Durham, and Lincoln, finally turning back westward to revisit Wilts, Somerset, and Dorset.

Reading accounts given by Leland leaves one somewhat perplexed at times. There are times when he goes into great detail about a town, significant aspects of an area, or simply images he sees. In other instances, he glosses over entire towns, making only the most general descriptions of them. Take for example the following excerpts from his initial entry into Somerset. The first passage describes the Roman town of Bath:

> The cite of Bath is sette booth yn a fruteful and pleasant bottom, the which is envirnonid on every side with greate hilles, out of which cum many springes of pure water that be conveyed by diverse ways to serve the cite. Insomuch that leade being made ther at hand many houses yn the toune have pipes of leade to convey water from place to place [Smith, p. 140].

Leland goes on for many lines speaking about the Roman baths as well as of several individuals of note, even describing the number and names of the gates leading into the town, the walls around it, and any number of specifics one might witness. He then continues to the city of Wells wherein lies the largest, most wealthy cathedral in England:

> From Bath to Palton al by hilly ground but plentiful of corne and grasse an eight miles.
> From Palton to Chuton by like ground about a 2. Miles.
> There is a goodly new high tourrid steple at Chuton.
> From Chuton to Welles by hilly ground but lesse fruteful partely in Mendepe about a 5. Miles
> The toune of Welles is sette yn the rootes of Mendepe hille in a stony soile and ful of springes, whereof it hath the name. The chefest spring I scaullid Andres welles, and risith in a medow plot not far above the est end of the cathedrale chirch, first renning flat west and entering into Coscumb water sumwhat by south [p. 144].

This is the only mention of Wells Cathedral in this description of Leland's trip through Wells. Although he mentions several other chapels, churches, and even hospitals in the area, as well as a description of the "right exceeding fair houses al uniforme of stone high and fair windoid in the north side of the market place," there is no further mention of Wells Cathedral, what would otherwise seem to be the high point of his visit.

This sort of treatment should not be taken as disinterest or negligence, however. In fact, he gives the town of Glastonbury the same sort of short treatment only a few lines later:

> From Hartlake bridg I passed by a low about a quarter of a mile: and then I consceneded by a litle and a litle to hilly ground a hole miles ryding, and so entereid into Glessenbyri.
>
> The chief streate and longest of the towne of Glessenbyri lyith by est and weste, and at the market crosse in the west ende there is a streate by flat south and almost northe.
>
> There is a market kept in Glessenbyry every weke on the Wensday [p. 148].

He goes on to describe St. John the Baptist church on High Street and much detail of the architecture and what he finds inside. However, there is no word of the great abbey just across the street.

Crossing the "bridge of stone of a 4. arches communely caullid Pont-perlus, wher men fable that Arture cast in his swerd," he went by the way of Bruton to Castle Cary, and then he arrived at Cadbury. There we get a lengthy description of the hill claimed to be the site of King Arthur's great fortress.

> At the very south ende of the chirch of South-Cadbyri standith Camallate, sumtyme a famose toun or castelle, apon a very torre or hille, wunderfuly enstrengtheid of nature, to the which be 2. enteringes up by very stepe way: one by north est, and another by south west.
>
> The very roote of the hille wheron this forteres stode is more then a mile in cumpace.
>
> In the upper parte of the coppe of the hille be 4. diches or trenches, and a balky waulle of yerth betwixt every one of them. In the very toppe of the hille above al the trenchis is *magna area* or *campus* of a 20. acres or more by estimation, wher yn diverse places man may se fundations and *rudera* of walles. There was much dusky blew stone that people of the villages thereby hath caryid away.
>
> This top wityn the upper waulle is xx. acres of ground and more, and hath bene often plowed and borne very good corne.
>
> Much gold, sylver and coper of the Romaine coyness hath be found ther yn plouing: and likewise in the feldes in the rootes of this hille, with many other antique thinges, and especial by est. Ther was found *in hominum memoria* a horse shoe of sylver at Camallate.
>
> The people can telle nothing ther but that they have hard say that Arture much resorted to Camalat [p. 151].

In this photograph taken from Cadbury Castle Hill, the most likely candidate for the historical Camelot, one can see Glastonbury Tor looming some miles distant. If this was the site of the legendary King Arthur's throne, he could in a sense have seen his own fate every day (photograph courtesy Sophie Morse).

From this excerpt, it seems that Leland put quite a great deal of stock in traditions regarding local legends, especially when it was a figure of some high esteem in British history. Regardless of one's stand on the historical nature of King Arthur, or the Cadbury hill fort as Camelot, this account serves to demonstrate Leland's vital role not only as a travel writer, but as a chronicler of what history and archeology was known at the time. In a historical investigation, any tidbit of information could be valuable, and as was the case with his account of Cadbury, Leland has some vital insights to offer us regarding our investigation of Glastonbury and its traditions.

When John Leland first visited Glastonbury in 1534, he commented on the great antiquity of the library he found there, and even reported holding the legendary lead cross that had once been found at the original burial site allegedly belonging to King Arthur, which had by the time of his visit been relocated to the great black marble crypt just to the west of the high altar. When he returned around 1543, he did not mention the abbey since it had already fallen to the Dissolution. He did, however, speak of it in fuller detail in his later work *De Rebus Britannicus Collectanea*, and also in his *Assertio*

Arturii, in which he claimed much of his information came from the fragmentary remains of Melkin's writing at Glastonbury.

William of Malmesbury originally dated the beginning of the ecclesiastical history of Glastonbury Abbey to the eighth century with King Ine of Wessex. However, after his time spent there, combing through the abbey's vast library of ancient histories and accounts, he revised that assessment, claiming that Glastonbury was much older, even hinting at sources that claimed a truly legendary beginning. It would seem that whenever historical writers visit Glastonbury, they come away with a completely different perspective than that with which they arrived. One might wonder exactly what could be found in the Glastonbury archives that would result in such a complete reversal. When John Leland visited Glastonbury, he was astounded at the great antiquity of the volumes held within. He made a now very famous and quite telling statement to this effect after his first visit.

> I was a few years ago at Glastonbury in Somerset, where the most ancient and at the same time most famous monastery in our whole island is located. I had intended, by the favour of Richard Whiting, abbot of that place, to refresh my mind, wearied with a long course of study, when a burning desire to read and learn inflamed me afresh. This desire, too, came upon me more quickly than I thought it would. So I straightway went to the library, which is not open to all, in order to examine most diligently all the relics of most sacred antiquity, of which there is so great a number that it is not easily paralleled anywhere else in Britain. Scarcely had I crossed the threshold when the mere sight of the most ancient books took my mind with an awe or stupor of some kind, and for that reason I stopped in my tracks a little while. Then having paid my respect to the deity of the place, I examined all the bookcases for some days with the greatest interest [Carley, *Manuscript Remains of John Leland*, p. 142].

Let us take a little time to dissect this statement, as it will become important later. He begins by saying he "was a few years ago at Glastonbury in Somerset," indicating he was referring to his first visit to Glastonbury, before it was dissolved by the king. He also says that he visited the library "by the favour of Richard Whiting." This is quite important to consider because by the time of John's second visit to Glastonbury, Abbot Whiting had already been put to death by hanging on Glastonbury Tor. He goes on to say that his mind had been wearied by a long course of study, indicating that it was only after a long time of travel that he had visited Glastonbury. However, it soon becomes clear that what he finds there is so inspiring that his passion for reading and study is rekindled.

He continues to make the statement that his purpose there was to "examine most diligently all the relics of most sacred antiquity, of which there is so great a number that it is not easily paralleled anywhere else in Britain." One might immediately think that Leland is referring to treasure or holy relics, such as the bones of saints or similar objects, but here he is referring to the library itself. He refers to the books housed therein as "relics," and not just relics but relics of "sacred antiquity." This would demonstrate that the books he found there were not just old, and not just ancient, but so ancient that they reached back to a much earlier time — potentially to the time of Jesus. Although this may seem a leap of faith, to describe a book as a "relic of sacred antiquity" is to say something very particular, pointing to a source and date of writing beyond what was customary for even such a seasoned antiquarian.

Finally and most telling, he states, "Scarcely had I crossed the threshold when the mere sight of the most ancient books took my mind with an awe or stupor of some kind, and for that reason I stopped in my tracks a little while." If we are to take this passage as truth, John is saying that the mere sight of the library at Glastonbury literally stopped him in his tracks, awestruck. Remember that in the sixteenth century, Glastonbury Abbey was an enormous, lavishly decorated, awe-inspiring place in itself. If John took the customary route through to the library, which was then held in the cloisters just beyond the southern wall of the nave, he had to pass through this vast and beautiful abbey to get to the library. If he bypassed that, only to find himself in an ecstatic state upon reaching the library, what he found inside must have been an antiquarian and bibliophile's heaven.

It is interesting that he reserved his most intriguing comments regarding the exact nature of what he discovered in the abbey library for other works that came after his famous *Itinerary*. Unfortunately, his later works have been erroneously discredited due to his failing health, which led to his eventual insanity. Let us now investigate these lesser known manuscripts and Leland's later fall from grace.

Even after the completion of his masterwork and its presentation to the king in 1543, Leland continued a lifelong pursuit of writing. Although he died before he could see his dream come to fruition, segments of his writings can be found in many other histories and compilations of scholarship that continued to be published through the eighteenth century. The first of these later works is called *De Rebus Britannicis Collectanea*, which was five volumes filled with notes regarding antiquities he encountered, lists of the books he found in the libraries he visited before the dissolution, and transcripts he copied from many of these.

> The *Collectanea* is made up of a group of what might almost be called commonplace books devoted, for the most part, to extracts from manuscripts Leland had seen. It is almost entirely Latin quotations from other authors. In the *Collectanea* Leland distinguishes between his transcription and his own opinions. He notes what an author has to say and then adds his own

judgment under a marginal entry marked with his name. In the marginalia he discusses other manuscripts he has seen of the work, conflicting opinions by other authorities, the script of the work, age of the manuscript, and so forth [Carley, *Manuscript Remains*, pp. 113–114].

From this incomplete work, we learn that John Leland was not only meticulous but also prolific in his desire to pass on all that he had encountered during his journeys. Published in its present form by Thomas Hearne in 1716 after Leland's death, the incomplete corpus of his writing was passed down through the generations, some donated to the Bodlean College and some damaged or lost, making it difficult to get the full picture even from such a wealth of information. However, it seems clear by this example that Leland was clear-minded and dedicated to the preservation of knowledge while writing the *Collectanea*.

Turning now to the text that has been more a bone of contention among scholars, we enter some of the gray area that is encountered all too often during an investigation of legendary events or figures. Formally named *Assertio Inclytissimi Arturii* (*Assertions of the Renowned Arthur*), this is a work devoted entirely to the life and deeds of King Arthur. The tone of this manuscript demonstrates that Leland's intent was to create a work of history, not a latter-day medieval romance. At one point, Leland even expresses displeasure with Polydore Vergil over what he considers his careless treatment of Arthur's history, making reference to Vergil's "Italian bitternesse."

In the beginning of his Arthurian treatment, Leland includes something of a bibliography — a list of sources which he titles "The Table of the names of those Authors, whose testimonies this present booke useth." Included in this list of sources are names familiar to Arthurian histories, such as Gildas Badonicus and Nennius. However, he also has listed names that some would question as historical. One example is Merlinus Caledonius, or the "Scottish Merlin." This demonstrates that he had at his disposal Geoffrey of Monmouth's *Vita Merlini*, in which is told the story of Merlin Wylt, a wild man of the Caledonian Forest who went mad after the battle of Arthuret. Norma Lorre Goodrich, in her book *Merlin*, suggests that this individual could be the Merlin of Arthurian fame, although others dispute this.

The name on the list most relevant to the present investigation of Joseph of Arimathea is Melchinus, the Latin version of a name with which we have already become familiar: Melkin. In Chapter 11, "The Antiquitie of Avalonia," Leland mentions this ancient source, speaking of the ancient nature of Glastonbury. (Some liberties have been taken with spelling for the sake of clarity).

> Melchinus the Brittaine makes mention of Avalonia and of the religious place there. Silvester Geraldus in his booke *De Institutione Principis*, thus speaketh. And the island which at this day is called Glastenbury, was called

> in auncient time Avalonia: For it is an Islande altogether environed with Moorish or fenny groundes: Whereupon in the Brittish tongue it is called Avalon, that is, an Island fruitefull of apples: For with apples (which in the Brittish tongue are called Aual) this place aboundeth [Leland, p. 55].

Many have made the supposition that Leland did what so many who came before and after him did, and simply intertwined history with accepted legend and literary accounts as written by some of the well known Arthurian writers of the day. However, one must remember that John Leland was more than just a writer; he was a chronicler. He was well familiar with the difference between fiction and history, as well as the difference between ancient texts and modern renditions merely derived from them.

If you are tempted to believe Leland was duped by some faked manuscript of antiquity, understand that those were not the days where cunning fakers aged the paper appropriately, used period ink, and distressed the paper to make it look the appropriate age. If someone in an abbey wanted to present a fake document as one of great age, all they really had to do was to say it was so. There was no carbon 14 dating or microscopic analysis for which the hoaxer had to account. It was all a simple matter of credibility. As one trained since youth in the study of antiquity and literature, it is fairly certain that he would not have been so easily fooled. In addition, he appeared to be of the most serious mind regarding England's antiquities. To him, passing off fiction as history would have been an abomination, and having taken Holy Orders at some point prior to his appointment by King Henry VIII, he also quite likely would have considered it a sin.

Leland's use of Melkin as a source of historical information in his own treatises is very important in placing some of the legends of Glastonbury Abbey in the realm of historical fact. John of Glastonbury stated in his *Cronica* that Melkin was a sixth-century Welsh bard who wrote a prophecy that told of Joseph of Arimathea being buried at Glastonbury. Since John of Glastonbury's credibility as a history writer is questionable, his reference to Melkin might have to be rejected were it not for the fact that Leland, writing some time later, made the claim that he also saw texts written by Melkin when delving into the library at Glastonbury Abbey. Surely Leland would not have simply looked at extant copies of the *Cronica* and made the claim that it was an ancient document. If he claimed to have seen fragmentary remains of Melkin's writings, potentially entire texts, he should be taken at his word.

> The most important pre–Dissolution witness to the tradition of Melkin is John Leland. Leland reported that he found in Glastonbury's library an ancient fragment of Melkin's *Historia* and that he took notes from it. From this statement it appears that there were in the library at least documents apart from John's *Cronica* which contained a record of Melkin and his writ-

ing. Moreover, in his examination of the fragments Leland discovered quite a number of facts, several of which do not appear in the prophecy itself. He says that Melkin was anciently known as one of the most famous and erudite of British writers; his later obscurity was a result of the Saxon invasions. Leland notes that Melkin was born in Wales, that he was trained as a bard, and that he wrote *Historia de Rebus Britannicis* (in prophecy form, typical of his country). He mentions Melkin's belief that Joseph of Arimathea was buried at Glastonbury, but adds that he does not himself believe this to be accurate. Finally, he notes that according to the extant information Melkin flourished before Merlin [Carley, *Chronicle*, p. liv].

There remains one outstanding question regarding Leland's familiarity with these mysterious texts. Were these texts carted off to join the thousands of others contained in King Henry's libraries, or did they fall to the fires that ravaged the monasteries during that time in British history? It seems certain that Leland had access to them after submitting his famous *Itinerary*. Both of the above-described later works were written after the completion of his task to inventory Britain's antiquities. Although he could have taken notes and transcriptions from them, it would seem by the depth of these works that he still had the original material to which he could refer.

It would seem clear that these texts remained among the holdings of King Henry's libraries. However, anyone who reads James Carley's *The Books of King Henry VIII and His Wives* will attest to the fact that no reference to Melkin can be found. In fact, it includes titles that could be considered the popular literature of the time. It is possible that some of the material in question was destroyed in a fire that ravaged one of the royal libraries, but considering the extensive lists of the books removed from Glastonbury after the Dissolution, it would seem that such material would have been listed at some point. It has also been suggested that they have not been lost at all but merely incorporated into other volumes, either by binding several smaller texts into one larger volume or by having been incorporated into later manuscripts under different names.

Although there are several possibilities for the eventual fate of these ancient texts, one remains uninvestigated. Could at least some of these have found their way into Leland's keeping?

> As in Eco's fictional world, the library constitutes a privileged area, not open to just anyone (Leland shrewdly brought a letter of introduction from the king himself), and in entering its precincts Leland was going into a private, even arcane, territory. It took Leland some length of time to go through the collection and he listed in his notebooks over forty titles; these reflect his own interests but also give us some insight into the last days of the library. Most of the books he saw appear to have been of a venerable age, and at least thirty could possibly date from pre–Conquest times. (Five

or six of these, moreover, still survive.) A majority of these texts which Leland described were historical, but he also noticed some English exegetical works and several vernacular items. A keen Arthurian, he was pleased to see Geoffrey of Monmouth's *Life of Merlin*, but what impressed him most was the Charter of St Patrick, of which he seems to have taken possession, and the garbled fragment of Melkin's prophecy. In the eyes of the monks, too, both of these items would have ranked among the greatest treasures of the library [Carley, *Chronicle*, pp. 142-143].

There is no definite evidence supporting this theory, but it is possible that, at least for a time, Leland had several choice manuscripts at his fingertips from which he eventually penned some of his later histories and accounts, including those describing the life and death of Arthur, as well as the antiquity of Glastonbury itself. However, as with John of Glastonbury, little can be known for certain regarding his claims of Melkin and his writing. It is said that in his later life, Leland became insane, and ultimately died of his affliction before he could complete his study of these materials.

John Leland died in 1553 after having been declared insane in 1550. An account of one who knew him stated that for a short time before this declaration he had "fallen beside his wits." What this means exactly is uncertain, but the account has marred the credibility of his later writings, rendering them untrustworthy. Dr. Carley disagrees with this assumption, stating that several years elapsed between Leland's citation of Melkin and the onset of his illness.

While it would certainly be easier to take his claims and references to Melkin more seriously if he had not been so afflicted, it should by no means follow that we cannot take these works into consideration. In fact it seems the other works he attempted after his *Itinerary* was presented are accepted as being completely valid. His list of British writers of note was eventually published under the title *Comentarii de Scriptoribus Britannicis* by Anthony Hall in 1709, and his *De Rebus Britannicis Collectanea*, published by Thomas Hearne in 1716, was notable for displaying Leland's dedication to scholarship and ability to separate his own thoughts from the base material, as stated previously. It is only his manuscript dealing with matters of Arthurian legend that is seen as questionable, due to an illness that would not affect him until some years later.

Considering that all of his works, including the *Itinerary*, were written in their final form in a period spanning no more than seven years, 1543-1550, is it possible that his condition worsened to the point that only one of his works was written with a sound mind? Possibly, but it would seem very unlikely that Leland would have been recorded as such a valuable writer and recorder of his time period if only one of his works could be considered entirely trustworthy. It is more likely that the same degree of scholarship and dedication to the truth of history was constant throughout his career and that the only role his mental illness played in his writing was to end it.

Whatever the verdict on John Leland's mental state may be, his love of the ancient and meaningful did serve one very valuable purpose that we as investigators of the Joseph and Grail legends can utilize. He mentions, almost in passing, a character who not only was contemporary with King Arthur but also knew enough of Glastonbury's history to provide a record of the final resting place of its founder. He confirmed that there were housed in Glastonbury's rich storehouses of knowledge texts of great age that spoke of its origins not in terms of legend, but as historically and archeologically verifiable facts.

Needless to say, the fact that Leland saw these fragments and that an actual, historical man named Melkin wrote them does not make the story true. This point is conceded. However, multiple people writing of Glastonbury's history made reference to him and what he wrote. That in itself makes this reference worthy of consideration. However, there is still the damning matter of doubt found in both John of Glastonbury's lack of historical credibility and John Leland's mental state near the end of his life. As tantalizingly close as the answer would otherwise appear, it still lies outside our grasp. It would be helpful to find some instance of the Joseph tradition at Glastonbury between the time of Melkin and its popularization in the Middle Ages. It would also be helpful if we could identify the exact point when the associations between Glastonbury and Joseph's Grail became the medieval romances known as the Grail Cycle. We can again look to Glastonbury in the twelfth century as the place and time where all these points coincide.

Chapter 9

Glastonbury's Warrior Monk

There is a saying among those who study the Bible, both as a religious text and as literature: "As above, so below." This phrase has two meanings. First, it means that often times in the Bible, stories are told from two perspectives, that of what is happening on Earth and that which is happening in Heaven. One example of this is found in the book of Revelations, in which the sequence of events happening on the Earth is repeated from the perspective of one witnessing those events from Heaven. It also means that as a religious text, the Bible seeks to instruct how to make Earth, both man and the world, more like they would be in Heaven. This means that man strives to be more Christ-like while struggling to make the world more a paradise of ideals and virtues.

Much of what is taught in modern Christianity deals with this concept. There cannot be good without evil, no Heaven without Hell, no joy without sadness, and no salvation without contrition. This paradoxical approach to spiritual enlightenment exemplifies our human nature. As the highest form of life on this planet, we are capable of great acts of madness and destruction, as well as great demonstrations of love and kindness. Anyone with a two-year-old child likely sees this play out daily. One moment two children will be fighting like bitter enemies and the next, they'll be sharing an ice cream cone.

There is a very similar binary aspect to the legends of Glastonbury. There are the romantic legends, characters, and events, and then there is the real-world history, archeology, and written record that sheds some light on the reality behind the stories. The Middle Ages are famous for their fanciful interpretation, and sometimes outright creation, of stories, traditions, and histories that we now know as little more than entertainment. However, this period is also rich with vital accounts that tell modern historians much about the life and times of this fluid period. Such is the case with the Grail legend, only the above phrase changes from "as above so below" to "as at court, so in the church." By this I suggest that the Grail romances, to some extent, draw a parallel between the Grail Castle and the Grail Chapel — places once thought to house the Grail, such as Glastonbury Abbey and another abbey in Spain. Therefore, when reading a Grail story in the future, I suggest the reader think less in terms of knights, kings, and castles and more in terms of monks, abbots, and churches.

The Holy Grail is not only the pinnacle of legend and the king of all historical mysteries, it is an exercise in duality. It is an object both Christian and pagan, physical and supernatural, a relic and its own quest. Most importantly there is ample evidence, circumstantial though it may be, to support the theory that the Holy Grail is a historical object as well as the subject of literary fantasy. It would seem that Glastonbury is a magnet for such split personalities, both as a place of historical significance but also famous for its spiritualism and legends. In fact, the same could be said for one little-known member of its community in the twelfth century.

Born Henri Etudes in 1101 to Stephen, the duke of Blois, and Adela of Normandy, daughter of William the Conqueror, this man proves to be the best link between Glastonbury and the literary origins of the Holy Grail legend. Bishop of Winchester and brother to the embattled King Stephen, he was also the abbot of Glastonbury Abbey during the twelfth century — the time that saw great change at Glastonbury as well as the birth of the Grail saga in Western society. It has been suggested that it was through Henry of Blois that the Grail story found its way to the high French court of Marie de Champagne, since Chrétien "might have visited England in connection with Count Henry of Champagne's uncle, Henry of Blois" (Cline, p. xxiii). Although this theory is contested among scholars, it introduces the link between Glastonbury and Chrétien de Troyes, who allegedly first wrote of the Holy Grail. It is thought that the sourcebook cited by Chrétien in the introduction to his famous manuscript originally came to Marie's court from Glastonbury, and was later given to Count Phillip of Flanders as a gift during his brief courtship with Marie following her husband's death. This migration most likely would have taken place due to Count Henry's visit to Glastonbury to see his uncle Henry of Blois.

This familial link between Glastonbury and the court of Champagne seems promising, but we still must answer the ever-important five questions. If there was indeed a sourcebook from which Chrétien fashioned his Grail story as he claimed, why did it end up in Count Henry's hands? If it did come from Henry of Blois, how did he come to have it in his possession? Where and when was it composed? Lastly, and most contentiously, who originally wrote it? To answer these questions, it would be prudent to take a closer look at the man who allegedly facilitated the birth of the Grail legend.

Henry of Blois was born into a world of wealth, prominence, and power. An American equivalent would be someone born into the Vanderbilt or Carnegie families. As such, it is not surprising that Henry's upbringing was equally privileged. Although his father died when Henry was still young, he quickly found himself in a world of knowledge. He was educated in the great Benedictine abbey of Cluny in the heart of France, which meant his life and education were geared not only toward the strictly religious but the intellectual as well.

Like Glastonbury Abbey, Cluny was known throughout Christendom as a place of learning as well as devotion, housing one of the world's most formidable libraries. There can be little doubt that these factors made Henry into the man he was. At Cluny Abbey, he by necessity learned a strict devotion to God and acquired an in-depth knowledge of church history, its founding fathers, and all their important writings. In addition to feeding his spirit, the abbey school gave his mind its fill of art, architecture, literature, and music. Combine this with the growing troubadour movement that would become so intertwined with literature and storytelling in medieval France, and we see that the man who emerged from his tutelage at Cluny Abbey was a true Renaissance Man — one best described as a warrior monk.

Henry was established as abbot of Glastonbury in 1126 at the age of 25. Three years later, he accepted the title of Bishop of Winchester, under the condition that he could stay at Glastonbury, which he had grown to love. It is important to remember that the abbey over which he presided was the older, pre–Norman church, the burnt ruins of which would later grow to the height of prominence in the sixteenth century. His Glastonbury included the full splendor of the older Great Church, as well as the original, then wood- and lead-shrouded wattle church that was allegedly built by Joseph of Arimathea himself. Included within this old church was the mysterious pattern of lines and geometrical forms mentioned by William of Malmesbury, as well as any ancient documents (such as the ones he used to write his *De Antiquitate Glastoniensis Ecclesiae*) that didn't survive the fire of 1184.

Henry's time at Glastonbury was not an easy one. Despite being one of the monetarily and intellectually richest times for the abbey, his brother, King Stephen, was responsible for creating one of the most turbulent periods in British history. Known as the Anarchy, Stephen's reign began when he usurped the throne from Matilda, daughter of King Henry I. Henry had named Matilda his successor if he had no male heir at the time of his death, and by all rights she should have inherited the throne of England. However, she was out of the country at the time of Henry's death, and Stephen took advantage of the opportunity, rushing to London to see that he was named king of England.

Henry of Blois used his power and influence to assist his brother in the succession to the throne—something he would later regret when Stephen ordered the arrest of several high-ranking bishops. However, Stephen's reign was as short-lived as it was turbulent. In 1154, Stephen signed the Treaty of Wallingford, in which he agreed to name Matilda's son as his successor upon his death, thus beginning the line of Plantagenet kings of England. It is clear to see that Henry of Blois was no humble abbot shuffling about in his robes, contenting himself with the goings-on of his own abbey. Many researchers maintain that Henry was the true power behind the throne during the more fractured times of Stephen's rule, making him for a time the most powerful and influential man in medieval England.

Despite the authority he wielded during his time as abbot, political ambition was clearly not among his priorities. It should be remembered that, despite being named bishop of Winchester, he did so only if he could remain the abbot of Glastonbury. Therefore it would appear that at Glastonbury, Henry found either a place he loved as his home or potentially a place that piqued his spiritual and intellectual interests to such a degree that he refused to leave despite being offered other more prestigious appointments. Historical accounts suggest it was not the abbey's established glory and magnificence that held him. In fact, it would seem quite the opposite.

> The next important abbot was Henri de Blois, an aristocrat and scholar, who ruled the Abbey for a very long period (1126–71). The buildings were in a state of collapse (reminding him of the dwellings of peasants), and he set about restoring them, together with the finances of the Abbey. He was responsible for many new buildings, including a bell tower, chapter house, cloister, lavatory, refectory, dormitory, the infirmary with its chapel, a castellum (a princely "castle"-like structure within the grounds), an outer gate, a brewery and stabling for horses [Rahtz and Watts, p. 46].

From this account, it would seem that Henry saw himself more as a small-scale Templar than a player in the never-ending battle of the kings of England. Considering he followed the bloody abbacy of Thurstin and that of Herlewin in which the abbey experienced its second "reboot" in twenty years, one could say that Henry was the greatest, most prolific abbot of Glastonbury since Dunstan in the tenth century. Henry was no pure saint, however. His dual nature could be seen in his love of the secular as well as that of the spirit: "He was a patron of William of Malmesbury and Gerald of Wales, and gave over forty books to the library. He had, however, a love of luxury ill-suited to the basic ethics of monastic life, which earned him the epithets of 'a rival pope, the old wizard of Winchester'" (Rahtz and Watts, p. 47). In fact, it is claimed that he felt the need for an archdiocese in the west of England, bringing him into conflict with the archbishop of Canterbury. When he later became a papal legate, or regional representative of the pope, he became more powerful than the archbishop, in essence becoming the most powerful man in the English church. Were he another sort of man, he might have become a type of dictator of medieval England — a single man who held power over both the secular and clerical world. However, as we have already seen, his ambitions seemed more focused on Glastonbury Abbey.

From the above quote we learn something else of vital importance. As evidenced by the beauty of the Winchester Psalter, commissioned by Henry of Blois, books were highly prized objects, not as objects of acclaim and wealth but as repositories of every kind of knowledge. By all accounts, he was as interested in architecture, mythology, and philosophy as he was in church history or ruminations on the Bible. The statement that he gave over forty books to the abbey at Glastonbury lacks the weight it would have closer to his time. First, the statement suggests that he introduced new texts to the abbey's library. This indicates that he had access to this many books not held at Glastonbury instead of simply ordering their transcription. Second, to produce a book during this time was a major undertaking. The printing press had yet to be invented, so all the work had to be done by hand, both the complex lettering and the intricate artwork that usually accompanied it.

Among these books for which he was responsible, several were famous works authored by individuals well known to students of the Grail and Arthurian legends. Possibly the most well-known of these works was William of Malmesbury's *De Antiquitate Glastoniensis Ecclesiae*. Although William officially credits the origination of Glastonbury Abbey to King Ine in the ninth century, he at least suggests that there is evidence to support an earlier foundation due to new material he encountered while at Glastonbury Abbey. It is quite likely that when Henry of Blois commissioned William to write this history of his abbey, he was aware of the ancient texts that William would encounter there and was sure it would truly challenge William's previous conclusions. It has been suggested that the edited version of William's *Gesta Regum Anglorum*, or *History of the Kings of England*, was inspired by material he saw while at Glastonbury.

It is also possible that Henry of Blois inspired another famous book associated with Arthurian and Grail legends. Chrétien de Troyes, named by some the father of the modern novel, probably wrote his story of the Grail called *Perceval, le Conte del Graal*, during the second half of the twelfth century. In the dedication of this Grail text, Chrétien claimed that the story came from a mysterious sourcebook given to him by Phillip, Count of Flanders. Most who accept the notion of Chrétien's sourcebook assume it came to Count Phillip from the court of Chrétien's former patron, Marie de Champagne. The theory states that Marie gave this book to Phillip during a short courtship after the death of her husband, Henry I "The Liberal." If this were the case, this sourcebook most likely came to Marie's court when Henry visited his uncle Henry of Blois when he was installed as bishop of Winchester.

Although this is far from established historical fact, it does stand to reason. Chrétien is viewed by most scholars of medieval literature less as a novelist and more as a redactor — an elaborator who takes an existing tale and expands upon it, making it into the sort of grand medieval romance one would expect from Chrétien. While not his only subject, Arthurian material seemed to have been his most successful subject, despite using an English protagonist in a story intended for a French audience.

It has been theorized that Chrétien accompanied Henry to Glastonbury while visiting his uncle. Many state that Chrétien's familiarity with English place-names and topography demonstrates that he was actually in England at some point prior to his writing. In addition, his signing his name "Chrétien de Troyes," that is "Christian *of Troyes*," suggests that he was not in France at the time. These claims have been countered by saying that the knowledge of England could have been acquired secondhand and that he didn't have to be in a different country to refer to himself as being from Troyes.

Regardless of whether Chrétien visited England himself, many agree that his Grail story did come from some previous source instead of purely from his own imagination. If this is true, the sourcebook most likely came from Glastonbury, the center of Grail and Arthurian myth in England, by way of Henry of Blois when Henry I came to visit him, later becoming the property of his wife Marie de Champagne. If so, what was this sourcebook? Was it one of the many valuable books held in Glastonbury's vast library, or was it something different? To answer these questions, we must attempt to glean as much information as we can from the brief description given by Chrétien in his dedication.

Besides saying the book was given to him by Phillip of Flanders, Chrétien says he was instructed to write his rendition of this story in verse, which means in poetic, rhyming form. He further indicates that this story is more than his average Arthurian tale. This is a story that requires the highest attention, seriousness, and diligence. By this, we may assume the original sourcebook was written in another form than verse. If this text actually came from Glastonbury, it would seem logical that the original story was written in another language than medieval French, most likely Latin, since that was the commonly used language of monastic writing during the medieval period. While it is possible that it was written in French, a book written at Glastonbury was less likely to be written in this foreign language. It is also unlikely that the book was written in a lesser known language such as Gaelic, otherwise there would have been the need for a translator, for which there is no historical evidence.

Therefore, if Chrétien's sourcebook came from Glastonbury it most likely would have been a text written in Latin, available to Henry of Blois when he became bishop of Winchester in 1129, and unknown to the French court of Marie de Champagne, which was a court famed for being a center for literary study. It would be tempting to make a connection between the mysterious lost writings of Melkin of Glastonbury and Chrétien's sourcebook, but in reading the confusing, broken Latin of Melkin's prophesy, one realizes that it is unlikely to be the source of a vast, sweeping medieval romance. There is one Arthurian/Grail text that nicely matches these requirements for the sourcebook in every way except two: the date of origin and the language in which it was written.

Typically dated to the first or second decade of the thirteenth century, the anonymous manuscript called *Perlesvaus* or *The High History of the Holy Grail* was supposedly written at Glastonbury, most likely by a devoted monk. This is the lengthy saga of Perceval, a Welsh youth willfully withheld from the knightly world by his mother, who we later discover was descended from none other than Joseph of Arimathea through a long line of Grail guardians, among whom is the wounded Fisher King. This story, full of incredibly complex allegory and imagery, follows Perceval from the beginning of his journey, as did Chrétien's tale, all the way through his quest until he finally achieves the Grail, later following it to a distant, otherworldly land where he is never seen again.

Aspects of this saga can be found in several other Arthurian and Grail texts, such as the *Fouke le Fitz Waryn* story, suggesting they share a common source. However, its dating to around 1220 places it near the end of the 30- to 40-year period that is responsible for the exponential growth of the Grail legend in Europe. This date has been called into question by some scholars, on the grounds that because the earliest surviving copy of the *Perlesvaus* dates to this period, there was probably an earlier copy from which this version was taken. One other aspect of this text seems problematic: Originally, this text was written in Early French. Although it is possible that an earlier copy of *Perlesvaus* could have been written in another language such as Latin, one controversial theory states that its language not only helps establish an earlier date of origination, but also suggests a specific name for the author.

Hank Harrison, famed for his association with the Grateful Dead and for being the father of Courtney Love, is also an accomplished author and historical researcher, focusing his attention on topics such as medieval history, archeo-astronomy, sacred geometry, and other forms of lost wisdom. His research on the history and evolution of the Grail legend produced the first of his treatises on the Grail, *The Cauldron and the Grail*, which connects the concept of the Grail to standing stone monuments found throughout Europe.

His second work (yet to be published at the time of this writing) has proven to be quite interesting in light of our investigation of Henry of Blois and his role in the continuation of the Grail legend.

In it, he makes the astonishing claim that the curious, late continuation of the Grail cycle, *Perlesvaus*, is neither late nor a continuation of Chrétien's unfinished work. He states that this misrepresented work was in fact either the very sourcebook given to Chrétien by Phillip of Flanders, or a close copy written later from the same original. Furthermore, he claims to know the name of its author. According to Harrison's research, the author of this curious, nearly metaphysical treatment of the Grail was none other than Henry of Blois, Glastonbury Abbey's "warrior monk" abbot. Although his theory flies in the face of conventional wisdom, he raises many points that prove to be quite intriguing.

In the true tradition of scholarship, Mr. Harrison made a pre-publication edition of his book available on his website (www.hankharrison.com) for anyone who wished to read it. The first chapter of this book opens with the following lines:

> The *Perlesvaus* may have been edited and highly modified in the thirteenth century at a time when the true Templars and Hospitaliers were still in power, as suggested by several scholars, but it was almost entirely based on an earlier book, now lost to us except as a fragment found recently in the ancient archives at Wells cathedral. This previous book — written in Latin in the mid-twelfth century — probably originated at Winchester or Glastonbury Abbey. Like its later redactions the book contained clues pointing to mysteries intrinsic to the abbey and the esoteric cults functioning there.
>
> More importantly the book reflects ideas intrinsic to the Cluniac-Benedictine cultus, ideas of freedom and independence hated by the Inquisition and the Palatine councils in Rome. The veiled author of the *Perlesvaus* lived in the golden age of the Troubadours and worked from the center of the fading Benedictine enlightenment. Moreover, based on the hospitals and churches he built, he must have been a member of the Knights Hospitalier. If I am correct in his identity, his life almost exactly spanned a period from the crowning of King Henry I (*Beauclerc*) 1101 to the death of Thomas Becket, and the unjust imprisonment of Queen Eleanor of Aquitaine in the early 1170s. Moreover, this monk from Glastonbury knew Thomas Becket, Beauclerc and Eleanor directly, and was acquainted with many other legendary figures of that era [Harrison, p. 10].

Harrison goes on to point out that the tone and nature of the text known as the *Perlesvaus*, or *Perlesvaux*, as he states it was originally called, indicates authorship by someone who sounds very much like the image of Henry of Blois as it is painted above. A man both holy and worldly, knowledgeable in both church teaching and art, architecture, and literature, does indeed sound like an out-of-place troubadour — one of the romantic bards of their era. He makes the assertion that, despite the agreed-upon dating of around 1220, "the body of *The Perlesvaus* was probably completed at Glastonbury before 1165" (p. 12).

Harrison also attributes the migration of the Grail myth from Glastonbury to France by way of Henry to the court of Marie de Champagne, however he claims the text follows a different path. Eleanor of Aquitaine has been called "the mother of courtly love, her court being a model for the courtly behavior made famous by tales of King Arthur and his court of honorable lords and ladies. However, one aspect of her life more closely mirrors Morgan la Fey's use of her son Mordred to overthrow the king. In 1173, King Henry II became embroiled in a revolt begun against him by his three sons and backed by his wife, Eleanor of Aquitaine. When this revolt failed, Eleanor was arrested and was eventually incarcerated for sixteen years in Winchester Castle. It is here that Harrison suggests the *Perlesvaus* from Glastonbury might have made its way into the hands of the French court.

> Also remember that Eleanor was not without reading materials during her imprisonment, and that until he died in 1143, Malmsbury was close to Henry Blois, both as a scribe and as an observer of all things Glastonbury. We know he traveled back and forth between Glastonbury and Malmsbury on many occasions. Thus — assuming the book was in the possession of Malmsbury before he died, or was even possibly edited by Malmsbury — it is highly possible, even likely, that a copy of the *Perlesvaus* could have been located at Winchester Castle or at Old Sarum Castle long before Eleanor's period of captivity and that she could have simply donated the book to Marie upon her release. Then too, Malmsbury was originally from Salisbury and was very famous during his life, making his works, and his collected manuscripts, available in many collections decades after he died [p. 173].

It would seem fairly reasonable to make this connection between Glastonbury and the court of Marie de Champagne, explaining how a British tale wound up in a high French court, but it is quite another matter to ascribe the *Perlesvaus* text to one person, especially an abbot of Glastonbury. However, if one attempts to engage in an act of true scholarship by abandoning preconceived notions, the least we can do is accept that it is a possibility. The dating of this text is based largely on its style and the discovery of King Arthur's grave. For this reason many assume it could not have been written prior to 1190. Since this mention comes as a footnote at the end of the text, one must concede that this may well have been a footnote to the main body of text that was added later, as was the custom of medieval scribes, who added notes and marginalia in existing texts.

Stylistically, the existing copy of the *Perlesvaus* would agree with the general time frame given to the text; however, to agree with this assessment, one must assume that there was never an earlier copy. The copy from which the dating has been drawn was originally written in Old French. As previously mentioned, this is an unusual language for a medieval romance to have been written in if it originated at Glastonbury, which is its accepted point of origin. Most things written at a Benedictine abbey in England would have been written in Latin. Although it was rare for something of this nature to be written in the "vulgar" English, it would be the natural second choice after Latin.

Even if the original copy of *Perlesvaus* was written in French, who better to write such a text than Henry of Blois, born in France and educated in Cluny Abbey? Although it would have been possible for him, of all people at Glastonbury, to write a Arthurian and Grail story in Old French, even Henry would most likely have written it in Latin, the language of the scholar. When one recalls Henry's penchant for commissioning books, adding no less than forty volumes to the already vast Glastonbury Abbey library, it would seem natural that he would take the legendary traditions centered at Glastonbury, probably drawing from ancient texts already housed there, and create this sort of highly moral, esoteric, allegorical tale. Almost an intellectual exercise in some regards, *Perlesvaus* presents a story whose purpose was much greater than to be a simple form of entertainment.

> The text also tells us that the author is no stranger to monastic isolation. In the *Perlesvaus* hermits lead us into and out of almost every adventure, and yet he portrays lavish court scenes as if he experienced them directly. He describes melancholy as a catalyst for one of the knights and yet he describes the joy of the contemplative life. His story unfolds, wrapped in the swaddling of the past, but the practiced eye can find him peering out from one of the castles or chapels he describes as if he built it himself.
>
> With focus, the reader will undoubtedly see the anonymous author as an enlightened soul, not so much for his monkish character, but for the books he must have studied, i.e., Ovid, Marcus Aurelius, the commentaries on the *Timaeus* of Plato by Saint Honorius, Hillary of Poitiers, Erigena and Peter Abelard, to name only a few. In addition, he must have been an architect because the reader is led through landscapes and buildings as if the author is a master mason holding a plumb and compass [Harrison, p. 15].

Saying Henry of Blois sounds like the sort of person who *would have* written the *Perlesvaus* does not mean that he was in fact the person who wrote it. There is no way to know for certain who wrote this story, nor when. The date of 1220 for this text still remains an unsolved issue, although it must be agreed that this date could be in error. However, the smoking gun, or more correctly in this case, the "autographed copy," might not be mythical.

> In the *Elucidation*, a three page introductory narrative appended to Chrétien's *Perceval* (BN mss# 12576s), the authorship of the original Grail book is ascribed, not to Chrétien, but to Master Blihos, who happens to be the

narrator of this short introduction. Here the name is almost shouting for revelation. It is a simple anagram for Blois.
> This anagram gives us two solid clues.
> First, we remove the letter H, from BLIHOS
> Which is silent anyway, and we see:
> BLIOS
> The next step is simply to reverse the two vowels
> (O & I) thus:
> BLOIS H
> Moving the H to the front yields:
> H BLOIS
> Now, as we read the Elucidation, we are probably hearing Henry Blois narrate his own book [pp. 111–112].

The concept of anagrams and hidden names written into a medieval romance might seem like something from a Dan Brown novel, but it was not uncommon for medieval authors to play these sorts of intellectual games with their readers. In addition, it must be remembered that even Geoffrey Chaucer wrote himself into his own *Canterbury Tales* as the narrator. In his case he made himself very clear, naming his character *Chaucer*.

Whether you believe that Henry of Blois was the anonymous author of the *Perlesvaus*, it is without question the most intriguing in the Grail literary canon. It presents the Grail as a Christian relic as well as a path of enlightenment while mixing in an air of mysticism that is very uncommon among most other medieval moral tales. However, what is possibly most interesting is how it stands out against itself. It is allegedly a continuation, yet it seems more coherent than the original. It suggests a level of complexity that would bar its authorship from any but the most unusual individual. Most of all, it is allegedly from a time in Glastonbury's history that would seem to preclude the writing of a romance of this intricacy.

Although the *Perlesvaus* is recognized as being from the early thirteenth century, a closer look at the history of Glastonbury Abbey during this time introduces the shadow of doubt into this supposition. A cleric at Glastonbury Abbey would have been working on this herculean treatise during a time of great turmoil and activity. Following the great fire of 1184, the Lady Chapel was consecrated a remarkable two years later after a period of nearly non-stop construction. From then on, Glastonbury saw a period of marked decline thanks to the heavy hand of King Henry II's chancellor, Ralph Fitzstephen, who was charged with the task of rebuilding the abbey, and the tension between the bishops of Bath and Wells.

This would not have been a time particularly well-suited to writing this type of exceptionally complex and allegorical story. In fact, the next period of relative calm that would allow for such writing was likely not until the fifteenth century. The more likely answer is that the *Perlesvaus* was written before the fire of 1184 and after the tumultuous, active period overseen by abbots Thurstin and Herlewin — specifically, during the abbacy of Henry of Blois. This was not only a time of calm; it was a period of rebirth, rebuilding, and growth overseen by a true intellectual and spiritual powerhouse with a love of the books.

Since the dating of *Perlesvaus* is based in no small part on the end-matter mention of King Arthur's grave, it is also worth noting that this is not the only place in the text where Arthur's burial place is mentioned.

> The King apparelleth himself for the pilgrimage, and saith that Messire Gawain and Lancelot shall go with him, without more knights, and taketh a squire to wait upon his body, and the Queen herself would he have taken thither but for the mourning she made for her son, whereof none might give her any comfort. But or ever the King departed he made the head be brought into the Isle of Avalon, to a chapel of Our Lady that was there, where was a worshipful holy hermit that was well loved of Our Lord [Evans, p. 163].
>
> ...
>
> There were three hermits therewithin that had sung their vespers, and came over against Lancelot. They bowed their heads to him and he saluted them, and then asked of them what place was this? And they told him that the place there was Avalon. They make stable his horse. He left his arms without the chapel and entereth therein, and saith that never hath he seen none so fair nor so rich. There were within three other places, right fair and seemly dight of rich cloths of silk and rich corners and fringes of gold. He seeth the images and the crucifixes all newly fashioned, and the chapel illumined of rich colours; and moreover in the midst thereof were two coffins, one against the other, and at the four corners four tall wax tapers burning, that were right rich, in four right rich candlesticks. The coffins were covered with two pails, and there were clerks that chanted psalms in turn on the one side and the other.
>
> "Sir," saith Lancelot to one of the hermits, "For whom were these coffins made?"
>
> "For King Arthur and Queen Guenievre."
>
> "King Arthur is not yet dead," saith Lancelot.
>
> "No, in truth, please God! but the body of the Queen lieth in the coffin before us and in the other is the head of her son, until such time as the King shall be ended, unto whom God grant long life! But the Queen bade at her death that his body should be set beside her own when he shall end. Hereof have we the letters and her seal in this chapel, and this place made she be builded new on this wise or ever she died" [pp. 190–191].

These passages say something important about the alleged discovery of King Arthur's burial. Some renditions of the text on the lead cross found in Arthur's grave state that the body of their son was indeed buried with them, but the name mentioned isn't Lohot, as he is named earlier in the *Perlesvaus*, it's Modred. Furthermore, this inclusion can be found in only one account, while the rest merely state variations on an epitaph for King Arthur himself and sometimes Queen Guinevere. More likely these passages simply reflect a tradition that King Arthur and his queen were buried at Glastonbury (the Avalon of Arthurian romance), instead of a direct knowledge of their burial site. In other words, the ancient writings previously mentioned that were kept in Glastonbury's library most likely indicated that these individuals were buried in the cemetery, but the grave site (authentic or hoax that it may have been), was yet to be discovered.

There is one other intriguing passage that would suggest the copy of *Perlesvaus* we have today is not the original. If this unusual romance was written by Henry of Blois as Hank Harrison suggests, it would be unexpected to find a passage reflecting the narrow and often intolerant view of the world and other cultures of which the Roman Catholic Church was sometimes guilty during his time. Such a "Renaissance Man" as Henry would certainly not pick out a group of people such as the Jews to vilify, as was the case during the Middle Ages. However, the *Perlesvaus* contains one story involving a mysterious vision of a creature named the Questing Beast. This strange vision is of a beautiful white animal that is later torn apart by twelve wild dogs that issued from its mouth when it lay down at the foot of a cross. It is later explained by a hermit Perceval finds in the woods that the white creature was Christ Himself, and that the twelve wild dogs that were vomited from its mouth were the twelve tribes of Israel, the Jews, who sought to tear the body of Jesus apart.

This clearly anti–Semitic story is unlike Henry of Blois as he has been portrayed here. Indeed the very inclusion of this culturally biased imagery stands out strongly amid a story of spiritual refinement and proving oneself worthy of Christ's special insight. The story of the Questing Beast is common in Arthurian literature, but it is usually a monstrous beast seen as an evil portent, in one case announcing the birth of Arthur's nemesis, Mordred. As out of place as this story is within the context of the *Perlesvaus*, it seems likely that this is a later addition by an overzealous editor wishing to introduce the medieval dislike for the Jewish people into an otherwise quite pious saga.

In the end, it is impossible to tell if the Grail story *Perlesvaus* was written by Glastonbury's paradoxical twelfth-century abbot, Henry of Blois. Certainly his character and actions would indicate he was the sort of person who might begin such an ambitious undertaking as this, having shown such pride and love for Glastonbury's library; however, the story's author will most likely remain forever anonymous. If some examples of Henry's writings were found, or any other example of his style were to be known, linguists and literary scholars might be able to make or dispute the case for Henry's being the author. Sadly, there is only one. The only record of his words are found in a speech he gave during a rededication ceremony for the Sapphire Altar, lost for many years only to be found behind a door in a nearby building. In this speech, recorded in Malmesbury's *De Antiquitate Glastoniensis Ecclesiae*, we have the only example of the man himself.

> Art is above gold and gems: The Creator is above all things. Henry, while living, gives gifts of brass to God: whom, equal to the muses in intellect, and superior to Marcus in oratory, his renown makes acceptable to men, his morals to the God above [Harrison, p. 268].
>
> ...
>
> The servant sent before him, fashions gifts acceptable to God: may an angel carry up to heaven the giver after his gifts. Let not England, however, hasten this event, or excite grief: England to whom peace or war, movement or quiet, come through him [Harrison, p. 274].

Whether or not you agree with the theory that Henry of Blois wrote the *Perlesvaus*, the allegorical complexity of this Grail manuscript makes it more than simply one among many medieval romances. This text both varies considerably from most other Grail romances of this time and introduces themes that can be found in later continuations of Chrétien's incomplete book. The *Perlesvaus* also exhibits the author's familiarity with Glastonbury Abbey. Among its pages are indications suggesting not only that the author came from Glastonbury, but that portions of the story came from there as well.

The author first outlines how the story of Joseph of Arimathea, good knight and soldier of Pilate as well as great-uncle to Jesus, was recorded by Josephus. It then goes on to tell that no other earthly king advanced the Law of Jesus Christ more than King Arthur. However, as the story begins, it seems that the great king has fallen into complacency. Chided by his wife Queen Guinevere, Arthur agrees to undertake a pilgrimage to the holy chapel of St. Augustine which is in a place called the White Forest. Accompanying him on his trip is a squire called Chaus, whom the king instructs to prepare himself and his horse to ride out at daybreak.

Chaus wakes to find neither King Arthur or his horse, and assumes the king found him sleeping and left without him. Quickly, he prepares himself and rides off after the king. Upon reaching a chapel and graveyard in the middle of an open area of land, he goes in thinking to find the king already in prayer. Instead, he finds a dead knight laid out for burial, richly arrayed and surrounded by many candlesticks. To prove his story to the king, he takes one of the costly golden candlesticks as a trophy to present to Arthur. However, a short time later he is stopped by a knight in the forest who challenges him for taking the candlestick. Chaus refuses to give up his gift for the king, and charges forth to joust with his opponent, but the knight stabs him deep in the side with a dagger.

Screaming in pain, he immediately finds himself again in the court of King Arthur. When Arthur and Quinevere hear his cry, they rush to his side only to find the dagger from his dream still embedded in his side. Asking for a priest to confess him before his death, Chaus relates the story to the king. When the dagger is finally removed from his side, Chaus dies and Arthur rides forth to avenge his squire upon this enemy knight. When Arthur finds the chapel of St. Augustine, he finds only a coffin containing the body of a good hermit who, he later finds, was named Calixtus. When he leaves the chapel, he hears the voices of demons and angels debating over the man's soul. Soon the voice of a lady, presumably the Virgin Mary, make the final argument for his salvation, and the chapel becomes silent.

Arthur spends the night in the adjacent hermitage and ventures ahead the next morning. He soon encounters a damsel under a tree who tells him that was indeed the chapel of St. Augustine. He rides back to the chapel only to be blocked from entering by some unseen hand. He is allowed to witness a holy vision taking place inside.

> Sore ashamed is the King thereof. Howbeit, he beholdeth an image of Our Lord that was there within and crieth Him of mercy right sweetly, and looketh toward the altar. And he looketh at the holy hermit that was robed to sing mass and said his "Confiteor," and seeth at his right hand the fairest Child that ever he had seen, and He was clad in an alb and had a golden crown on his head loaded with precious stones that gave out a full great brightness of light.
>
> On the left hand side, was a Lady so fair that all the beauties of the world might not compare them with her beauty. When the holy hermit had said his "Confiteor" and went to the altar, the Lady also took her Son and went to sit on the right hand side towards the altar upon a right rich chair and set her Son upon her knees and began to kiss Him full sweetly and saith: "Sir," saith she, "You are my Father and my Son and my Lord, and guardian of me and of all the world" [Evans, p. 14].

This account is similar to a legend known around Glastonbury. In the area known as the Beckery, there is a site called Bride's Mound where there once stood a series of chapels, over time progressing from a simple wooden structure to a stone one. According to legend, it was here that King Arthur had a vision of the Virgin Mary and the infant Christ. In addition, there was once a tradition that pilgrims on their way to visit Glastonbury Abbey would first stop and spend the night at Bride's Mound.

It is worth noting that this story of Chaus, variously called Cahuz, is also present at the end of a later, less familiar medieval Arthurian story called

Fouke le Fitz Waryn—an early fourteenth-century text allegedly derived from a now-lost, late thirteenth-century original.

> For in this country was located the beautiful chapel of
> Saint Augustine [of Canterbury],
> Where Cahuz the son of Yvain dreamed
> That he stole the candlestick,
> And that he met a man
> Who wounded him with a knife,
> And wounded him in the side.
> While asleep Cahuz cried so loud
> That King Arthur heard him.
> And when Cahuz awoke from his sleep
> He put his hand to his side;
> There he found the knife
> Which [in his dream] had wounded him.
>
> This is all recounted in the Grail story,
> The book of the Holy Vessel.
> We also learn therein how King Arthur
> Recovered his health and his valor,
> When he had lost all
> His chivalry and his power [Evans, pp. 190–191].

This clear reference to the story first seen in the *Perlesvaus* makes one very interesting parallel. Here the book from which this story of Cahuz was taken is called "the book of the Holy Vessel" and is said to be the Grail story. From this reference, one may infer that whatever original text both the *Perlesvaus* and *Fouke le Fitz-Waryn* were taken from was considered the original Grail text—an assertion also set forth by Sebastian Evans in his introduction to his edition of *The High History of the Holy Grail*.

The next similarity between *Perlesvaus* and Glastonbury is in its description of the area around Glastonbury in the time when it was considered "the Isle of Avalon." When Sir Gawain first encounters the Grail Castle, or Castle of the Fisher King, he is told that it is a land surrounded by great waters and abundant in all good things, where only the best knights may be sheltered. In Chrétien's *Perceval*, the Grail hero first meets the Rich King Fisherman as he is fishing in a boat in the waters around what he would later discover to be the Fisher King's castle—the Grail Castle.

These details could also be used to describe Glastonbury when it was an island completely surrounded by marshy waters. It has been said that the inhabitants of the Glastonbury Lake Village survived during the summer months primarily by fishing the waters around their man-made island. Looking then at the patch of land that stood out from the marshes, Glastonbury has been known for its rich soil, most especially for its apple orchards. Despite its seclusion and seemingly hostile environment, anyone inhabiting this land during Arthur's time might have seen it as a paradise, not only in its bounty, but also in its sacredness, thus making its reputation as being a truly magical place.

The *Perlesvaus* also includes one story that seems simultaneously sacred and profane, both qualities harkening back to one tradition of Glastonbury. The story of the Grave-Yard Perilous is quite curious amid the already astonishing array of strange stories found in this particular Grail text. In this story, Perceval's sister says she must go to the Grave-Yard Perilous to retrieve a piece of the cloth that covers the altar in the chapel she will find therein. Only with this cloth, she is told, will the knight who wars against her mother and their family castle be defeated. Later she gives Perceval a piece of this cloth before he reclaims the castle for his widowed mother and his sister.

> XIV.
> The damsel goeth her way all alone and all forlorn toward the grave-yard and the deep of the forest, all dark and shadowy. She hath ridden until the sun was set and the night draweth nigh. She looketh before her and seeth a cross, high and wide and thick. And on this cross was the figure of Our Lord graven, whereof is she greatly comforted. She draweth nigh the cross, and so kisseth and adoreth it, and prayeth the Saviour of the world that was nailed on Holy Rood that He would bring her forth of the burial-ground with honour. The cross was at the entrance of the grave-yard, that was right spacious, for, from such time as the land was first peopled of folk, and that knights began to seek adventure by the forest, not a knight had died in the forest, that was full great of breadth and length, but his body was borne thither, nor might never knight there be buried that had not received baptism and had repented him not of his sins at his death.
> XV.
> Thereinto entered the damsel all alone, and found great multitude of tombs and coffins. Nor none need wonder whether she had shuddering and fear, for such place must needs be dreadful to a lonely damsel, there where lay so many knights that had been slain in arms. Josephus the good clerk witnesseth us that within the grave-yard might no evil spirit meddle, for that Saint Andrew the apostle had blessed it with his hand. But never might no hermit remain within for the evil things that appeared each night all round about, that took the shapes of the knights that were dead in the forest, wherof the bodies lay not in the blessed burial-ground [Evans, p. 132].

Here we are told two things about the Grave-Yard Perilous that point back to the old Cemetery at Glastonbury Abbey. First, the passage above states, "from such time as the land was first peopled of folk, and that knights began to seek adventure by the forest, not a knight had died in the forest, that was full great of breadth and length, but his body was borne thither." It has been said of the cemetery at Glastonbury that ancient pagan kings shared the same holy ground as holy men who abided in the abbey. Therefore, both the Grave-Yard Perilous and the old cemetery at Glastonbury Abbey share the tradition of holding the honored dead of old.

The second similarity is that the ground itself seems sacred. The above quote states that no one who could be considered profane or unholy could be buried in the Grave-Yard Perilous. Indeed the same was once said of the cemetery at Glastonbury. A tradition was held that no one could as much as spit in the old cemetery lest some ill fate befall them for their sacrilege. There is also the story of Rainald of Marksbury who, upon traveling to the Holy Land, was captured by the sultan of the time and was only released when he retrieved a small amount of soil from the cemetery at Glastonbury, which even the sultan knew was made sacred by all of the holy individuals buried therein.

The *Perlesvaus* also includes one story that seems simultaneously sacred and profane, both harkening back to one tradition of Glastonbury. The story of the Grave-Yard Perilous is quite curious amid the already astonishing array of strange stories found in this particular Grail text. In this story, Perceval's sister says she must go to the Grave-Yard Perilous to retrieve a piece of the cloth that covers the altar in the chapel she will find therein. The cloth is described in the story as follows: "The cloth is of the most holiest, for our Lord God was covered therewith in the Holy Sepulchre, on the third day when He came back from death to life" (p. 132). Only with this cloth, she is told, will the knight who wars against her mother and their family castle be defeated. Later she indeed gives Perceval a piece of this cloth before he reclaims the castle for his family.

> The damsel beholdeth their sepulchres all round about the grave-yard whereinto she was come. She seeth them surrounded of knights, all black, and spears had they withal, and came one against another, and made such uproar and alarm as it seemed all the forest resounded thereof. The most part held swords all red as of fire, and ran either upon other, and gashed one another's hands and feet and nose and face [Evans, p. 132].

Relics play a big part in both the history of Glastonbury Abbey and the story of *Perlesvaus*. If the legend of the Holy Grail once being held at Glastonbury is true, it must have been sent away at some time of trouble in which the relics might have been placed in jeopardy. If Joseph brought with him the two cruets of Jesus's blood and sweat, as he is often depicted, whatever became of them? When the castle of the Fisher King was overtaken, the holy relics housed there vanished and only returned when Perceval reclaimed the castle. Similarly, just before he left the Grail Castle for the last time, the Grail was translated to a different, otherworldly place and the remaining relics were distributed around the countryside to local hermitages.

Indeed, many relics that once were housed at Glastonbury Abbey have found their way to other holy houses in the surrounding areas, although this was mostly thanks to the Dissolution. However, there have been many stories telling of relics from Glastonbury being removed for safety. One example is the foundation of the Grail tradition regarding Nanteos Manor in Wales. It is said that several monks from Glastonbury fled when the abbey was in danger of capture and eventually wound up in Strata Florida in Aberystwyth, carrying with them a wooden cup that had been hidden in the abbey walls. Although the infamous Nanteos Cup appears to be nothing more than a medieval bowl, its story and that of the Glastonbury monks still lives in the area around Nanteos Manor.

Similarly, several possible contenders for Joseph's cruets have surfaced around Britain and beyond. In Shropshire a small onyx vial, verified as a Roman scent jar or *unguentaria*, has been found and associated with the Grail legend. Similarly, many claim that Joseph's vial once went to Rosslyn Chapel in Scotland, begetting the Grail tradition there. Along those lines, a Roman vial similar to that allegedly found in Shropshire, also claiming to be the original Holy Grail, came to the world's attention in years past thanks to a man named Rocco Zingaro, a member of a modern-day Templar sect in Rome.

Although these are all intriguing similarities between history and legend, none compare to the feature found in the *Perlesvaus* that is unique to that story—the tomb belonging to Joseph of Arimathea.

> Perceval cometh nigh the castle in company with his sister, and knoweth again the chapel that stood upon four columns of marble between the forest and the castle, there where his father told him how much ought he to love good knights, and that none earthly thing might be of greater worth, and how none might know yet who lay in the coffin until such time as the Best Knight of the world should come thither, but that then should it be known. Perceval would fain have passed by the chapel, but the damsel saith to him: "Sir, no knight passeth hereby save he go first to see the coffin within the chapel."
>
> He alighteth and setteth the damsel to the ground, and layeth down his spear and shield and cometh toward the tomb, that was right fair and rich. He set his hand above it. So soon as he came nigh, the sepulchre openeth on one side, so that one saw him that was within the coffin. The damsel falleth at his feet for joy. The Lady had a custom such that every time a knight stopped at the coffin she made the five ancient knights that she had with her in the castle accompany her, wherein they would never fail her, and bring her as far as the chapel. So soon as she saw the coffin open and the joy her daughter made, she knew that it was her son, and ran to him and embraced him and kissed him and began to make the greatest joy that ever lady made.
> XXIV.
> "Now know I well," saith she, "that our Lord God hath not forgotten

me. Sith that I have my son again, the tribulations and the wrongs that have been done me grieve me not any more. Sir," saith she to her son, "Now is it well known and proven that you are the Best Knight of the world! For otherwise never would the coffin have opened, nor would any have known who he is that you now see openly."

She maketh her chaplain take certain letters that were sealed with gold in the coffin. He looketh thereat and readeth, and then saith that these letters witness of him that lieth in the coffin that he was one of them that helped to un-nail Our Lord from the cross. They looked beside him and found the pincers all bloody wherewith the nails were drawn, but they might not take them away, nor the body, nor the coffin, according as Josephus telleth us, for as soon as Perceval was forth of the chapel, the coffin closed again and joined together even as it was before [pp. 135–136].

Here the story introduces Joseph's tomb almost as a character. Not only does it show the lineage of Perceval from Joseph, it also shows the body in the tomb as that of Joseph himself. In yet another odd display of this story's dualistic nature, the tomb is also present at the castle belonging to Perceval's family. The following passage is found early in the text, when the Grail hero's peculiar name is explained:

"Sir," saith she, "When he was born, his father was asked how he should be named in right baptism, and he said that he would he should have the name Perlesvax, for the Lord of the Moors had reft him of the greater part of the Valleys of Camelot, and therefore he would that his son should by this name be reminded thereof, and God should so multiply him as that he should be knight. The lad was right comely and right gentle and began to go by the forests and launch his javelins, Welsh-fashion, at hart and hind. His father and his mother loved him much, and one day they were come forth of their hold, whereunto the forest was close anigh, to enjoy them. Now, there was between the hold and the forest, an exceeding small chapel that stood upon four columns of marble; and it was roofed of timber and had a little altar within, and before the altar a right fair coffin, and thereupon was the figure of a man graven. Sir," saith the damsel to the King, "The lad asked his father and mother what man lay within the coffin. The father answered: 'Fair son,' saith he, 'Certes, I know not to tell you, for the tomb hath been here or ever that my father's father was born, and never have I heard tell of none that might know who it is therein, save only that the letters that are on the coffin say that when the Best Knight in the world shall come hither the coffin will open and the joinings all fall asunder, and then will it be seen who it is that lieth therein'" [p. 18].

It is strange here to note that Perceval's home and the castle of the Grail, as well as that of the Fisher King, are clearly meant to be seen as one and the same place. This would support our previous mention of the "as above, so below" motif. Perceval's family castle is the earthly face of the mystical, spiritual realm that is the enchanted castle of the Fisher King where the Grail and the other relics of the procession are seen. Therefore, when Perceval finds the Grail Castle, he is in essence coming home, demonstrating his destiny to be the Grail's guardian. This is important to our investigation of the Grail tradition at Glastonbury for one very important reason: Like the Grail Castle, Glastonbury once had a small, simple chapel standing just away from the site of the Old Church that allegedly held the remains of Joseph of Arimathea.

According to archeological evidence, the small chapel called St. Michael in the Cemetery, previously mentioned as being rebuilt and rededicated by Abbot Chinnock in 1382, contained the relics of many a holy man and saint once buried in the cemetery, chief among whom was Joseph of Arimathea. Prior to Abbot Chinnock's restoration efforts, the chapel was said to be "ancient and ruinous," dating from a time so far distant that none could recall its creation. At the time the *Perlesvaus* was written, this chapel was still in its ruinous state, and if those at Glastonbury held the tradition that Joseph's remains were under the altar, this would fit the description in the *Perlesvaus* of the Grail Castle's chapel quite well.

Although we have no direct description of this chapel in the cemetery at Glastonbury Abbey, it represents the greatest among our parallel references between history and literature. This tomb containing the mortal remains of Joseph indeed stood between the Old Church of Joseph and the "wilderness" that lay just beyond the abbey grounds. From the above literary account, it sounds as if the writer was aware that Joseph's tomb was present in this chapel, but not necessarily its contents, with the account of letters and bloody pincers being simply the elaborations of a hopeful ecclesiastical mind imagining that abundant treasures of Christianity might lay hidden inside. Today we have neither the remains nor any sealed letters detailing their authenticity, but like a thief who gives away his identity by leaving behind his fingerprints, so too is the presence of this small, little-known chapel at Glastonbury left as evidence by the unknown man who wrote the *Perlesvaus*.

The final parallel drawn between Glastonbury and the accounts outlined in *Perlesvaus* is not one of historical evidence, but one speaking to the profoundly spiritual nature of Glastonbury Abbey and the effects it seems to have on those who journey there, looking either for knowledge or a place of peace amid the chaos of earthly pursuits. At the end of our story, there is a passage stating that after Perceval departs the Grail Castle for another realm, his castle falls into ruin but still retains the palpable sacredness that the relics once housed there left behind.

> When it was fallen into decay, many folk of the lands and islands that were nighest thereunto marvel them what may be in this manor. They dare a many that they should go see what was therein, and sundry folk went thither from all the lands, but none durst never enter there again save two

Welsh knights that had heard tell of it. Full comely knights they were, young and joyous hearted. So either pledged him to other that they would go thither by way of gay adventure; but therein remained they of a long space after, and when again they came forth they led the life of hermits, and clad them in hair shirts, and went by the forest and so ate nought save roots only, and led a right hard life; yet ever they made as though they were glad, and if that any should ask whereof they rejoiced in such wise, "Go," said they to them that asked, "thither where we have been, and you shall know the wherefore."

In such sort made they answer to the folk. These two knights died in this holy life, nor were none other tidings never brought thence by them. They of that land called them saints [pp. 248–249].

Even after this Holy House had fallen to ruin, it brought a change on any who entered its remains. Whether it was Henry of Blois, the great warrior monk, holy knight, and ecclesiastical troubadour of Glastonbury Abbey, William of Malmesbury, great historian and researcher, or John Leland, Royal Antiquarian, chief librarian, and forerunner of the Dissolution, anyone who spent any appreciable time at Glastonbury came away a changed individual. It is almost as if they were touched by something unseen — secrets of a past so ancient that only legend can record their origin.

Whether it was written by Henry of Blois or by a simple scribe and monk, the Grail text *Perlesvaus* seems to be a manuscript that harkens back to the earliest writings taking place at Glastonbury pertaining to Joseph of Arimathea and the Grail. As such, either as Chrétien's sourcebook or as a derivative work based on earlier, previously unknown texts, it represents a rare window into the pre–Chrétien Grail tradition and its genesis at Glastonbury Abbey. However, the Grail legend is more complex than just its origin. It is also important to see how it became the elaborate tapestry of medieval mysticism that it is today. Therefore, the next stop along our pilgrimage in search of the Grail leads us to what some would call its birthplace. Now we must further investigate Chrétien de Troyes and his mysterious sourcebook.

Chapter 10

The Book of the Grail

The word "genesis" means different things to different people. Say it to a group of people and the meaning that comes to each person's mind would certainly vary widely, ranging from the biblical reference to a pop group to a plot device for a series of *Star Trek* movies. Whatever mental associations we may form, the root of it has always referred to beginnings. Genesis refers to the point of origination, whether it be of the universe, a person, a group, or a story. Tracking one's genealogical origins involves using what information is available, filling in gaps from a variety of sources, sometimes finding that previous information is wrong, and sometimes understanding that a small amount of guesswork and inference may be in order. Finding the genesis, the point of origination, for a legend is really no different.

Historical research, whatever the subject might be, is always made more difficult by the lack of reliable information and the unintentional muddling caused by those who came before you. You must first determine what is evidence and what is opinion, and then see where that information fits into the larger picture. Once all the secondary information has been removed, what is left can be used to determine which direction through the past you should look. At that point, the real task of historical research begins. As convoluted as this method of reduction may seem, it makes the study much easier. It's a bit like reading the ripples in a stream to determine what kind of fish jumped out of the water upstream and around a bend. With a little knowledge of angling and surroundings, you can make a very close guess, but unless you were there to see the fish for yourself, you really can't know for sure.

As I mentioned in the introduction to this book, there can be no real proof, not of the Grail, nor of anything requiring an investigation, for the simple reason that we weren't there to see it for ourselves. However, we agree to accept some things as proof on the basis that the evidence is good enough. Agreeing that something is "good enough" also means different things to different people. A measurement that is off by one eighth of an inch might be acceptable in construction, whereas it might not be in furniture-making, and most definitely not in brain surgery. Similarly, what we agree to be acceptable evidence varies according to the weight of what asks to be accepted.

While medieval literature cannot be used as definitive proof to validate the Holy Grail as a historical object, it can be used as evidence which, when combined with other pieces of evidence, slowly makes a case for a historical Grail. An FBI profiler can provide evidence that someone is either more or less likely to be responsible for the commission of a crime, but this evidence must be combined with other evidence such as fiber evidence, fingerprint evidence, DNA evidence, and perhaps even eyewitness testimony to finally convict or acquit the suspect. Therefore we must similarly take the historical evidence, recorded personal accounts, and archeological evidence previously presented and now combine it with what we can learn from the medieval romances written about the Grail.

What pieces of the historical Grail were left behind in references made by various Grail writers? Is it possible that the medieval romances with which we have become so familiar today contain the whispered echoes of a long forgotten history? The simple answer is yes. As authors today frame their purely fictional stories in real-world settings, using real-world references, medieval authors surely never gave a second thought to basing their stories within a familiar framework based in truth.

To put it into a context familiar to us, consider a recent fictional work, *The DaVinci Code*. Whatever other historical inadequacies of which one might accuse the text, clearly it was not written as a historical treatise on the European automotive industry. With that in mind, imagine yourself a historical researcher a few hundred years from today, investigating the rise of a curious little energy-efficient automobile now known as the Smart Car, specifically whether or not it was in production prior to 2010. Since we are contemporaneous to the Smart Car, this may seem a ridiculous analogy. However, depending on the importance of the subject matter at hand, how widely known it was, and the survival of original documentation, five or ten years' variation in its history can be both quite common and quite significant. Since the heroine of the story, Sofie Neveu, drove a Smart Car in the book, it can be demonstrated that this type of car existed as early as 2005, when the book was published. Granted, it doesn't give a specific year of origination for this particular model of car, but the simple mention of a Smart Car in a book published prior to 2010 can be used to prove the researcher's thesis.

To learn more about the origin of the Grail legend in Western culture, the first task is to investigate its foundation text, *Perceval, ou le Conte del Graal*, as well as its author Chrétien de Troyes. Scholars agree that this is the text and writer responsible for introducing the concept of the Holy Grail to the European imagination. Although he never specifically states that the Grail was an artifact of Christ's Passion, his story created its image as the magical, mythical lost cup of the Eucharist that we understand today. Some call Chrétien de Troyes the father of the modern novel and a medieval French master, while others call him a simple redactor — an elaborator planted somewhere between a copyist and a poet.

Very little is known for certain about the "father of the Grail legend." It is even uncertain whether he was born in Troyes or simply began his career there. Troyes doesn't really recognize him as a particularly celebrated figure in its history. Urban Holmes in his 1970 book, *Chrétien de Troyes*, states that Troyes was an important center of Jewish commerce and learning in the twelfth century and that Chrétien might have been a converted Jew, citing a document dated 1172 that mentions a poet called Cristianus who served Henry and Marie's court. All that is known of Chrétien is that he was a trouvère (the northern version of the better-known troubadour), and that he worked in the court of Marie de Champagne from 1160 to 1172 and afterwards for Prince Phillip of Flanders.

We can draw a bit of detail regarding his character from one of his Arthurian romances called *Lancelot, the Knight of the Cart*. Chrétien allegedly left this work incomplete, and it was finished by another court poet, perhaps an apprentice. It has been conjectured that he did not agree with the adulterous tone of the story, and refused to finish it, moving on to write *Yvain, Knight of the Lion*. Although this assertion is far from certain, it is well known and has become widely accepted. From this, we can gauge Chrétien as a pious man upholding the honorable courtly ideals set forth by his patrons.

There exists no record of his early years or training, although it is clear he was familiar with the Latin and Greek classics that were typical of the time. Besides his Arthurian works, Chrétien is known to have authored several other works. Once erroneously thought to be the author of the medieval romance *Guillaume d'Angleterre*, a story about the life and times of another legendary king of England, Chrétien is known to have written several poems based on Ovid's *Metamorphoses*, of which his *Philomena* is the only surviving example. Although copies no longer exist, he references several other of his unrelated works in his better-known Arthurian poems.

Accompanying Ruth Harwood Cline's translation of *Perceval*, she presents a wonderful introduction regarding Chrétien de Troyes, his career, and his patronage. It contains two noteworthy points pertaining to our present investigation.

> Urban T. Holmes, Jr. speculated that Chrétien might have visited England in connection with Count Henry of Champagne's uncle, Henry of Blois, who became Abbot of Glastonbury and Bishop of Winchester (in *Chrétien*

de Troyes [New York: Twayne Publishers, 1970], p. 24.) Holmes speculated that Chrétien might have visited Nantes in Brittany for the investiture of Godefroy, brother of Henry II, as Duke of Brittany, in 1158 [Cline, p. xxiii].

As mentioned in an earlier chapter, if Chrétien accompanied Henry of Champagne to England, he might at that time have acquired the mysterious sourcebook from his uncle Henry of Blois. Cline suggests another possible aspect of Chrétien's history that could have impacted what source material was made available to him:

> There has been speculation, but no proof, that Chrétien de Troyes might have been in holy orders: Nitze and Holmes note that in 1172 the Count and Countess of Champagne awarded the benefice of Saint Maclou to a Chrétien who may have been the poet, and there is also a record of a Chrétien who was a canon of the Abbey of Saint-Loup in Troyes, in Holmes, *Chrétien de Troyes*, pp. 22–23, and Nitze, *Perceval and the Holy Grail*, p. 282. In addition to the possibility of travel in Nantes and England, ... it is possible that Chrétien de Troyes accompanied Count Philip [*sic*] of Flanders [p. xxiv n. 5].

This possibility not only speaks further of Chrétien's mindset and character, it also illustrates that he was no simple traveling minstrel or bard. He was a career author who likely had a wealth of source material from which he may have drawn inspiration for his many works. In addition, if Chrétien was a member of a holy order, it would have made him privy to material that was likely not available to any simple court poet. However, these points introduce an interesting question.

Was he first exposed to this sourcebook when it was given to him by his second patron, Phillip of Flanders, or did he see it during his patronage under Marie de Champagne? In the introduction to his famous *Conte*, in which he allegedly outlines the story of the Grail for the first time, he very clearly states that his story is taken from Phillip's sourcebook. However, if the story of the Grail originally came from Britain decades earlier, why did he credit Phillip of Flanders and not King Henry, husband of Marie de Champagne? Then this raises another question. If Chrétien was initially exposed to the sourcebook early, shortly after his potential visit to England, why was it still incomplete at the time of his death? In truth, the answer to these questions may be more complex that one might first imagine.

Since most of Chrétien's classic works took place while in Marie's court, we should first consider his time writing in what some have called the medieval "Court of Love." Marie's model of the high French court began with her embattled mother, Eleanor of Aquitaine, who has been seen as the creator of the idyllic system now known as chivalry. Eleanor, one of the most powerful women in the medieval period, is famous for participating in the Second Crusade — she and her retinue embarking on their journey dressed in armor and carrying spears and shields. Despite her obvious sense of adventure and independence, she is most well known for her court at Poitiers. There it is said that the very best of honor, grace, and intellect met in one place to form a court like none other before it. Her marriage to Henry II of England was popularized by the 1968 motion picture *The Lion in Winter*.

Eleanor's Court of Love was continued by Marie, countess of Champagne, daughter to her and her first husband, Louis VII, and half sister to King Richard I (the Lionheart) of England. It could be said that Marie was a child destined for greatness despite the contentious and difficult times into which she was born. Known for her Cathar sympathies, she was a member of a growing intellectual elite that questioned the views and power of the Church as well as traditional roles for women. Marie was also well known for maintaining her own sizeable library and serving as benefactor to many of the best poets, writers, and thinkers of her day.

Eleanor and Marie's Court of Love was an oasis of calm in a politically and spiritually fevered time, allowing the blossoming of many forms of art and literature that survive into this day. Embodying many of the controversial ideas of the time such as gender and cultural equity, this idea of patterning life after a nearly mythical level of honorable, "courteous" behavior defined our view of such high moral tales as can be found in Arthurian literature. However, Eleanor and Marie's influence did more than paint the background setting for chivalrous stories. Their court was actually responsible for generating quite a few of the stories themselves.

The high court of Marie de Champagne and her husband Henry I, "The Liberal," played an important role in the perpetuation of many ancient texts in a variety of languages, and served as host to several well-known romancers and bards of the time. The troubadour movement that was taking place during the time of Marie's court was not a separate and foreign event. In fact, it was at the very heart of it. All of the highly controversial ideals one could find in Marie's Court of Love were an intrinsic part of the troubadour movement. As one might expect, this meant that several notable troubadours such as Bertran de Born, Conon de Bethune, Bernart de Ventadorn, and Gautier d'Arras passed through the court of Champagne. Even the unknown romancer known as Marie de France appears to have frequented the court, since "the influence of Marie de France has also been suggested in the works of Chrétien de Troyes. Stefan Hofer has concluded from a comparison of the prologue to the Lais of Marie and that of Chrétien's Erec that Chrétien must have known Marie's work" (McCash, p. 3). Troubadours were more than just writers; their role was more like unto a bard, taking a simple story and transforming it into a performance piece. Many poems, songs, and even short plays have been ascribed to this group, and have been called some of the greatest masterpieces of their time, still performed today by groups such as the Boston Camarata. Although the troubadours and trouvères are typically thought of as a French phenomenon, their influence spread all across medieval Europe, stretching into Spain, Portugal, Italy, and Germany.

Among all these troubadours, one stands out as being of particular interest to this investigation of the Grail legend. Named Rigaut de Barbezieux, this mysterious troubadour is not known for his exceptional work, nor for his role in the court of Marie de Champagne. In fact, very little is known about him other than that he was famous for a series of poems, fifteen of which survive. The exact time of Rigaut's writing has been debated, some saying he thrived from 1170 to 1210, while other say he was one of the earliest troubadours, dating him from the first half of the twelfth century. This earlier date is due to an association made by Rita Lejeune, in her treatise "Le Troubadour Rigaut de Barbezieux," between Rigaut and the writings of a Rigaldus de Berbezillo, suggesting that Rigaut's work should be dated between 1140 and 1157. While this assertion has been met with resistance in the scholarly community, it seems there is sufficient evidence to back it up.

> It is possible, of course, that the Rigaldus identified by Lejeune is not the same person as Rigaut the troubadour. There does, however, seem to be enough overlap between the historical and literary evidence to warrant further consideration of the question. For example, both the Rigaldus of the documents and the Rigaut of the vida entered a monastery. The documents cited by Lejeune show that Rigaldus was in the entourage of Guillaume Taillefer, counter of Angouleme in January, 1157. This information is compatible with that of the vida, for the count of Angouleme was a cousin of Jaufre Rudel, with whom he was on good terms, and it is the daughter of Jaufre Rudel who is identified in the vida as Miels de domna, the woman to whom Rigaut addressed a number of his songs. It is also significant to note that she is cited in the vida as the wife of Jaufre de Tonnay, a name associated with the court of Eleanor of Aquitaine and Henry II, which provides an intriguing link between the poet Rigaut and the court of Queen Eleanor [McCash, pp. 3–4].

Although this flies in the face of conventional wisdom regarding this lesser-known troubadour's writing, it does introduce a very interesting possibility. If this Rigaut and the early troubadour Rigaldus de Berbezillo are in fact the same writer, this would create a very unexpected twist on the point at which the Grail story enters into the European popular imagination. In his Chanson III, or third poem, *Atressi con Persavaus*, he compares his astonishment upon seeing the beauty of his *"Miels de domna"* (best of ladies) to Perceval's shocked silence upon first seeing the Grail procession in the castle of the

Fisher King. In so doing, he illustrates either that he lived long enough to see Chrétien write the story of Perceval and the Grail, or that the story's genesis took place before Chrétien's *Conte del Graal*. Considering that the period during which Rigaut flourished as a troubadour is hotly debated, the answer to this question makes all the difference.

If the first option is true, Rigaut wrote his third poem after 1190, the latest accepted date for Chrétien's writing. At this point, he was either around 70 years old, judging by McCash's assessment, or another Rigaut dating from an entirely later period. Considering the similarities between Rigaut de Barbezieux and Rigaldus de Barbezillo, both in name and in history, it is most likely that these individuals were one and the same. Therefore, if Rigaut/Rigaldus waited to write his third chanson until after Chrétien had first written about Perceval, he had yet to write many of his poems, and he would have been of a fairly advanced age — a time at which he had purportedly declined in activity and retired to a monastery.

It would seem much more likely that Rigaut's third chanson was actually written significantly earlier than Chrétien's tale about Perceval and the Grail. If this were true, it would strengthen the notion that the original story came from around the time of Henry's visit to his uncle Henry of Blois earlier in the twelfth century. Since the most likely time of this visit was when Henry became Bishop of Winchester, the earliest point at which the Perceval story entered the court of Champagne was in 1129. Turning back now to Rigaut and his encounter with the story, we must recall that the time during which he seemed to be most active was roughly 1140 to 1160. This pushes the date at which he is exposed to the story of Perceval and the Grail to around the middle of the twelfth century. If we accept the notion that Rigaut was writing his third poem near the beginning of this period of activity, his mention of the Perceval character would indicate that he had a familiarity with the story some forty to fifty years before the latest possible time of Chrétien's writing *Le Conte del Graal*, and thirty to forty years before the most widely held dating for his work.

Judging from this information, it is possible that the story of Perceval and the Grail might have been around in the court of Champagne, gaining in popularity among the court poets and minstrels for a decade or more before Rigaut made his telltale mention of it in his famous love poem. This of course puts the notion of Chrétien as the father of the Grail legend in serious jeopardy. Although the traditional dating of Chrétien's Grail saga is not likely to change anytime soon, this unexpected link does beg one to contemplate the possibility that the Grail legend comes from someplace other than this one man's colorful imagination.

However, merely accepting an earlier date for the introduction of the

Grail story into popular culture does nothing to tell us how Count Phillip of Flanders came to give the alleged sourcebook to Chrétien, nor anything concrete about the sourcebook itself. To learn these answers, we should see what else we can find about Phillip and his relation to the sourcebook. What led him to give this text, the greatest story in Christendom, to his newly acquired poet, Chrétien de Troyes? Why was such importance placed on this book? Finally, is there any information illuminating the book itself?

If we attempt to use Chrétien's own words as a guide, we get little assistance. He spends nearly all of his prologue heaping praise on the name of his new patron, Phillip of Flanders; however, of the sourcebook itself, he says only this:

> Chrétien shall gain, since he has striven
> at the command the count has given
> and made endeavors manifold
> to rhyme the best tale ever told
> in any royal court: this tale
> is called the *Story of the Grail.*
> The count has given him the book;
> now judge what Chrétien undertook [Cline, pp. 3–4].

Scant information that it is, this paragraph can tell us two things. First, Cline's footnote to the line "The count has given him the book" asserts that this line suggests a Latin original since Chrétien's source for his earlier *Erec and Enide*, to which he referred in a similar manner, was a Latin treatise — Macrobius's commentary on the *Dream of Scipio*. Second, it demonstrates that the original was written in prose. Chrétien's statement that Count Phillip commanded him "to rhyme the best tale ever told" illustrates that he had to convert his sourcebook's information into the rhyming couplets found in his *Conte*.

Taking all of this information as a whole, it would seem likely that the sourcebook was a Latin book of some importance that existed in the early twelfth century. It is interesting here to remember the subject of the previous chapter. If we are to look for a Latin book containing a story of great worth about an artifact now called the Holy Grail, accessible to a pious medieval writer who might have taken Holy Orders, likely originating in Glastonbury, we must realize that Hank Harrison's theory regarding the Grail romance called the *Perlesvaus* meets all of these requirements. Unfortunately, this description could also include thousands of other books that might have been found in the twelfth century. Therefore, if we are to learn more about Chrétien's mysterious sourcebook, we will have to look at what other writers have to say, both about this curious book and as their own work.

Those who wrote the "continuations" of Chrétien's Grail romance seemed to have done little to illuminate the sourcebook from which the story sprang.

While some clearly used a degree of artistic license to complete the tale in their own way, some seemed to complete the story in keeping with its original tone and style. It has even been suggested that some of his continuators had access to some, if not all, of Chrétien's original source material — in theory, including Phillip's sourcebook. Investigating the four continuations of the *Conte del Graal* can actually yield some important information about the materials one might have found on Chrétien's writing table at the time of his death.

The first attempt to complete Chrétien's Grail story has been dubbed the "Pseudo-Wauchier" continuation, after Wauchier de Danain, who was once thought to have been its author. This text represents the very first attempt to complete the interrupted story of Arthur's knights and their search for the Holy Grail, only this story focuses on Gawain's adventures. The first Grail romance to outwardly introduce the concept of the broken sword, it also suggests that the author had access to the story in its earliest and purest form.

> As a sequel to Chrétien's poem, moreover, the adventure of Gawain at the Grail castle is preposterous, for its author, as already said, contradicts his predecessor on every essential point. It is hard to understand how Bruce and other commentators could have believed that he knew and was inspired by Chrétien's account and in "a legitimate attempt to gain the effect of mystery" produced a scene totally irreconcilable with his model. The effect on readers who remembered Chrétien's story must have been blank bewilderment, for our ancestors were not totally wanting in a sense of continuity and harmony. One can only conclude that Gawain's visit to the Grail castle had a source quite different from Perceval's and combined quite different strands of tradition [Loomis, p. 74].

Although Loomis credits these "different strands of tradition" to the Irish *echtrai*, or "mythical adventures," it is possible that the story of the Grail simply originated from another Christian text that first came to light earlier in the twelfth century.

The remaining continuations seem to be derivations from the original *Conte* and other Grail stories that existed at the time. The second continuation, actually written by Wauchier de Danain, exhibits a familiarity with Chrétien's original and the First Continuation (the "Pseudo-Wauchier" continuation). The next, that of Gerbert de Montreuil, seemed to incorporate themes present in Robert de Boron's retelling of the Grail's origins. The last of the four, called "Manessier's Continuation," endeavors to finally end the story of the Grail by returning to its original Grail hero, Perceval. Curiously, this final continuation mirrors the account of Perceval's final years as it was presented in the *Perlesvaus* saga, in which Perceval retreats to a hermitage deep in the woods where he lives out the remainder of his days in contemplation surrounding the Grail. Upon his death, the relics he reclaimed — the Grail, the Lance, and a great silver platter, depart from the Earth.

Although these first additions to Chrétien's originating text can help us learn more about the source material that was used to create the Grail story, none of them mention the mysterious sourcebook given to Chrétien by Phillip. Among these, only one seemed to make a conscious effort to tell us about the sourcebook in more detail. Traditionally seen as a later continuator, Wolfram von Eschenbach was the author of the early thirteenth-century Grail romance entitled *Parzival*. He made the intriguing claim that his interpretation of the Perceval myth was the more correct, and was more true to the source material than that written by his French counterpart, Chrétien de Troyes. He claimed that an individual he named as Kyot de Provenz (or Kyot of Provence) provided him with information regarding the source material that led to his conclusion that Chrétien did not do the original story full justice.

While Wolfram does not provide full disclosure about from when and where this source came originally, he does at least further claim that Kyot originally heard the Grail story in Toledo, Spain, which is just south of Madrid. From this, one may assume that this Kyot from Provence may have carried the story across the Pyrenees into France during his travels, but this is of course mere conjecture. In fact, the person of Kyot is somewhat under debate itself. While some identify him with Guiot de Provins, another trouvère of some popularity during the twelfth and thirteenth centuries, many scholars now question this assertion, leaning more toward the idea that Kyot was merely a dramatic creation used to lend authenticity to Wolfram's claims.

It was not uncommon for medieval writers to claim their writings were due in part to a source of greater antiquity, written by someone of higher acclaim. This was done not only to make it seem that their work was born in sources so old as to be beyond incredulity, but also to defray criticism. If someone happened to be offended by the story or disliked the message in some part of it, the author could then simply say that these were not his words, and that he was merely repeating what the great thinkers of the past had said. Although this sort of literary device was often used in the middle ages, it does not preclude the possibility that some writers may have actually had some manner of source material from which they drew their final work.

One notable example is William of Malmesbury, who used the wealth of historical documentation at Glastonbury to write his history. Geoffrey of Monmouth also claimed to take part of his much disputed *Historia Regum Britanniae* from a source he describes as a "certain very ancient book written in the British language." Much like the ever-present claim of hoaxing, the veracity and authenticity of such previous sources have always been questioned in the scholarly community. It seems that unless there is an extant copy of the sourcebook in question, the claim must be concluded to be a fraud. However, this sort of rush to judgment seems to be an all-too-common "get out of jail free" card thrown down when the subject matter strays into an area seen as non-scholarly. We must therefore question for ourselves whether such claims are worth a second look.

If an answer is to be found regarding whether Chrétien's sourcebook existed and, if so, what its story might be, one must go directly to the source, so to speak: Phillip of Flanders. Since Chrétien specifically states that the sourcebook he used to write his *Conte del Graal* was given to him by Phillip, investigating him and his history should yield some information telling us not only whether or not this was an actual historical and literary artifact, but potentially where and when it originated. How did this relative newcomer to the court of Marie de Champagne obtain the sourcebook he later gave to Chrétien? What prompted Chrétien to leave the court in which he had done the majority of his most notable writing? Why did he credit his Grail romance to Phillip when there is ample evidence suggesting he had already been exposed to the story of Perceval while in Marie's service? Most importantly, what does this all tell us regarding the origin of the Grail story?

While one theory suggests that Phillip obtained the book from the Cistercian Melrose Abbey in Scotland while trading for wool, this appears to derive from the abbey's association with the Templars, such as its being the final resting place for the heart of Robert the Bruce, allegedly buried in a silver casket somewhere on the grounds. As common as it may be to look to the mysterious Templars as the source of the Grail legend, a more tantalizing link can be found closer to home. Chrétien de Troyes served Marie de Champagne from roughly 1160 to 1172, writing most of his Arthurian works during this time. However, in 1172, he suddenly left the court of Champagne to write for Phillip of Flanders. Some ten years later, Phillip proposed marriage to Marie, only to inexplicably break off the courtship a year later to marry Mathilda of Portugal. According to the most commonly accepted timeline, he gave Chrétien the all-important sourcebook some time between 1172 and 1191 when Phillip died while on crusade. It is commonly thought that Phillip had received the sourcebook as a gift from Marie during their short-lived engagement. However, this theory does suggest a bit of a conundrum. If Phillip didn't present Chrétien with the sourcebook until around 1182, why then did Chrétien leave his previous patron in 1172?

The answer may be found in a most unexpected place — Spain. In Joseph J. Duggan's study *The Romances of Chrétien de Troyes*, he makes the statement that Phillip "journeyed as a pilgrim to Santiago de Compostella in 1172" (p. 20). This may seem an unimportant coincidence at first, but when one relates the pilgrimage path through Spain from France to the Grail legend, one very important connection becomes immediately apparent. Along the southern leg of the pilgrim's path to Santiago de Compostella lies the town of Jaca, well known among medieval pilgrims and for being a place rich with relics in its own right. On a remote mountainside nearby stands the monastery known as San Juan de la Peña, officially founded in the tenth century, but the site of hermitages long before. It is here that the Santo Caliz, claimed by some to be the true Holy Grail, was housed during the medieval period. It was common for pilgrims on their way to Santiago de Compostella, the resting place for the relics belonging to James, the patron saint of Spain, to take several smaller side pilgrimages to sacred sites along their journey. For anyone traveling the full distance from France to the west coast of Spain where the pilgrimage ended, San Juan de la Peña quite commonly was included.

Along the winding path that the Grail researcher travels, many alleged ties to the Grail can be found. Therefore, one may wonder, what is the significance of one more monastery that claims to have been the resting place of the Holy Grail? Although Chrétien doesn't tell us much about his curious little sourcebook, he can possibly answer this question. Chrétien tells us in his *Conte* that the Grail is made of pure, fine gold and set with precious stones of many kinds, the richest and most precious in the earth or the sea. This description matches the image of the Grail as we have inherited it today; however, the real connection to Spain can only be appreciated when one first sees the Santo Caliz, the relic that is set onto an elaborate reliquary — a stem, handles, and foot made from fine gold, set with precious gems from the earth and pearls from the sea.

Chapter 11

England to France, Spain to Germany

The one abiding edict of historical research is to follow where the information leads you. Although it is deep in the human condition to take control, feeling you know how to find the answer yourself, it is necessary to sometimes relinquish control and simply go where you are taken. Imagine yourself walking along a mountain trail that leads to a magnificent waterfall. If you hear water running somewhere off to the side of the trail, you typically would not just push through the woods assuming you've found a shortcut. You would probably follow where you are led, keeping to the path that leads to your ultimate goal. Looking for the Grail in history is much the same, only the path is not so well worn. You have to search for it, picking up the broken trail as it presents itself.

Research has led the author to the conclusion that the Grail story emerged not from one historical object, but from several — each once containing the blood of Jesus recovered both from the Crucifixion and the tomb in which He was interred. It appeared that medieval romancers took the stories of multiple artifacts and melded them into one master legend. As complex as this theory sounds, it now appears that the truth of the matter is not so simple. In fact, it now appears that the story of the Grail as we understand it today came from a melding of multiple medieval legends that were created based on the stories of these multiple objects.

The legend of the Holy Grail is inexorably bound to that of King Arthur, the great warrior king of England. When people imagine the secret hiding place of the holy chalice, they naturally think of an overgrown stream hidden by lush green ferns and grass, or a deep, lost, inaccessible crypt under a mossy gothic church. Few would expect to find it high on the side of a mountain, secreted away inside the red rock of an ancient Aragonese monastery. This is the sort of environment where the intrepid adventurer would more expect to find the Ark of the Covenant than the Holy Grail. However, this unusual twist to the story has done more to shape our literary conception of the Grail than even its verdant home at Glastonbury.

Legends traveled as readily as trade goods in the ancient and medieval world. Due largely to wealthy individuals traveling abroad for the first time during the Crusades, it is thought that new stories, new practices, and new ideas began to find their way into Western Europe. Just as Welsh bards wrote texts that helped formulate stories in England that became popular in France, traditions from a remote Spanish Pyrenean sanctuary likely became known to a traveling writer in Toledo who later passed it to a poet from Germany. Perhaps Chrétien's sourcebook, nearly as legendary as the Grail itself, is only part of the story. Two often forgotten factors along the path toward a historical Grail might just be the key to understanding the whole journey — a well-known but little-considered relic and a continuator relegated to obscurity.

Famed for his Grail text *Parzival*, the inspiration for the Richard Wagner opera *Parsifal*, Wolfram von Eschenbach was a twelfth- to thirteenth-century *Minnesinger*, a German poet-musician, who is thought to have been from Bavaria, although the exact place of his birth is uncertain. It has been suggested that although he was a landowner of minor proportions, he was relatively poor, possibly due to being a second son. He made his living as something of a migrant poet, traveling to different kingdoms in search of patronage. It seems he wrote his more famous works in the court of Hermann of Thuringia; however, after his patron's death in 1217, Eschenbach either died himself or simply stopped writing.

His last great work, *Willehalm*, was left incomplete due to his death, much like that of his rival Chrétien de Troye's *Conte del Graal*. Wolfram was much better known for his first two texts, *Parzival* and *Titurel*. His *Titurel*, which served as a sort of prequel or introduction to *Parzival*, tells the story of Sigune and Schionatulander, a romantic tale briefly treated in *Parzival*. This story was later elaborated into *Der Jungere Titurel* by an anonymous author who until recently was thought to be Eschenbach himself.

Wolfram is known in Arthurian and Grail circles for writing his story of Perceval and the Grail in a very different, almost metaphysical fashion. The hero Parzival is mesmerized by the sight of blood spreading through fresh snow. His mother's name, Herzeloyde, means "heartache." His brother is described as being striped or spotted black and white to show his descent from mixed Christian and Moorish parentage. This mixing of the sacred with the surreal extends to his description of the Holy Grail as well. Wolfram equates the Grail with what he calls the *lapsit exillis*, which has been considered the Philosopher's Stone, able to perform any manner of transmutations such as turning a base metal into gold. One of the most interesting facets of Eschenbach's Grail story is not the curiosity of its tones and themes, it is the claim he makes regarding its source.

Like Chrétien, he makes the assertion that this story is not his original work. He states he took it from an older book in which the original story was outlined. What makes it most curious is that the sourcebook he allegedly used is the same, or at least from the same source, as that used by Chrétien. Wolfram goes further to state that his French counterpart did not do the original story justice. According to him, the story that he wrote was more correct and closer to the original than Chrétien's, and should therefore be taken with greater credibility. Although the almost surreal feel of the thirteenth-century text makes this difficult to accept, his story does in fact answer several questions about the earliest origins of the Grail legend, as will become apparent by the end of this chapter.

According to Eschenbach, he learned of the story from someone he names Kyot, another writer who allegedly was familiar to both him and Chrétien de Troyes. He claims this Kyot first heard the story in Toledo, Spain, although he does not indicate when or how.

> Kyot, the master well-known, found the foundation of this adventure in Toledo, written in heathen script and discarded. He first had to learn the ABC of the writing, except for the cunning of necromancy. It was a help that baptism was with him: otherwise this story would still be unheard. No heathen cunning could assist us in revealing the nature of the grail and how one is initiated to its secrets.
>
> A heathen, Flegetanis, earned high praise for his knowledge. That same scholar of nature was born of Salomon, begotten of Israelite kin in the old days before baptism became our shield against the fire of hell. He wrote about the grail's adventure. Flegetanis was a heathen on his father's side, and he prayed to a calf as if it were his god. How can the devil bring such mockery on such wise people that they did not and do not separate it from Him Who wields the Hand Supreme and to Whom all wonders are known? Flegetanis the heathen could tell us much about the going down of every star and its future coming back, and how long each of them goes around before it stands at its endpoint again. By the circular movement of the stars all human nature is regulated. Flegetanis the heathen saw secrets hidden among the stars and spoke of them with caution. He said there was a thing called the grail, whose name he had read among the stars, without question as to what it was called [Lefevere, p. 121].

In this passage we see Wolfram trying to demonstrate that his source, Kyot, was a reliable, upstanding Christian man who braved the perils of what was at the time Moorish Toledo to delve into the secrets of the original text written by Flegetanis. It is difficult to ascertain what exactly was meant by the statement that Flegetanis read the Grail's name among the stars. It is possible that this is supposed to mean that Flegetanis saw the Grail in a vision, much as the Wise Men from the story of Christ's nativity learned of His birth from signs in the stars. Others have suggested that Wolfram is alluding to the idea that the Grail is actually an emerald that fell to earth from Lucifer's crown.

This does beg the question: exactly what sort of Grail was Wolfram envisioning? The nearest thing to an answer we may find is provided by a hermit of great holiness, much the same as in *Perlesvaus*.

> *The hermit proceeds to explain the meaning of the grail and the rituals connected with it. He says:* "You say you are yearning for the grail: I must pity you, you stupid man, since nobody may search for the grail except if he is known to heaven and called to the service of the grail. I must tell you this about the grail: I know it and I have seen it as true." Parzival said: "Were you there?" The host said to him: "My Lord, yes." Parzival was altogether silent about the fact that he had been there too. He asked the hermit for knowledge: how things stood about the grail.
>
> The host said: "It is well-known to me that many a warlike knight lives at Munsalvaesche with the grail. For the sake of adventure they always go on many travels, these same Templars, whether they are looking for care or praise: they endure it for their sins. There dwells a warlike host. I shall tell you about their food. They live off a stone. Its nature is very pure. If you have not recognized it, it will be named for you here: it is called *lapsit exilis*. Through that stone's power the phoenix burns up so that it turns to ashes, but those ashes bring life to it. Therefore the phoenix throws off its molt and gives off a very bright glow afterwards, so that it becomes more beautiful than before. Also, never did such illness overcome a man that if he sees that stone one day he cannot die during the week that comes soonest after it. Also, his color never deteriorates. They must admit that his skin is of the same color as when he saw the stone, man or woman, as if his or her best years had just begun. And if he were to see the stone for two hundred years, nothing would change, except that his hair might turn gray. Such power does the stone give to man that his flesh and bone receive youth without delay. The stone is also called the grail [Lefevere, p. 124].

It is interesting here to note that Wolfram does not capitalize the word "grail," seemingly to illustrate that it is more of a descriptor rather than the term by which it is known. Also here it is made very clear that the grail and the stone are one and the same object. It is stated that the Templars, specifically named as "warlike" knights, use the stone/grail as their sustenance, harkening back to more traditional tales of the Holy Grail providing food to the brave knight of his favored type and in great abundance. It also parallels the Grail's alleged ability to restore and prolong life to those who partake of it.

If we recall Wolfram's claim that this story originally came from a Moorish source in Toledo, Spain, it becomes somewhat less uncharacteristic to call the Knights Templar, warrior-monks and guardians of pilgrims to the Holy

Land, a group of "warlike" knights. If the original story were written by a Moor, the Templar and indeed all Christian pilgrims were their opponents, and would have been viewed in such a less-than-flattering light. We may find more examples in this description that further suggest an Arabic origin to this text. Many have suggested that the medieval pseudoscience of alchemy came from the crusaders' exposure to the new cultures, new religions, and new traditions that they found in the East. The magical properties described by Eschenbach may have derived from a Christian's interpretation of early Muslim accounts of such metaphysical objects and practices.

The idea that the Grail of Arthurian legend is actually a stone seems quite foreign to us indeed. It is easy to see how much more alien the concept would have been to the medieval Christian mind. If one considers the stone less as a physical object and more as an allegory for a transformational process, the concept begins to seem less outlandish. The traditional stories of Perceval and the Grail are ones in which a simple man becomes not only a great man, but a holy man as well. This seems to be the thrust of all Grail texts — the transformation from the simple to the sublime.

Students of alchemy sought to perform this same type of refinement, although traditionally on a more material level. Along with early forms of medicine, this study sought not only to turn lead and other common forms of metal into gold, but to learn how some materials interacted with other materials in order to yield a more valuable end result, much like modern chemistry. Some modern scholars who have studied alchemical texts have found this similarity, and claim that the medieval alchemist's goal was simply to further human knowledge. However, considering how closely the physical and the spiritual worlds were tied in the Middle Ages, it is also thought that this study included the ultimate desire to make the baseness of the human body, which naturally included the soul, into something more heavenly, thereby attempting to be more like God. Therefore the typical claim made of medieval alchemists, that their desire was to turn lead to gold, may well be put into different terms. They may have also wished to turn the clay from whence came our human flesh into air, or the divine breath of God Himself.

The search for the stone by which this physical and spiritual transmutation might occur, the Philospher's Stone, was referred to as the "Great Work," and was undertaken by many great thinkers and early scientists of the time such as Sir Isaac Newton. Wolfram's comparison of the Grail and the stone seems more plausible when one considers the claim that the stone grants everlasting youth and vitality. The Philosopher's Stone was thought to produce another mythical substance known as the Elixir of Life, with which one might achieve immortality. It seems fairly clear that Wolfram von Eschenbach was trying to make an association between the Grail and the alchemical Philosopher's Stone, although the use of the term *lapsit exillis* does not specifically draw the reader to that conclusion. Although this term may seem unusual to us, it is quite possible that the term would have been quite familiar to his intended reader.

> A.E. Waite, in his work *The Holy Grail: The Galahad Quest in the Arthurian Literature* [most recent edition: (New Hyde Park: University Books, 1961)] gives the variants *lapis exilis* and *lapis exilix*, for it seems that the spelling differs according to the manuscript; and he also points out that according to the *Rosarium Philosophorum* (citing Arnold of Villeneuve), *lapis exilis* was for the alchemists one of the designations of the "philosophers' stone" [Guenon and Fohr, p. 279, n. 1].

Wolfram provides one description for his grail/stone that does not match any other description of the Philosopher's Stone known to date. He outlines how upon the rim of the stone, an unseen hand scribes the name of the individual who is chosen to protect the grail. This same sort of supernaturally affected object can be found in the fifteenth-century text *Morte d'Arthur*, written by Sir Thomas Malory. In this work the Siege Perilous was a single seat left empty at King Arthur's Round Table. According to the story, any knight who attempted to sit in the Siege Perilous was swallowed up, never to be seen again. Eventually, the Grail hero Galahad arrived at King Arthur's court and, safely sitting in the empty seat, demonstrated that he was the knight intended to achieve the Grail.

It turns out that the Siege Perilous and the stone that Wolfram von Eschenbach called the grail share more than just this one likeness. In fact, each seat at Arthur's Round Table had the name of the one knight who was destined to sit in it inscribed by the invisible finger of God. Like the grail/stone in *Parzival*, this motif of objects' being marked by the hand of destiny was not that uncommon in the Grail legend. Some think the idea of names marked on the seats of the Round Table simply shadows the Round Table at Winchester on which the names of Arthur's knights are written around the outer rim, marking each knight's place at the table.

It is quite likely that this kind of supernatural scribbling is simply a literary device, much like stories of a saint being set adrift in a ship with no sails and no rudder, meaning that the person arrived in a certain location thanks to the Hand of God alone. It is simply a way for the writer to demonstrate that an individual, or an action, or a place is marked out by God to play a special part in the events about to unfold. In a similar manner, the place where the Grail manifests itself is shown to be a special place. The Grail Castle, the castle of the Fisher King, is a location that inspires awe both in name and in appearance. Wolfram's take on this place is no different. Like those who came before him, he makes it very clear that this place, where the intrepid Grail Knight must go to achieve his final reward, is a place unlike any other he has ever encountered.

When one reads Wolfram's description of the Grail Castle in *Parzival*, it sounds as if he has simply picked up the description from an earlier Grail romance and copied it into his own. The Grail knight Parzival finds an old fisherman in a boat probing the waters surrounding an imposing castle. The fisherman tells the knight to ride on to the castle and request a night's lodging. Parzival does as the fisherman tells him, and although he is well greeted by his host, he witnesses a peculiar sight. He sees a bleeding lance and a holy vessel amid a luminance the likes of which he has never seen before. Despite his obvious curiosity over such a spectacle, he does not inquire about any part of it, remembering the advice given to him by the elder Gurnemanz not to ask too many questions. Once the procession ends, the great dining hall empties and upon the morning, Parzival leaves the castle alone.

On the surface, it seems this familiar story can tell us little new information regarding the possibility of a historical Holy Grail. However, several specific pieces of information offered by Wolfram can point us not only toward a historical Holy Grail, but from a quite unexpected direction. Like the Grail Castle from Chrétien's *Conte del Graal* or the anonymous *Perlesvaus*, Wolfram paints a picture of a great, glorious castle in the midst of what might be called the "wild wood"—a paradise in the wilderness. What is unique about Wolfram's Grail Castle is its name, *Munsalvaesche*.

Odd sounding as this name might be, alone it does not tell us a great deal. In addition to this peculiar name, we are provided with two other interesting pieces of information. The first of these is the very specific mention of the Knights Templar. Wolfram states quite clearly that the Grail is guarded by a group of knights whom he names as being the Templars. It isn't merely insinuated by giving them a red cross on their surcoats; they are mentioned by name. There seems to be no evidence that Wolfram was a Templar or that he owed any particular fealty to them. Therefore, one may wonder why he made such a definite association.

Finally, the account of Parzival's half-brother Feirefiz and his baptism is yet another aspect of Wolfram's Grail Castle that will later prove to be telling. Leading a large Saracen army, Feirefiz first encounters his brother Parzival in a heated battle, only to be later invited to join Parzival on his quest. In keeping with the overall air of strangeness we find in Wolfram's romance, Feirefiz is described as being piebald, spotted black and white due to being the child of a European father and a Moorish mother. Because he is Moorish, he cannot see the Grail at first. Partly to see the Grail, but mostly to marry his lady love and Grail bearer, Repanse de Schoye, he agrees to be baptized as a Christian. Immediately upon being baptized, he finds he can see the Grail just as his brother Parzival does. It is later said that Feirefiz and Repanse return to his native lands to the East, later giving birth to the legendary Christian king in pagan lands, Prester John.

The requirement that one is to be holy enough to see or touch the Grail is not at all uncommon in Grail literature. In fact it is almost a requirement that those who are too worldly or are holding on to a particular sin, such as Lancelot refusing to give up his love for his king's wife Guinevere, will never witness the Grail procession even if they succeed in finding the Grail Castle. So, what does the story of Feirefiz's baptism, or in fact any of these aspects of Wolfram's Grail Castle, offer us in the way of finding the historical Holy Grail? Why is his *Parzival* anything other than a curious side note in our investigation of the Grail as an archeological relic? Quite simply put, its value is that it points to one place that matches Wolfram's descriptions at a time in which a historical relic that has been called the Grail resided there. *Parzival* not only tells us this, it may also provide a link back to the Grail tradition in literature founded by Chrétien de Troyes and possibly back to its source in Glastonbury.

Let us first consider the curious name Wolfram gives the Grail Castle: Munsalvaesche. Janice Bennett seeks to provide a real world location for Wolfram's curiously named Grail Castle: "In Wolfram von Eschenbach's *Parzival*, the Grail is kept in the castle of Munsalvaesche, which is surrounded by a wild forest. *Salvaesche* is from the Old French form of *sauvage*, meaning 'wild' (in Latin *silvaticus*)" (p. 156, n. 8). Bennett goes on to state that the rugged woods surrounding the mountain monastery of San Juan de la Peña near Jaca Spain certainly matches the description of the Grail Castle being a paradise set amid the wilderness. However, she does not rely on this aspect of the ancient site alone to justify her assertion that this was the place Wolfram called the Grail Castle. Instead the most convincing evidence comes from the ancient language of the Pyrenees.

Wolfram calls his Grail Castle *Munsalvaesche*. Judging from the claim that this term derives from the French word for "wild," we might assume that "Munsalvaesche" might well mean something like "wild mountain." Although this would be a fitting description for the wooded area surrounding the San Juan de la Peña monastery, there is another more intriguing interpretation for the name. According to Bennette, the name "Munsalvaesche" can be translated from the old Occitan language of the French and Spanish Pyrenee Mountains into a name more familiar to the area. In modern Spain, the mountains near Jaca in which the San Juan de la Peña monastery is housed are referred to as San Salvador — "Munsaelvaesche" in Occitan.

In this regard, Wolfram's Munsalvaesche might be better translated as "the Mountain of Salvation." If so, this would be an appropriate name for a

11. England to France, Spain to Germany

place that was considered holy since long before the first monastery was built into a giant natural cave in the eleventh century. This mountain was the location of many hermitages and, according to legend, the place where a local holy man and saint named Juan de Atares spent the last years of his life in solitary contemplation, allegedly dying with a cross clutched to his breast. This also corresponds to the description that Wolfram's Munsalvaesche was surrounded by several other tiny hermitages.

If we refer back to the passage in Wolfram's *Parzival* in which his half-brother Feirefiz is baptized in order to see the Grail and marry its protector, we can find another link between the Grail Castle and San Juan de la Peña. Deep in the monastery, there is a niche in the wall where the Grail is thought to have been kept. Above and to the left of this niche, there is evidence that a natural spring once ran down the wall from a small opening near the chamber ceiling, leaving behind the mineral deposits that are commonly found where water once flowed. Again it is the specific wording Wolfram uses that points to this as the chapel of the Grail.

> *The next morning Parzival and Anfortas lead Feirefiz to the baptismal font in the castle. Parzival reminds Feirefiz that he will have to renounce all his gods.* "Whatever I have to do to get the maiden," spoke the heathen, "shall be done and it shall be shown that I have done so with loyalty." *The baptismal font was tilted a little toward the grail. Suddenly it was full of water, neither too warm nor too cold* [pp. 221–222].

From this passage we can infer a number of things in relation to our new-found Grail Castle. First, the passage said "the baptismal font was tilted a little toward the grail." This description would seem to indicate that the baptismal was near the Grail as is the case with the niche and spring in the wall of San Juan de la Peña. Since the spring is both above and to the left of the niche, one could imagine that a small basin may have once collected the water that flowed from the spring, and if it were tilted toward the niche, the water would have indeed flowed into or at least near the Grail. Second, the passage says "suddenly it was full of water, neither too warm nor too cold." The water that runs from a natural spring down a stone wall and into a cup would likely be a little cool to the touch, but neither cold nor warm.

These aspects of the San Juan de la Peña monastery are tantalizing to be

Opposite: The mountain monastery of San Juan de la Peña near the city of Huesca in Spain. This medieval monastery is ancient indeed, but older still are the numerous cave hermitages dotting the cliffs and mountainside around it. These mountains were called *Munsalvaesche* in the medieval local dialect known as Occitan. *Munsalvaesche* was also the name given to the mountain land of the Grail Castle by German Grail romancer Wolfram von Eschenbach in the early thirteenth century (photograph courtesy Janice Bennett).

sure, but they are not conclusive. Although it appears quite likely that Wolfram von Eschenbach used San Juan de la Peña as a model for his Grail Castle, it is also possible that it was merely a place with which Wolfram was familiar, using it as a backdrop for his Grail story. However, there is further evidence that this location was thought to have some relation to the Grail. Wolfram had a continuator of his own for the work he began in his *Parzival*, a later writer named Albrecht von Scharfenberg. In 1272 Albrecht took Wolfram's incomplete romance *Titurel* and turned it into a work all his own which he called *Jungere Titurel*.

Renowned Grail researcher John Matthews took a particular interest in the Albrecht account of the Grail Castle, claiming it bore an uncanny resemblance to the "Takht-i-Taqdis," or "Throne of Arches," which served as the seat of power for the Persian king Chosroes II. According to Matthews, the onyx lake on which it is built and the arches that surrounded it match Albrecht's description of the Grail Castle.

> Even more conclusive evidence of a dependent relation between Albrecht's Grail Temple and the Takht-i-Taqdis is furnished by an engraved bronze salver, in the Berlin Museum, which is either very late Sasanian or early post–Sasanian. For this shows in elevation a domed palace which is elaborately decorated with symbols of fertility — trees, great blossoms, jars of the living water.
>
> This building, depicted by the line engraving in the center of the salver, has been identified, by an intricate complex of internal evidence paralleling the literary records, as the Takht-i-Taqdis. A striking confirmation is that the rollers on which, according to Persian accounts, the building was set, are clearly shown in the drawing on the salver, a most unusual kind of foundation.
>
> The building itself was interpreted by Strzygowski as an emblematic representation of the Holy Grail to which, when he reaffirmed it at the Second International Congress for Persian Art (London, 1931), Professor Sarre replied with great vigor that not one line of evidence has been produced — only affirmations. But Strzygowski's guess was apparently correct, for with Professor Wolf's publication of the more accurate Albrecht manuscript the two were virtually conclusively linked. For on the salver the central building is surrounded by twenty-two arched panels, each framing a decorative tree; and in the revised version of the Albrecht poem the rotunda of the Grail Temple is surrounded by twenty-two arcaded chapels, each decorated with an ornamental tree [Matthews, pp. 339–340].

Although Matthew's argument is compelling, the value to this investigation of the Grail is the tradition, put forward by Eschenbach's continuator, that the Grail chapel was surrounded by arches. Conventional thinking relating to this tradition is that it was the building, the Grail Chapel, that was encircled with arches. However, if we take it literally that the Grail Chapel itself was surrounded by arches, we find another link to San Juan de la Peña.

Today tourists and pilgrims can visit the chapel where a replica of the Grail is kept in a glass case on an altar. This is the chapel where the holy relic was allegedly venerated when it was actually at San Juan de la Peña. What immediately strikes the visitor when they enter this chapel is that it is completely surrounded by arches. There are three main arches that form the front of the high altar, which consists of three smaller chapels or chambers. In each of these three semispherical chambers, the walls are ornamented by a curtain of carved arches. In the center chamber, there are a total of seven arches adorning the back wall, and in both the left and right side chambers, there are five carved arches. In addition to these, there are two more arches that form "doorways" from the central chamber to either of the side chambers.

These specifics of the high altar chambers at San Juan de la Peña draw a quite unexpected parallel to Albrecht's description of the place where the

The medieval chapel of San Juan de la Peña. Here is where the Holy Grail in the form of the Santo Caliz was venerated, and even served as a holy relic over which Spanish "proto–Templar" knights swore their oath of allegiance. Where the modern replica of the Santo Caliz now stands, the true relic could be seen in the twelfth century when Prince Phillip of Flanders likely visited while on pilgrimage, possibly passing its description down to Chrétien de Troyes. Note the arched altar area — an intriguing twenty-two arches in total (photograph courtesy Roberto Abizanda).

Holy Grail was kept. He claimed the Grail Castle was surrounded by arches, twenty-two to be precise. It is intriguing here to note that there are also a number of arches present in the high altar at this obscure Spanish monastery. When one adds them all together, three arches at the front, two arches leading from the center chamber to either of the side chambers, seven arches on the back wall of the center chamber, and five arches on the back wall of both side chambers, we discover that the total number of arches is the same as that mentioned by Albrecht, twenty-two in all. Although this compelling information does not prove a definitive link between Albrecht and San Juan de la Peña, it does suggest that Albrecht, Wolfram von Eschenbach's continuator, derived his information from the same place that Wolfram apparently used as inspiration for his *Parzival*— San Juan de la Peña.

A mysterious medieval monastery perched high on a holy mountain is certainly the stuff of the Grail legend, and could well have been the seed of truth behind the image of the Grail Castle. However, this still does little to justify the notion of the Holy Grail of legend being anything other than an artfully crafted fiction based on some real-world locations or stories. To prove the existence of the Holy Grail within the confines of history, we need a bit more corroborative information than just this. Fortunately San Juan de la Peña fulfills this requirement as well. Not only does this monastery fit the descriptions of the Grail Castle given by Wolfram von Eschenbach and Albrecht von Scharfenberg, it also offers a relic that quite nicely fits the descriptions of the Holy Grail itself given by Wolfram and his French predecessor, Chrétien de Troyes.

The grail that San Juan de la Peña once housed is today called the Santo Caliz of Valencia. This ornate object, now kept in Valencia Cathedral, is claimed by those who protect and venerate it to be the one true Holy Grail. The Santo Caliz is a red agate cup, supposedly dating to the time of Christ, that sits atop an elaborately decorated gold and jeweled reliquary monstrance that forms its base, stem, and handles. This object of obvious value and significance certainly meets with our Western view of what the Holy Grail would be; however, its appearance is only one feature of this small cup that lends itself to the claim that this is the true Cup of Christ. Guarded and passed down through generations, this cup touts a well-documented history that none of the other potential Grail cups around the world can claim.

According to tradition, this cup was the very one used at the Last Supper and later caught Christ's blood at the site of the crucifixion. Later recovered by the disciple and first pope, Saint Peter, the Santo Caliz served as the first cup of the Eucharist used in the Christian Church. The Santo Caliz was allegedly used for the purpose for roughly 200 years until religious persecution in Rome caused Pope Sixtus II to entrust the relic to his deacon St. Laurence.

Before his own death, St. Laurence gave the cup and several documents testifying to the object's authenticity to a fellow Spaniard, and sent it to his family's homeland in Huesca, Spain, for safekeeping. There it remained for nearly 300 years until it was moved to the recently completed Cathedral of Huesca. For the next 150 years, the Santo Caliz was safely housed in Huesca, until the year 711, when an invading Moorish army caused the relic to begin a long journey of obscurity, being secreted away in several tiny monasteries throughout the Pyrenees.

The Santo Caliz was known to be in the monastery of San Pedro de Siresa in 830 where it became the center of relic worship and acquired royal sponsorship that lasted several centuries. However, in 1071, the cup was taken to the mountain monastery of San Juan de la Peña, where it remained for nearly 300 years. Although it wound up in Valencia after having again gone into hiding during the Spanish Civil War, it is this time at San Juan de la Peña that

The Santo Caliz of Valencia. The closest thing to the Holy Grail, this ancient vessel has travelled down through the ages from Rome to Spain, resulting in the classic image of the Holy Grail that we know today. Likely viewed by Count Phillip of Flanders while on pilgrimage to Santiago de Compostella in the late twelfth century, this is basically the same image he passed down to the troubadour poet Chrétien de Troyes. From his *Conte del Graal* came the story of the Holy Grail into Western culture, including his description that it was of the purest gold and adorned with the finest jewels found on the land or, most importantly, in the sea (photograph courtesy Janice Bennett).

is of particular interest to us in this investigation of the Grail and the evolution of its legend. Sometime between the late eleventh century and early fourteenth century, this red agate cup was transformed, not just physically but also literally, into the Holy Grail, the sacred chalice of high medieval romance.

Let us now investigate how a small stone cup became the Holy Grail of legend, beginning with an investigation of the cup itself.

Before Antonio Beltran's archaeological study of 1960, next to nothing was known about this precious relic, other than what has been contributed by tradition. At times it has been vaguely described through the epochs by various authors who often struggled with words, and at other times it was deliberately omitted from the document as the only defense against theft. Nevertheless, Beltran affirms that the upper cup is indeed from the first century, and maintains that archaeology has found nothing that would be opposed to its authenticity.

Gaspar Excolano, in the seventeenth-century *Decada primera de la Historia de la Insigne y coronada Ciudad y Reyno de Valencia*, describes it in the following manner: "*The entire cup of the Chalice is made of a single precious stone, similar to what they call chalcedony, according to what Pliney, in book thirty-seven, chapter seven, relates that the ancients prided themselves on making chalices of those stones* [Bennett, p. 28].

Thus considering the agate cup on its own, we find that such costly cups of semi-precious stones were common in Roman times, typically the property of the wealthy more than the commoner. In fact, there exist in the British Museum several cups of Roman origin made of almost identical materials, exhibiting the same shape and dimensions right down to the slight engraving around the lip. Once we remove the gold and jeweled reliquary, we are left with nothing more than a simple if costly Roman drinking vessel of a type that was common in the first century A.D.

The fact that this cup is of the highest quality and probably the possession of one who could afford such costly finery likely precludes the possibility that it was simply a cup carried by Jesus as He traveled across the land spreading His message. Therefore, if this cup was not in the possession of Jesus or any of His disciples, we must conclude that it first belonged to the same person who owned the house in which the Last Supper was held. This high-status ritual item can provide some insight into the people who hosted the critically important Seder meal. The purported location, today called the *Cenacle*, is a room in Jerusalem that has obviously been touched by the medieval hand of the western Crusaders. What visitors to the Cenacle see today is nothing like what it might have looked like at the time of Jesus. Some have even suggested that if the Last Supper was a historical event at all, there is no evidence supporting this site's claim to be the actual location.

The medieval remains of this space can be deceiving. In fact, there is evidence that the Cenacle has been the site of pilgrimage since at least the fourth century A.D. It is thought that this is the site of the early Christian church known as the Church of the Apostles, where many of the first Christians met. Not only is there a long-standing tradition that the upper room now called the Cenacle was the actual site of the Last Supper, other early accounts go a step further, ascribing a name to the location. According to

Bennett, "one testimony is that of Theodosius, who speaks of the Cenacle of Holy Sion when describing his visit to Jerusalem around 530 A.D. He says: *Ipsa fuit domus Sancti Marci Evangelistae*, or 'This was the house of the Evangelist St. Mark'" (p. 43). It has long been thought that the upper room in which the Last Supper was held belonged to the family of Mark, specifically his mother Maria, whose family was more wealthy than the average Jewish Israelite. It has even been suggested that Mark's family owned olive trees and presses (Bennett, p. 44).

If this was the actual house in which Jesus and His disciples held their famous last supper on the night of Passover, this would certainly explain the tradition that the Holy Grail was the cup of the Last Supper in which Jesus began the ritual of the Eucharist. However, it has always been questioned how a cup from the upper room found its way to the Crucifixion. It is possible that since this was the last place the group met before Jesus's arrest, trial, and crucifixion, this was the only place where they might have obtained vessels in which to catch His blood, as was the tradition of ancient Hebrew funerary practice. However, there is another option that harkens back to the Last Supper itself that might explain this act.

The answer can be found in the Bible in the book of 1 Corinthians 11:25 in which Jesus says, "This cup is the new covenant in my blood." Although specific words might have changed as they have been passed down throughout the centuries, the meaning remains the same. As He hung on the cross, his followers would have no doubt remembered these recent words spoken by Jesus, and felt it was important to retrieve the actual cup He held as He made this statement, using it to fulfill their tradition of collecting the lifeblood of their beloved dead. It was tradition to entomb this collected blood with the body, but it may have been kept among his followers, in remembrance of their fallen master. Whether the cup was left in the tomb with the body or kept protected among His followers, the cup containing the blood of Christ would have acquired new significance when they found His tomb empty, and were admonished to continue His teaching throughout the world.

> The Eucharist, as a new concept for the Apostles of the newly formed Christian Church, would have been indelibly engraved on them for its transcendental significance. Communion as a Eucharistic feast had been just established as a rite, and it is inconceivable that the receptacle that served to consecrate the wine into the blood of Christ would have been lost. Because the owner of the Cenacle was also a disciple of Jesus, he certainly would have balled the cup even more for having been the object of such unexceptional use, but even if that were not the case, the cup was an expensive piece of fine stone that was part of his property. And certainly, as a disciple of Jesus, it is logical to think that the owner of the Cenacle would have entrusted the relic to St. Peter as head of the Church. Peter

even calls Mark his son (1 Pet 5:13), which implies a long-standing and deep relationship, and supports the hypothesis that Mark gave the precious cup of salvation to the first Pope. Although it is not possible to find documentary proof of something so remote in time, most would agree that the sacred vessel had to have been preserved. That such a significant relic would have been buried or lost is impossible according to most Christian writers, simply because it was so important for the early Christians to use their relics in the liturgy, and certainly, if the cup was in the possession of St. Peter, it would have gone to Rome, just as tradition maintains [Bennett, pp. 44–45].

The Santo Caliz entered the monastery of San Juan de la Peña with these prestigious credentials, a fact attested by an 1134 document kept in its archives and preserved by Canon Juan Agustin Ramirez in his writings on the life of St. Laurence. It has been suggested that the acclaim over the arrival of this relic began the story that would become the Holy Grail legend. Certainly the time is right, since the Holy Grail entered popular myth and culture around the end of the twelfth century according to traditional interpretation. In addition, the time in which the Grail sprang up to become the subject of so many medieval romances spanned a period ending in the mid-thirteenth century. We must consider the possibility that the Santo Caliz of Spain is the object that spawned the Holy Grail tradition in western Europe. Convenient timing and claims from the early papacy do not cement this one relic as the Grail of medieval romance. However, the description given by the Grail romancers provides the corroboration we require.

Looking again to Wolfram's Grail, we are told two things: first, that it is a stone of some form, and second, that it apparently has transformative powers, most likely in a metaphysical sense. Both of these descriptions fit the Santo Caliz in various ways. Obviously it is made of semi-precious stone, which would potentially account for one interpretation of his term *lapis exilis* as meaning "slight, small, or insignificant stone." The stone cup is relatively small, certainly no *krater* as in the Greek tradition. It is also made of agate, which although a beautiful stone, it is not as rare or valuable as something like emerald or ruby. Although the exact meaning of this phrase is debatable, the one thing we can know for certain is that Wolfram wanted to make it very clear that his Grail was made of stone.

In addition, the lapis exilis has also been likened to the Philosopher's Stone, which transforms the common or base into something of greater worth. Similarly does the ritual of the Eucharist transform a simple wafer into the flesh of Christ. Likewise it transforms the sinner into a divine being, closer to God in the taking of Communion. In a physical sense, the cup that is the true relic of the Santo Caliz has a particular appearance in the eyes of the medieval alchemist. It has been said that the red agate has the appearance of fire, especially when turned at different angles. This natural phenomenon is a characteristic peculiar to this type of stone. Being translucent and red in hue, the veins of varying color resemble dancing flames when viewed against the light. Since fire is a basic, primal element, a requisite for any form of alchemical formulation, this cup would have been seen as something almost supernatural in form—a cauldron of fire in which the Great Work might be wrought.

Wolfram also makes the curious statement in his Grail romance that at times, mysterious writing appeared on the grail/stone as if by the finger of God. Although this sort of divine communication could very well be nothing more than creative license, it also sounds curiously like another little-known aspect of the Santo Caliz. On the base of the ornate monstrance, there is an enigmatic bit of Arabic writing. Although this base is not part of the relic associated with Jesus and His Crucifixion, it has a mysterious history all its own. Research has indicated that it could be nothing more than an offering dish, but the inscription itself is telling.

The Kufic, or old Arabic, lettering spells out something akin to "allabsit as-sillis," which could itself explain Wolfram's use of the name "lapis exilis." There have been several translation attempts made which include phrases such as "For the flourishing one," "For He who flourishes," and "For the Bright One." It would seem that whatever the specific wording is, the inscription refers in some way to God or Jesus. Dr. Antonio Beltran, who originally researched the Santo Caliz translated the inscription as "he who shines" (Bennett, p. 180), which is the same term Wolfram used to describe God. For these reasons it would seem very likely that the early thirteenth-century author of *Parzival* not only knew about the Santo Caliz and San Juan de la Peña, but used both as models for the creation of his Grail text.

If these similarities are not convincing enough, Wolfram provides one final link between his *Parzival* and the Santo Caliz at San Juan de la Peña. He specifically states that the Grail at Munsalvaesche is guarded by a group of Templars. Although the Spanish monastery is not known among the hundreds of medieval structures associated with the Knights Templar, there is a reference to a group of knights who date back to the Templar order's earliest days. Alfonso I, "The Battler," king of Aragon until his death in 1134, is said to have gone to San Juan de la Peña so that his group of proto–Templar knights could swear an oath of loyalty before the Santo Caliz. In fact, King Alfonso allegedly bequeathed all his lands to the Templar order after his death. Therefore, Wolfram's description that the Grail was watched over by the Knights Templar was quite likely a reference to King Alfonso's act of dedication before their Holy Grail—the Santo Caliz.

There now seems to be a strong indication that Wolfram von Eschenbach and later his continuator Albrecht von Scharfenberg built their Grail literature upon the history and tradition present at San Juan de la Peña; however, all this really tells us is that this branch of the Grail legend originated there. It does not follow that the entire body of medieval Grail romances, including the earlier originating text *Le Conte del Graal*, had anything to do with the Santo Caliz. For this, we need evidence that other Grail authors knew about this Spanish Grail and drew upon its legacy to create their own romances. Fortunately, we have such information, and as luck would have it, we are led back to the founding father of the Grail legend, Chrétien de Troyes.

When Chrétien describes the Grail, he states that it was made of pure gold and decorated with precious stones of many kinds, the richest and most precious in the earth or the sea. These specific words are a dead give-away. Although our image of the Grail would surely include fine gold and jewels, the inclusions of precious jewels from the sea can refer to only one thing: pearls. Pearls are the only jewels found in the sea. Therefore, Chrétien is telling us that the Grail about which he is writing is adorned with gold, jewels, and pearls. Looking at a picture of the Santo Caliz of Valencia, the eye is immediately drawn to the row of pearls around the bottom edge of the base. Therefore, it would seem quite likely that Chrétien was aware of the Santo Caliz when he wrote his description of the Grail. However, this assertion all comes down to a matter of timing.

If Chrétien wrote his *Conte* sometime between 1170 and 1190, we must determine if the original relic of the red agate cup was joined to the ornate gold and jeweled base during this period. There is a great deal of documentation surrounding the Santo Caliz and its time at San Juan de la Peña, but unfortunately there is nothing that specifically mentions when this transformation takes place. It is fairly certain that the agate cup entered San Juan de la Peña as a separate cup, and was known to be in the form the Santo Caliz takes today when it left the monastery in the fourteenth century. Therefore at some time between these two dates, the rich reliquary was added to the cup, but the question remains, when?

Michael Hessemann, German writer, historian, and Grail researcher, has studied the Santo Caliz and its associated documentary evidence for many years. He claims that "in a document of the year 1135, the 'chalice of precious stone and a dish of similarly precious stone' are still listed as two separate items. In that year, King Ramiro II of Aragon commissioned his goldsmiths to set them into a single object which corresponded much more with the mediaeval idea of a chalice" (p. 18). The 1135 document he mentions is a request made by King Ramiro II of Aragon for both the red agate cup and the other dish of "similar precious stone." According to this document, both relics were sent to King Ramiro in that year, and that this was the only time the relic ever left San Juan de la Peña until it was permanently removed in 1399. He further states that the gold work on the stem and handles of the Santo Caliz is typical for twelfth-century metalworking (Hessemann, personal communication March 9, 2011). It is interesting to note that King Ramiro II ruled for only a few years following the death of his brother Alfonso I, retiring to the abbey of San Pedro in Huesca where he died in 1157.

Given the parallels between Wolfram's *Parzival* and the events that took place at San Juan de la Peña in the early to mid-twelfth century, it seems almost certain that this very unconventional take on the Grail legend was based on the Santo Caliz as it was seen in the medieval Spanish monastery. The location would seem to match. The name of the Grail Castle, *Munsalvaesche*, is the medieval Occitan name for the mountains now called San Salvador, where the monastery of San Juan de la Peña is found. The monastery exhibits several features mentioned in *Parzival*, such as a spring which once ran very near to the niche where the Grail could have been kept, matching the description of the baptismal font in which Parzival's moorish brother was baptized. It also holds a sanctuary altar where the Santo Caliz was venerated featuring twenty-two decorative arches as mentioned by Albrecht von Scharfenberg, a later Grail romancer who based his work on that of Wolfram von Eschenbach.

If these links were not convincing enough, there are even more correlations between Wolfram's Grail and the Santo Caliz itself— the Holy Grail of Spain. The Grail in this text is said to be a stone of peculiar quality, just as the Santo Caliz, which is made of beautiful if not rare red-brown agate. This grail/stone is likened to the alchemical Philosopher's Stone, which takes something base and refines it into something pure and of greater value. In a similar manner, the cup of the Eucharist is traditionally seen as the centerpiece for a ritual in which a miraculous transformation occurs, changing the mass wafer and wine into the very flesh and blood of Christ. Similarly, the act of taking the Eucharist transforms our fallen state into that of one who is closer to Christ for following His commandment to do so in remembrance of Him. The link between Wolfram's "lapis exilis" and the Santo Caliz is more firmly established when one discovers that *Parzival* states the Grail has mysterious writing upon it inscribed on it by God, "the Shining One." On the Santo Caliz, there is just this type of writing, inscribed on the foot. The ancient Kufic writing is read by some as "allabsit as-sillis," which sounds nearly identical to "lapis exilis," and has been translated as "For the Shining One." Finally, history indicates that the Santo Caliz was venerated by, and was the center of a holy oath sworn by, a group of Spanish knights, "proto–Templars," who followed King Alfonso during the time that it was being kept at San Juan de la Peña.

For these reasons, it seems fairly certain that Wolfram's grail romance found its origin in this high Spanish monastery. However, since Wolfram claims the same source as that used by Chrétien de Troyes for his *Conte del Graal*, one may wonder how it made the leap from Spain to Germany to France. In actuality, this compelling Spanish genesis story is only one branch leading back to the Grail's origins. Just as the objects which can all be called grails likely merged into one object in legend, it seems that the legend in literature came together from two separate traditions that literally criss-crossed medieval western Europe. As far reaching, and seemingly far-fetched, as this notion may seem, it is all brought tidily together in one place with which we have already become familiar — San Juan de la Peña.

Much like the Crusades to the Holy Land, pilgrimages to different holy sites brought the wealthy and itinerant alike together along a common course. Such was the theme of Geoffrey Chaucer's beloved text, *Canterbury Tales*, in which knights, royalty, clergy, and commoners all rubbed elbows on their way to the shrine of Thomas à Beckett in Canterbury. These medieval pilgrimages were something like a church social, a vacation, and a work-release program rolled together into one melting-pot event. Here was an occasion for people of different backgrounds and traditions to speak, learn, teach, and share a common experience. Given the popularity of pilgrimages to Santiago de Compostella on the west coast of Spain, one can justly imagine this as a place where many men and women of note throughout history came together to leave their mark on medieval myth and fable.

It has been previously mentioned that San Juan de la Peña was often included along the pilgrims' path to Santiago de Compostella as a kind of spiritual "extra credit." Among these are two names of special note from our study of the Holy Grail. The first of these was the medieval "Renaissance man" from Glastonbury, Henry of Blois. Hank Harrison, who studied Henry's history in detail for his unpublished book *Crown of Stars*, states that Henry of Blois went to Santiago de Compostella, possibly to follow Peter the Venerable in his 1140 pilgrimage. If Henry also saw the Santo Caliz while visiting San Juan de la Peña, it undoubtedly would have had a deep impact on him considering he was himself the steward of a site rich with its own Grail tradition. The second person of interest to this study who likely saw the Santo Caliz at San Juan was Chrétien's patron, Count Phillip of Flanders, who "journeyed as a pilgrim to Santiago de Compostella in 1172 and to the Holy Land in 1177–1178" (Duggan, p. 20).

It is my belief that this link between San Juan de la Peña and Phillip of Flanders by way of his pilgrimage to Santiago de Compostella is all-important to the growth of the Grail legend as we know it today. It has been demonstrated with reasonable certainty that the Santo Caliz was not only present during the time of Phillip's pilgrimage, but also in the form one can see it today in Valencia. If there was an existing tradition regarding the Grail legend originating from Glastonbury, as evidenced by the reference to Perceval and the Grail procession by early troubadour Rigaut de Barbezieux, Phillip's seeing a chalice purportedly used by Christ at the Last Supper as well as the Crucifixion would provide an ending to an otherwise incomplete tale. As fabulously entertaining as the story of Joseph bringing the Grail to Britain was, people would still crave a resolution. They would no doubt want to know what had happened to the vessel containing Christ's blood that had once been on England's pleasant pastures green.

The scallop shell is the symbol for the pilgrimage route to Santiago de Compostella, or the "Way of St. James." Church Square in the town of Jaca in Spain features a brass scallop shell embedded in the pavement. The symbolism of this image is to say, "Though there are many paths for the pilgrim, they all converge at the tomb of St. James" (shell provided by Janet Griffin; author photograph).

If we endeavor to see the story in its possible entirety, from the beginning of the historical events that inspired a legend to the tales of mystery in a distant land that became the myth, we can finally take two separate traditions and see how they fit together. Imagine for a moment that Joseph of Arimathea did in fact journey to Britain after the Crucifixion, carrying with him some kind of vials or cruets containing a small portion of Jesus's blood, which was to the first-century Jew the seat of the soul. If that event became the centerpiece of devotion at Glastonbury, resulting in the growth of the monastic community present there until the Dissolution in the sixteenth century, it would have become a fully developed, rich tradition which was just hitting its peak during the twelfth century, when the story of the Grail apparently entered Western culture proper. Chrétien, the author and father of the Grail legend, would have been privy to all of the bountiful volumes present in Glastonbury's ancient library by way of King Henry and Marie de Champagne's affiliation with Henry of Blois, abbot of Glastonbury at the time. From these he could craft his high medieval romance full of flowery illustration and imaginative rendering. However, the one thing he could not provide was a resolution — an ending to his story.

Fast-forward to 1172 when Phillip went on pilgrimage to Santiago de Compostella and San Juan de la Peña, seeing the Santo Caliz in its full gold-, jewel-, and pearl-encrusted glory. When Phillip was told it was the Cup of Christ, and was shown the historical documentation present in this high mountain monastery, he was in effect given the answer to the mystery of the lost Holy Grail. Arthur's quest, and that of his knights, had finally been completed, although not in the misty vales of Avalon, or on England's soil at all, but in a different house of God. In San Juan de la Peña, near the place where the body of St. James the apostle and brother of John the Beloved is housed, this cup which was venerated and protected by the early church fathers had rested in relative obscurity for centuries, the centerpiece of their devotion. With the same sense of wonderment and discovery we all would feel, Phillip must have known that he had found the Grail, himself becoming the Grail Knight and hero.

When he returned with his tale, and likely with copies of the historical writings about the Santo Caliz that he himself had seen, it is easy to see how Chrétien would have felt compelled to follow him, assured that he had the answer to the lingering question, "Whatever became of the Holy Grail?" For this reason, it is most likely that the sourcebook to which Chrétien refers in the introduction to his Grail romance, and for the recovery of which he fully praises and credits his then-patron Phillip of Flanders, was a book containing the story of the Grail derived from San Juan de la Peña, and not the original story of Joseph's relic derived from Glastonbury from which he began working on his *Conte del Graal*. Although Chrétien credits the entirety of his *Conte* to Phillip, it is likely that his attempt to reconcile the British Grail tradition with the Spanish Grail tradition led to the unfortunate state of incompletion in which it was left at the time of his death. One can imagine how difficult it would have been for Chrétien to realize their relation without the wealth of historical records and geographical sense that we have at our disposal today — knowing for certain these two stories were related, but beyond the hand of God alone, not being able to fully understand how.

Although it may be difficult to accept this conclusion at first, we must remember two things. First, it is very likely that the tradition of Joseph of Arimathea at Glastonbury was available to the French court through Henry of Blois and his relation to King Henry. If there was evidence suggesting this biblical figure so close to Jesus Himself had not only been to southern England, but had founded the church at Glastonbury, it surely would have been a large part of Glastonbury's identity as a place of Christian devotion. Second, it would appear quite likely if not certain that Wolfram von Eschenbach and those who continued in his tradition viewed the monastery of San Juan de la Peña as the place where the Holy Grail resided. As in the French Grail romances, these German Grail stories spoke of the Grail being kept in a castle which existed both in the physical world and that of the spirit. If one imagines the Grail Castle as a magnificent structure built by man but rich with the Holy Spirit, what better place than the powerful and imposing "Castles to God," the monasteries of Glastonbury and San Juan de la Peña?

Recalling also that Wolfram von Eschenbach claimed to have knowledge of the same source material as that used by Chrétien, and the fact that he apparently based his Grail Castle on San Juan de la Peña, it becomes more likely that the fabled sourcebook was a book containing the story of the Spanish Grail, the Santo Caliz. If this is the case, it in no way invalidates Glastonbury as the source of the legend. Instead, it confirms it. This connection finally defines the line between the Grail of history and the Grail of legend. Both locations claim, I believe rightly, the possession of a relic that can be called the Grail. However, it is Glastonbury alone that can be the source of the tales of Joseph of Arimathea and his role in bringing the Grail to Britain from which the French court almost assuredly first learned of the tradition. Similarly, it can only be from Britain and Glastonbury that we have the association of the Grail with King Arthur and the knights of his court.

But in Glastonbury we cannot find a beautiful gold and jeweled chalice to call the Grail. We only have the story, carried forward from their distant past, of two humble vials that once contained the blood and sweat of Jesus, and sadly, not the relics themselves. Then at San Juan de la Peña we find an existing cup — the relic from the time of Jesus that is said to have once held His blood, and to have been used in the holy rites of the Eucharist by the first popes. There we have the golden chalice of legend, surrounded by Templar-like knights in a place that at least one medieval romancer sees as the place where the Holy Grail is kept. Thus we can see how this holy relic, the Grail, which vanished after it was acquired by the Welsh Grail hero Perceval, had again resurfaced on Earth in the faraway, secret monastery in Spain, just waiting there for the intrepid Grail knight to find after proving himself worthy through quest and holy devotion.

In the Santo Caliz, it would seem we have matured as Grail questers and proved ourselves worthy to achieve our goal — finding the cup, used by Christ at the Last Supper and which caught his blood at the crucifixion, the golden chalice adorned with the most costly jewels on the land or in the sea, held in the high hermitage of Munsalvaesche in Spain. From what has been accepted as a quaint story woven for the benefit of tourists, we can finally find some answers. Criss-crossing the European continent, we can finally begin to understand how a French romance based in Britain and a German romance drawn from Spain tie together historical objects from Jerusalem with the medieval fantasy of Grail literature. However, this book isn't called *San Juan de la Peña and the Grail*, it's called *Glastonbury and the Grail*. As exciting as it is to find this link between the Santo Caliz and the Grail legends, one must come to terms with its source to fully understand the Grail as a historical artifact. Therefore let us end where we began — in the wattle church at Glastonbury with Joseph of Arimathea and his two cruets of Christ's blood.

PART IV

The Case for Glastonbury and the Historical Grail

Traditionally, the Grail Legend is seen as a medieval myth. Reason suggests that the objects of such fantastic tales as this could not possibly exist, and certainly should not be considered actual historical relics. However, for all of man's intelligence, he doesn't quite know everything. Man was once sure the Earth was flat. Man once thought it impossible to travel faster than the speed of sound. Once the very concept of a human being walking on the moon was absurd. Today, all of these are old news. In short, man has been certain that a great many things were impossible only to be proven wrong by those few who wanted to see for themselves.

The final section of this book is devoted to demonstrating that the legends of Joseph of Arimathea at Glastonbury and a true, historical Holy Grail are anything but mere legends. Both are in fact very possible. Given the evidence at hand, I would go so far as to say that both are actually quite likely. While examining this evidence, the reader must walk the tightrope—be critical but willing to consider. Although nothing that I have offered herein could be called definitive proof, it should at least serve to challenge the accepted disbelief.

Chapter 12

Making a Case for Glastonbury

Many months ago when I started making the outline for this book, I began with the end, so to speak. I knew the manner in which I wanted to end my argument supporting the Joseph of Arimathea traditions at Glastonbury and the existence of an historical Grail. Knowing I would never be able to provide definitive proof of the Holy Grail as a historical fact instead of an example of man's wish for the fantastic, I realized I could only make a case for the *possibility* of such — to draw into question the certainty that the Grail never existed outside of medieval literature. While understanding that "anything's possible," I wanted to do more than just hang my theory on a cliché. I wanted to show plentiful evidence supporting the fact that, although technically impossible to prove beyond a shadow of a doubt, there is plenty of reason to think that both Joseph of Arimathea and the Holy Grail at Glastonbury were very real, historical possibilities. While it would seem attempting to *prove a possibility* is a mediocre pursuit for a book, the truth is that proving a possibility is the most one can ever really hope to achieve. One can never prove anything definitively outside the realm of mathematics and chemistry, and even then the certainty they promise sometimes fails in truly bizarre circumstances.

Toward this end, I have tried to devise a way to present this evidence in the best manner possible, allowing for the inevitable uncertainty, but leaving as little margin for doubt as possible. First attempting to employ the scientific method to perform this proof in as scholarly an approach as I thought possible, I found that this approach relied too heavily on empirical evidence, hard facts, to execute its function. As there are too few facts in any given legend to go on, I soon realized this method was not a good match to the subject matter. I then settled on pursuing a "court case" style of argument to support my theory. Of course this would support my desire to make a case for Glastonbury.

12. Making a Case for Glastonbury

In true Perry Mason style, I could make a convincing argument supporting the historical nature of the traditions at Glastonbury while accepting there would be some lingering doubt and definitely no "yes or no" answer.

I found this approach most compelling. I would not try to put Joseph of Arimathea on trial, trying to prove he was at Glastonbury during the first century, nor that he held in his possession the Holy Grail. Instead I chose to put on trial the traditional certainty that the stories behind the Holy Grail and Joseph of Arimathea are nothing more than stories, with no foundation in truth. I, taking the role of the defense, would provide evidence supporting the tradition that Joseph indeed came to Glastonbury, founded the church there, and by extension could well have brought with him relics that would later become the Holy Grail of legend. Therefore the jury (you, the reader) could not say beyond a reasonable doubt that the story of Joseph and the Grail was mere fiction. Of course the argument to this approach would be, has always been, "You can't tell me to prove something didn't happen. It's your job to prove that it did!" This is quite true. You can't prove something didn't happen, though this is actually the stance taken by many over the years — "The Grail story can't be in any way true because there is no evidence showing that it is." Unfortunately, more emphasis has been put into debunking the medieval romance than considering the possibility of the Grail as a historical object. While it is certainly true that you can't prove something didn't happen, you can prove that there is reason enough to say, it could have happened.

In the attempt to outline exactly how this court case might function, I found that the prosecution (scholar-skeptics in this case) would make their argument first, which I as the defense would rebut. I would then have my turn, presenting my case which the prosecution would then rebut. Add in the provocative opening statements for either side and the persuasive closing statements, and there I would have my quite convincing court case to prove my theory sound. However, I quickly found a problem in my tactics: I could not make a substantive case for the prosecution. I could not provide substantial arguments to make a convincing case supporting the skeptical claims that the Grail story is nothing but a myth. I could only present the same allegation for each point, that there is no proof. There is no proof Glastonbury was ever considered Avalon before the Middle Ages. There is no proof Joseph of Arimathea ever came to Britain, nor existed at all outside the Biblical context. There is no proof of Melkin the Bard or his writings prior to John of Glastonbury's fourteenth-century *Chronicle*. There is no proof the Holy Grail ever existed outside of the medieval romances written about it. As damning as all that sounds for my position, there really is no evidence to support these allegations beyond hearsay and popular opinion.

It then occurred to me that the prosecution is critically hindered in its attempt to support their claim of fiction vs. history. Scholarship, for all its benefit and reward, is limited only to accepted facts. Definite statements can only be made using accepted facts. When the facts stop, the scholar can go no further, leaving out inference, intuition, probability, and all the other intangibles that most often pave the way for new discovery. If there is still a question, that means there are insufficient facts to fully answer the question, and if that is the case, you can't really prove anything. In other words, unless you know for a fact that the event in question isn't possible, you can't prove it didn't happen. You can only present circumstantial evidence, often bordering on mere suggestion and suspicion, not proof. Take for example the discovery of King Arthur's gravesite. There is physical evidence there was a grave on that site at an appropriate depth, and there are multiple historical accounts detailing eye witness testimony to the existence of Arthur's leaden cross — a situation almost identical to documented burials at Wells. However, due to the propitious timing and the monetary advantage such a discovery would have offered the supposedly floundering abbey, it has been assumed that the event in question was a hoax. Little heed is paid to the idea that if the Church (the "capital 'C'" Church) wanted to make the claim that they had found King Arthur's grave, all they really needed to do was to present some bones and a convincing story. They didn't have to actually dig, they didn't have to hang curtains around the site, they didn't have to create a fictitious lead cross recounting the validity of the discovery. All the Church needed to say to make their claim was, "We say it was so."

That having been said, the defense, in the form of an amateur scholar with no such rules to abide by, is allowed the lenience to consider what is possible, instead of just what is already known. With this indulgence, it becomes possible to ask, "What if?" When the correct sequence of "what ifs" are strung together, the task then becomes the finding of any evidence to suggest that is what actually happened. Then, like a lively game of *Clue*, you no longer require firsthand proof of the murder, you don't need to be inside the refrigerator to see the light go out, and you don't need to have witnessed the events in question. Instead, you can piece together enough circumstantial evidence to surmise what actually took place. With the understanding that you can never say for certain that something was or was not in these cases, you can say with some reasonable certainty that something *most likely* was or was not. While one can never make a circumstantial case completely watertight, (barring an emotional confession following a hot cross-examination), it is possible to take an open-and-shut conviction of a fictitious legend and turn it into an acquittal. Therefore, pursuing the theme of a court case trying the traditional stance that the legends of Joseph of Arimathea at Glastonbury, and by extension that of the Holy Grail, are nothing but medieval literary fabrications, I present the following summary to serve as the defense's case.

Whatever else the aim of this investigation may be, one question must ultimately be asked. Is there enough evidence to suggest that the traditions of Joseph of Arimathea and the Holy Grail are based in truth? Simply put, yes. To demonstrate this assertion, we really need ask only three questions:
1. Could a man from Palestine travel to Britain in the first century?
2. Could a first-century artifact from Israel find its way to Britain?
3. Was Glastonbury in Somerset the sort of place where both could have arrived?

The answer to all three questions is yes. The land now called Britain has been a part of European trade and migration throughout history. There is evidence that it was part of the Phoenician trade routes: the stone anchors of their sailing ships have been found on British shores. The people whom the Romans found when they arrived in Britain, the Celts, were for the most part not native to the island, and in fact migrated from other locations such as Gaul, what is now France. Similarly, foreign goods have been found in the graves of Britons since long before the arrival of the Romans. Although the Roman occupation came only slightly later than the time period in which we are interested, fine Roman wares have been unearthed in excavations at Tintagel Castle in Cornwall. It is clear that Britain was not a place so far removed from the European continent that it never came into contact with other cultures.

One may now ask, was the area in Somerset now called Glastonbury a place where these foreign transplants might have gone? This location has a singular characteristic that makes all the rest possible: access. By way of the Severn Sea and the River Brue, people and goods arriving in Britain could venture deep inland before ever stepping foot onto British soil. This area in the south of England was home to many religious and cultural centers. People wishing to trade or those simply moving in from foreign lands would not have landed in the hostile, harsh climate of the wild north country but in lush, fertile plains full of abundance. This was not yet a land torn by war, feuds, and struggles for power. For the most part, there were not enough strains on available resources to make it a place dangerous to outsiders. To a Roman metal merchant, this was the land of opportunity. Ore was rich and plentiful, and being in such a remote location, this was a great untapped resource.

When one strips away all the legend, all the tradition, and all the modern treatments of both, all you have left are these three questions. Since it is now clear that a man from the far-away Middle Eastern Roman province of Judea could have very easily migrated to Britain in the first century, the big question really becomes another question entirely. Is that what happened? At that point, it becomes a matter of probability. Was Joseph likely the sort of person who could have traveled that distance? Was the object in question likely in his possession? Was Glastonbury the most likely place he would have gone? To answer these questions, we must of course dig a bit deeper. Therefore let us begin with the man on whom the remainder of this argument rests.

Joseph was described in the Bible as being a wealthy man from the land of Arimathea. Although there has been much debate over where exactly Arimathea was, for our present discourse it is largely inconsequential. What is important is this description of his social standing. When a first-century Jew in Roman-controlled Palestine was called "wealthy," it means something very particular. It meant he was very likely a merchant of some kind. If he were a member of the priestly class, it would not have been worded in this manner, nor if he were a skilled tradesman such as a mason or metalsmith. To be called a wealthy man, he would have to be neither royalty nor commoner. As a merchant he would have occupied a very special place in his society. He was still subject to Roman authority but would have been granted some small freedom and allowances by those over him. Also, he potentially would have worked in similar circles as the Roman royalty and the priests of the Temple, depending on his trade. As such, he was able to do what few among his people could. He was able to afford a few luxuries, such as a new tomb in which no body had yet lain. It is thought that he was a member of the Sanhedrin and so likely came into contact with the Romans.

Joseph was wealthy enough to make a better life for himself and his family, but the question remains, who was his family? Who else might he have cared for? It has always been assumed that the reason Joseph gave his own tomb for the burial of Jesus was simply out of devotion and reverence for his fallen Lord, but it is possible there was another reason. The Bible also states that he went boldly to Pilate, the Roman prefect, to ask for the body of Jesus at the Crucifixion. This story has become so commonplace for us, it is easy to overlook several key details in this simple statement. By "boldly" going to Pilate, he exhibits some degree of authority and social standing in relation to such a powerful Roman. A common potter or smith would not have walked right up to a Roman of his standing, but would have requested an audience with him and likely would have met Pilate on his hands and knees, possibly resulting in the same fate as Jesus.

By asking for Jesus's body, he tells us one more thing of great importance. It was the practice of the time that the next of kin would request the body of the condemned man, if it had not yet been cast into the garbage heaps on the outskirts of the city. This suggests Joseph had some relation to Jesus, specifically the eldest male member of his family. Jesus's father Joseph had died prior to the Crucifixion, and since his brother James did not request the body, one can only assume that the responsibility fell to Joseph to make the request. It should also be remembered that the other followers of Jesus were in hiding, fearing their own arrest, trial, and crucifixion. If Joseph were simply another among Jesus's followers, it would have been unlikely for him to have approached Pilate with such a request, and even less likely for the request to be granted.

So far, this provides means and motive for Joseph to act just as legend suggests. However, it still doesn't fully justify the theory that Joseph went to Britain, to Glastonbury, carrying anything but the clothes on his back for the journey. To prove these points, it becomes necessary to delve into the particulars of his trade as a merchant, specifically the tradition that states Joseph was in the tin trade. Metals such as tin and lead were of vital importance to the Roman Empire, such as for use in their famed aqueducts, bath houses, and fountains. As a metal merchant, his travels would have surely included the Mendip Hills region of Britain, which served as one of the chief suppliers of tin and other valuable metals during Roman times. Archeological evidence in the area shows that tin mining and panning for tin ore along river and creek shores has gone on for centuries. Thus, the peaceful, green fields of the British countryside might have been an inviting place for Joseph to bring the young Jesus, both as a change of scenery during troubled times and as a precaution in light of the circumstances of his endangered birth. It has been suggested that even the flight to Egypt undertaken by Joseph, Mary, and the infant Jesus might have been orchestrated by Joseph of Arimathea thanks in part to his connections to the Egyptian metal trade.

If Joseph visited Britain with Jesus in the years leading up to His ministries and death, it could also account for why Joseph went to Britain following the crucifixion. If he was familiar with the area, it would have been easier to settle among its people and to spread the teachings of his master and nephew Jesus. Called the "Great Commission," one of the final commandments set down by Jesus to his followers was to bring his word to distant, "gentile" lands, as did many of the disciples after His death. The Apostle Peter went on to be the Rock on which the Catholic Church was founded. Saint Andrew became the founder and first pope of the Church of Byzantium. John apparently went into Ephesus to spread the Gospel. Phillip was sent to Greece and Syria, while Bartholomew preached in Albania and possibly as far as India. Matthew went into Africa to preach in Ethiopia, and Thomas (commonly known as "doubting Thomas") traveled to India to minister to a small Jewish population there. James possibly went to Egypt and Thaddeus, also known as Jude, went into Syria. Although the ministries of the Apostle Simon are disputed, some possibilities include Armenia, Syria, Egypt, and Persia.

Finally, St. James is the Patron Saint of Spain, although he died in Judea. According to legend, James went to Spain to preach the Gospel, only to witness an apparition of the Virgin Mary which caused him to return to Judea where he met his fate.

If Joseph was sent, or according to some traditions banished, to a foreign land to continue Jesus's teaching, it would seem only logical that he would go someplace with which he was familiar. Although his travels as a metal merchant would have taken him throughout the Roman Empire and surrounding areas, he may have chosen Britain due to its distance from Rome and Israel, as well as for potentially sentimental reasons. Based on his familiarity with the area and surely his ties to the people with whom he traded, Britain would have been the most likely choice of a new home in which he would spread the Gospel. From this we can see that Joseph not only had a logical reason to travel to Britain, but one might say he was sent there by Jesus Himself. Having now answered two of our three questions, we must answer the third and most important of these. Did he carry with him any vessels containing blood relics of Jesus? For this, we must turn to the only account of how his journey out of Judea began.

The *Gospel of Nicodemus*, a portion of the fourth century apocryphal Biblical text *The Acts of Pilate*, relates the story of Joseph asking for the body of Christ, and placing it in his own new tomb. This act resulted in Joseph falling from grace with the Sanhedrin, landing him in prison in a sealed cell under Roman guard. When his accusers returned to question him further, they discovered that the cell was still sealed, but no longer contained their prisoner. When they found he had returned to his native Arimathea, they decided a gentler approach might be in order, and requested his presence to discuss the circumstances of his escape. Joseph then related how he had been freed by God Himself and translated to his house under the instruction not to leave for forty days and nights, while Jesus returned to his followers in Galilee.

In this text, there is no mention of banishment or exile on a ship with no rudder or sail. However, Robert de Boron elaborated on the *Gospel of Nicodemus* in his thirteenth century book about Joseph of Arimathea and his role in the Grail saga. Here, Joseph is kept imprisoned for many years, maintained by a single mass wafer each day served from none other than the Holy Grail. When he is finally freed, he and his companions take the holy vessel to Britain. The story of exile, and his association with Mary Magdalene, allegedly doesn't come into the picture until the ninth century with Archbishop Rabinus Maurus's *Life of Mary Magdalene* in which the more commonly known version of Joseph's journey to France and on to Britain is outlined.

It would seem the closer the Joseph story comes to that of the Grail, the later in time the texts are written. Although a ninth-century account of Joseph and Mary, Martha, Lazarus, and a host of others certainly predates the traditional dating for the origination of "Joseph Mania" in Great Britain, it certainly falls short of the first century. However, one mustn't forget the other accounts of Joseph written by early church fathers. Eusebius wrote in the fourth century that the Gospel had already been brought to Britain before A.D. 222. In fact, Hippolytus, who lived in the late second and early third centuries, specifically stated that Saint Aristobulus accompanied Joseph to Britain, becoming the country's first bishop.

While on the subject of the legendary exile and ship with no rudder nor sails, it is interesting to note that, although the traditions of Joseph in Britain and Mary Magdalene are very separate and geographically distant traditions, both appear to be very old, nearly from the time of Christ Himself, and would in many ways appear quite similar. The use of the ship bereft of any means of self-guidance serves to illustrate that both individuals were brought to the distant lands on which they found themselves and serves to show that they were in essence guided there by God's hand alone. Mary's legend ends in southern France, near Marseilles, resulting in the alleged discovery of her body with her ever-famous alabaster jar. Joseph's legend is similar, but differs in a few very important ways. His is better known, obviously the root of a vast medieval legend, while her story remained relatively obscure until the publication of *Holy Blood, Holy Grail* in the 1980s. Most importantly, however, both stories include small vessels that supposedly once contained the precious blood of Jesus — a sort of personal relic around which their ministries could grow.

We have now answered all three fundamental questions. Joseph of Arimathea could have very easily traveled to, and settled in, Britain in the first century. As a metal merchant, Somerset would have been the very sort of place where he might have chosen to begin his new life as a minister to the Britons. Finally, as someone who played a critical role in the recovery of Jesus's body and entombment, he would have been present to collect His blood in whatever manner, and in whatever vessel, that was appropriate to his time. As such, any blood relics that were preserved following the discovery of the empty tomb could have, and almost certainly did, come into his possession. Now that we see the traditions of Joseph bringing the Grail to Britain could in fact be entirely legitimate, we must determine if there is any evidence supporting the suggestion. This evidence can be found at only one place — Glastonbury. Though this is a place conventionally called a "hoax factory," one can easily find evidence to the contrary. In Glastonbury we find a small town full of ancient traditions. Today those who act as modern pilgrims to the little town find many indications that they treasure their mist-covered past. Green Men peek out around every corner. Fairies line the streets. Mystics vie for space along the two main streets through the center of town. Most of all, everywhere one can see images of the mysterious stair-stepped Tor found a short distance away. It is clear that this is an ancient place. However, you really don't have to take the tourism board's word for it. Instead consult the archeology.

The Glastonbury Lake Village was constructed only a short distance away. Wooden trackways once criss-crossed the marshy landscape, leading from one patch of elevated dry land to the next. Standing on a main road between two Roman ritual sites, Glastonbury and St. Joseph's Well were likely an important stopover where Romans could pray to their gods for safe travels, or perhaps a sick loved one. Archeological evidence supports the idea that Glastonbury was not only alive and active in Roman times, but long before, potentially back to the age of the hunter-gatherer.

Many today assume that the title of "Avalon" for Glastonbury is also a relatively modern creation, possibly associated with John of Glastonbury. However, it would seem that Glastonbury has been associated with the idea of Avalon, if not the name, for many centuries. Called Ynis Witrin, Appolonia, the Glass Isle, or Glastingebury, it seems the idea of Avalon as the sacred isle amid the mists of the Somerset moors indeed originated here. If Glastonbury were considered to be Avalon, this alone could account for one of the more interesting and enduring mysteries of the Grail legend.

The idea that the Grail may be a historical truth may seem implausible at first — a magical, flying chalice granting both food and eternal life, won by a demonstration of innocence instead of wisdom. However, the medieval story belies one question that would stump the skeptic more than any of the Grail's magical properties. Why would the Dark Age Briton king Arthur be associated with the story of a relic from Christ's Passion, which happened a world away in Israel? The answer is very simple. As with many legends, multiple threads are over time woven, or perhaps more correctly beaten together, into one solid, contiguous whole. What we have today is merely the end result of this amalgamation process. Thus, King Arthur and his knights going in search of the Grail, or Sir Percival's acquisition of the Grail, is nothing more than one legend flavoring another.

If we assume that there was a King Arthur and that he was in some way associated with Glastonbury, through pilgrimage, patronage, or burial, and we further assume that there was a tradition that some object relating to the Crucifixion and Jesus was housed at Glastonbury, taking into account the amount of time passing between Arthur's time and the writing of the medieval stories, voilà! We have Arthur and the Grail. Taken literally, the story of Arthur being translated to the Isle of Avalon, that being Glastonbury, near the time of his death might have been a last-ditch effort to save his life after being mortally wounded, hoping that his life could be saved by a holy relic. It could also be that Glastonbury, a holy house on the Isle of Avalon, could have been seen as a place where the truly miraculous could happen, such as bringing the dead back to life. Anything might have happened, but if Arthur did end up at Glastonbury, the Joseph of Arimathea tradition there surely played a part in his association with the cruets later identified as the Holy Grail.

Whether one chooses to believe the accounts of King Arthur's burial, or Joseph of Arimathea's arrival at Wearyall Hill as they have been presented herein, there is one piece of evidence that must be reckoned with. William of Malmesbury himself states in his 1135 *Antiquitate Glastonie Ecclesie*, "There are numerous documents of no small credit, which have been discovered in certain places to the following effect: 'No other hands than those of the disciples of Christ erected the church of Glastonbury.'" It has been mentioned that his original work was elaborated and expounded upon by later monks or other writers, but that the original and these later additions can for the most part be separated with close inspection. This passage is thought to come from Malmesbury's original work. In addition, it must be remembered that after his time spent at Glastonbury, Malmesbury wrote a second edition of this previous work, *Gesta Regum Anglorum Libri Quinque*, outlining the chronology of the Kings of England in a way suggesting he had been privy to source material far older than he had previously cited.

In fact until fairly recent history, the church at Glastonbury was accepted as being the oldest in Christendom, set above those in Rome and Spain. It was this claim which no doubt aided Glastonbury in becoming one of the richest, most powerful, and most superbly endowed in both relics and writings of great antiquity. Setting aside our own skepticism momentarily and taking a look at the history, writings, and evidence alone, one cannot help but wonder if the traditions of Glastonbury relating to its foundation by Joseph of Arimathea might just be true. In so doing, one must invariably ask a rather difficult question, similar to that of Arthur and the Grail as listed above.

If Joseph of Arimathea did not come to Glastonbury in the first century, why does the tradition to this effect exist at all? Granted most believe this came from the fertile imaginations and ever-hungry coffers of the Middle Ages, but as the William of Malmesbury quote above demonstrates, this idea is much older than the time during which it was capitalized upon. If there is no truth behind it, why then is there a story at Glastonbury that this particular man came to the area with two relics from the Crucifixion? Understandably, an argument cannot be made which effectively justifies itself. However, it is a reasonable question. Where did the Joseph tradition at Glastonbury come from? After all, if there is no suggestion of their truth, why do these legends exist at all?

These were not the times of fanciful stories and fairy tales. In the Dark Ages, daily life consisted mostly of trying to survive, or perhaps in the abbey's case, trying to come as close to God as you might before your time came to depart this mortal stage. Since it involves someone from the Bible and Christ's time, it can't be a hallmark of the land's pre–Christian past, as some claim with the Grail legend. It doesn't seem the sort of thing the Romans would have brought with them as few were Christian upon their arrival in Britain. This would seem to indicate that the Joseph tradition is, if not justified, at least worth an honest, scholarly second look.

The portion of the Joseph tradition that is not in question is the existence of the wattle church, the Ealde Cirche of early historical writings. Although it cannot be proven definitively that Joseph or his followers built the wattle church, there is no question whatsoever that it existed until the great fire of 1184. While the fire destroyed the structure itself, it was unfortunately the creation of the crypt under the Lady Chapel that truly erased the wattle church from the historical record. A small amount of burnt daub exists in the Abbey Museum of the sort that would have been used in this oldest structure, but there is no way to be sure it came from the actual Old Church itself.

King Ine of Wessex is credited with building the oldest historically verifiable structure at Glastonbury, but there is ample evidence suggesting the small wattled chapel existed before he built his stone church in the eighth century. The foundations of his Anglo-Saxon church that have been unearthed under the western end of the much later Great Church exhibit a different, more correct east-west alignment than that of the Lady Chapel. Since the Lady Chapel supposedly reflects the footprint of the original wattle church, this suggests that these two buildings were built at different times. In addition, the first alteration to King Ine's stone church was the creation of a courtyard or atrium to the west of Ine's church, in effect joining the wattle church to another structure on the site for the first time. If the Old Church did not pre-date Ine's church, we are left with two peculiar and equally unlikely possibilities. Either the atrium was built for no apparent reason several years after the church (at most including St. Joseph's Well) or the wattle chapel was built at the same time as the eighth-century stone church. This presents an unusual problem. If the wattle chapel was built by Ine at this time or by someone else later instead of earlier by Joseph, the planners built the wattle structure on a different alignment than the stone church for reasons unknown.

Obviously a structure made from wood, mud, and thatch could not last over a thousand years without the assistance of someone who sought to protect it. Surely a structure of this importance would have been cared for and restored many times between the first century and its destruction in the twelfth century. Although there is a tradition of the original church falling into some form of disrepair within a few generations of its construction, it obviously survived to become the heart of the ecclesiastical community at Glastonbury. St. Paulinus reputedly covered the Old Church with boards and lead in the seventh century, the same time period as the creation of the *Vallum Monasterii*—the ditch and bank earthwork that once outlined the boundary of the church grounds. All this information strongly indicates that the wattle church existed long before the traditional dating of the church at Glastonbury.

The wattle construction that would appear to be the earliest construction on the site shows signs that it has been venerated and protected, being reconstructed and restored for centuries before Malmesbury's history was written. However, there exists other evidence showing that this structure was altered in other ways during its life, also recorded by Malmesbury. In his history of the church at Glastonbury, he mentions a strange pattern on the floor of the Old Church that he himself cannot entirely comprehend. It is traditionally held that this pattern was nothing more than a tessellated mosaic floor of some kind, made from the same sort of geometrically shaped tiles with which these floors were usually composed. Although there are many strange patterns suggesting some kind of hidden meaning that might fit this description, one must wonder why such a learned man would not have described such a floor pattern simply as a "mosaic floor." Surely Malmesbury was familiar with this type of flooring. What form of mystery would he have seen in a mosaic floor? It is possible that the pattern was of a Mithraic zodiac design. This would certainly reflect the "spheres of prophecy" mentioned by Melkin, but Mithraism did not become popular in Roman Britain until approximately the third century. While this doesn't preclude such a floor from existing in Malmesbury's time, it does mean that it probably wasn't created by Joseph, his followers, or likely *their* followers.

It is possible that someone later built a Mithraic zodiac into the floor of the Old Church; however, the question then becomes, why? Some have said that the Cult of Mithras was an early contributor to the bourgeoning Christian religion; however most believe Mithraism was a competitor to Christianity— merely another early mystery religion. In addition, it would seem that the early church at Glastonbury held more mainstream Judeo-Christian beliefs, meaning that such a marginally pagan design likely would not have been used in a building of this sanctity. It is also possible that another geometric design more in keeping with the Judaic roots at Glastonbury, called the Kabbalist Tree of Life, was the design Malmesbury found in the mystery floor. Although the Tree of Life is composed of lines forming triangles and squares as he describes, it too is from later centuries, and the idea is questionable at best.

Whatever secrets Malmesbury's floor design held, they were lost in 1184 when the fire that devastated the abbey reduced the wattle church to ashes.

If it were not for Malmesbury's history of Glastonbury Abbey, much of what we know about the Old Church would remain lost in the murky waters of legend. As an act of devotion in stone, the Lady Chapel was built in a mere two years after the fire, and was immediately consecrated even before the chapel was fully completed. According to archeological evidence and written accounts, the Lady Chapel was not merely an exquisite example of Norman architecture, it was a resplendent jewel unparalleled.

One might wonder why opulence was given to this one relatively small building when there was so much work to be done in rebuilding the entire abbey. A simple and quite likely answer was provided by a staff member and historical reenactor at Glastonbury Abbey. It was noticed that, if one imagines the Lady Chapel detached from the rest of the abbey, and again topped by its once A-framed roof which was surrounded by four turrets (only two of which survive today), the chapel takes on the appearance of a classical medieval reliquary casket — an elaborately ornamented box in which holy relics such as the bones of saints might be kept and exhibited before the eyes of faithful pilgrims. Why then might the builders of the Lady Chapel have chosen this particular style in which to embellish what was only a small portion of a truly massive church?

At this point it is beneficial to remember that the Lady Chapel is said to reflect the size and shape of the wattle church. It was not simply built on the same site, but instead it was built specifically to contain it — to enclose it. Recalling the wording inscribed on the plaque which once stood affixed to a pillar at the point where the Lady Chapel and Galilee joined, the Lady Chapel was willfully constructed to contain and record the memory of the wattle church for all time. It should also be remembered that the Lady Chapel was constructed within a span of time short enough to be seen by those who had firsthand knowledge of the Old Church from only a few years before, not hundreds of years in the past. Even the wattle chapel's unusual, slightly off-direction alignment was preserved in the Lady Chapel, when it could have easily been corrected by its builders.

When one considers all of these factors while trying to get into the minds of those who chose the form in which the Lady Chapel would be built, it becomes quite easy to see why it was built to resemble a reliquary — because it *was* a reliquary. Until it was joined to the rebuilt Great Church some time later, the Lady Chapel stood apart, alone, almost on display in the eyes of those who came to view the great abbey, reborn from the ashes of its former self. Beautifully ornamented, and crowned by turrets, the Lady Chapel served as a container for what remained of the wattle church. Since there were likely few physical remains, it likely held whatever the abbey could salvage that reminded the monks and abbots of the lost building and its history. Mostly it served as a humble echo of the once great edifice that stood on the site previously, created by the hands of Joseph himself. The wattle church was not simply seen as an out-building to a great church; it was the heart and soul of Glastonbury Abbey, the very thing that formed its identity. When it was lost, it surely came as a devastating blow to not only the community there, but the entire township. Therefore in an attempt to honor the Ealde Cirche, the Lady Chapel was built not only as its replacement, but as its shrine — a reliquary to the remains of the sainted chapel built by Jesus's disciple.

The antiquity of the wattle church is almost without question. It was there in ancient times, it was held in the highest honor, it was protected, and once lost, its memory was sanctified in the very form of the new chapel that replaced it. However, is its creator as indisputable? Was Joseph present in England to be responsible for the wattle church's construction? What evidence is there to support this claim? Although there is much circumstantial evidence to which we may turn in defense of this tradition, there is one that is more substantial than all the rest. The prophecy of Melkin, which speaks directly about Joseph and his burial at Glastonbury, would seem to serve as definitive proof that might put this question to rest. However, as is the case with nearly every aspect of Glastonbury's colorful past, nothing is as clear cut or certain.

Many assume Melkin and his writings were simply the fanciful creation of John of Glastonbury, whose reputation is ruined as a historian because he mixed legendary accounts and history as if they were the same. While today that is fairly damning testimony, one must remember that the sentiment of scholarship was not the same then as it is today. There were some things writers of the time felt could be assumed, because traditions set down by church leaders could be accepted as fact, even if you didn't have the source documents right before you to corroborate them. Therefore, before writing off John of Glastonbury to the pile of untrustworthy yarn-spinners who have set their own take on the topic, it may do the reader well to consider the following.

It is a confirmed fact that there were writings in the library at Glastonbury Abbey ascribed to an ancient writer called Melkin. They were witnessed and attested to by John of Glastonbury, John Leland, and potentially in a tangential way by William of Malmesbury. Then the question is asked, how old is "ancient"? To us today, ancient is truly ancient, while to the medieval mind, it could have simply been several hundred years old. Therefore, for these writings to be called "ancient" means nothing more than they were significantly older than the time of John's writing. However, if one digs only a little deeper, it isn't difficult to find evidence suggesting that Melkin and his writings were old enough to fit even our modern definition of "ancient."

The tone and language used in the prophecy suggest an origin much older than a simple medieval forgery. The text of the prophecy indicates the writer had an intimate knowledge of Glastonbury and its history to a degree much deeper than even a skilled student of the Middle Ages. The difficult Latin in which it was written, perhaps flavored with Welsh familiarity, suggests a writer who, although familiar with the language of the church, was not entirely fluent in it. Using a limited knowledge of this form of writing mixed with his own created a dialect that proves quite difficult to disentangle for the modern investigator trying to find direction in his mysterious wording.

One possible historical character who would fit this description is one whose name is quite similar to Melkin. Maelgwyn, the sixth-century warlord and king of Gwynedd in Wales, apparently put down his warlike ways to become a monk and learn Latin as well as the history of the earliest church fathers. However, according to Gildas, his contemporary and potentially a fellow student, Maelgwyn allegedly went back to his prior ways. It is unknown whether this means he turned away from the church to again become a warlord or simply that he did not agree with the Roman Catholic Church and became a hermit and bard of his own accord. The fact that he supported the growth of the monastic system in Wales throughout his kingdom suggests that his years as a servant of God were not lost on him.

Further evidence pointing to a truly ancient dating for the enigmatic Melkin and his texts can be found in the unusually high density of references to a "Welsh Bard" or "British Soothsayer" who apparently has a great deal of insight as to the history of Glastonbury and the whereabouts of its long-dead inhabitants. Consider the number of historical texts and accounts that claim to come from a nameless source who wrote "in the ancient British tongue." Consider the account of the discovery of King Arthur's grave, its location divulged by a British soothsayer. Consider also the chronicles of Helinand, which speak of such a Welsh bard and indeed of the Grail itself. It would seem that either several hoaxes were perpetrated relating to one place and a similar time, all based on nonexistent writings of a British/Welsh historical source, or there was an actual Welsh/British historical source who was responsible for writings from which information relating to Glastonbury was taken.

It has been suggested that the concept of Joseph of Arimathea being at Glastonbury is a relatively recent phenomenon created by medieval writers trying to lend some kind of historical credibility to their fictional stories. While interest in Joseph of Arimathea reached its peak at Glastonbury during this time, it is almost certain that this tradition stretches back long before this fervor ever gained ground. If the writings of Melkin were as ancient as medieval accounts and previous evidence suggest, this would place the tradition of Joseph at Glastonbury in a period predating the twelfth- to sixteenth-century "Joseph mania" by several hundred years. Joseph of Arimathea being mentioned in an allegedly sixth-century source, outside of a time when such a claim would be beneficial to the wealth and acclaim of a thriving medieval monastery, would effectively take the Joseph tradition out of the realm of legend and soundly into the realm of history.

It seems that Melkin's writing was taken as fact at one vital point in Glastonbury's history. When John Blome petitioned the king for permission to search Glastonbury for Joseph's burial site, it was done in nothing but an air of true historical and archeological interest. In 1345 when this search was undertaken, the golden age of Joseph veneration had yet to occur. Therefore, one may wonder what led Blome to his interest in Joseph's grave. It was before, if only slightly, the 1350 publication of John of Glastonbury's semi-historical text, in which Melkin's prophecy was first published. Blome was aware of the account dealing with the location of Joseph's burial site. Allegedly, Blome began his search for Joseph's grave after reading "ancient writings" detailing the grave's whereabouts. There can be little doubt that these "ancient writings" he mentions are one and the same as those allegedly written by Melkin.

When one accepts the possibility of Melkin's being an historical figure and an actual source of information regarding Glastonbury, then a number of potentially powerful possibilities open up. If Melkin knew about the great number of pagans who were laid to rest in the area around Glastonbury Abbey, and if he knew about Joseph and the place where he was buried, he must have known about other significant historical events taking place in at least that area of southern England. Therefore it seems logical to assume that he also knew enough about the historical individual who inspired the Arthur legend to record some dates and facts about his actions, where he met his fate, and where he was ultimately laid to rest. Melkin may have been a source of information for the earliest writers who mentioned Arthur, such as Gildas, who may have actually known this historical Melkin.

According to one writer of the sixteenth century, Melkin did indeed record some facts of the historical King Arthur's life. John Leland, who visited Glastonbury Abbey to survey its spectacular library just before the Dissolution, is famous for writing his *Itinerary*, which outlines his travels throughout the length and breadth of England and Wales, allowing historians the clearest image of Tudor Britain available to them today. Few people realize that he was also responsible for writing several other voluminous works dealing with various histories and notable writers. Among these was his *Assertio Inclytissimi Arturii*. In this text dealing with the life and times of King Arthur, Leland cites many authors as his source of information. Among these, listed under Welsh writers, Leland specifically names Melkin (written as *Melchinus*).

The Melchinus to which Leland referred in his citations is certainly the same Melkin that John of Glastonbury mentioned in his fourteenth-century history. It is thought that Leland had access to much of Glastonbury's library long after it had left Glastonbury, whether it was for personal study or as part of his role in King Henry VIII's kingdom. Although nothing is ever specifically mentioned about Melkin's writings among the Glastonbury cartularies, it is possible they were simply folded in with other works or anthologies and never mentioned by name. Many have thought that Leland's text on King Arthur, presented more in the form of a history than a medieval romance, was the result of Leland's failing mental stability due to the brain disease which ultimately claimed his life. However, Professor James Carley, a John Leland and Glastonbury scholar, firmly asserts this is not the case, stating the *Assertio* was written a decade before Leland's death in 1552.

Unless the actual writings of Melkin are ever found, either in some south England attic or hidden in the binding of another book, it is impossible to know for certain if these writings were actually written in the sixth century. However, most would agree that Melkin's mention of Joseph of Arimathea and his burial at Glastonbury is at the very least quite intriguing. Like the Grail tablet from *Indiana Jones and the Last Crusade*, we suddenly find a marker pointing a very clear direction away from fantasy and toward history. Over the years the largest argument against the validity of the Melkin text has been that no one has ever found Joseph's body. The appropriate response to this suggestion would be, *au contraire!* It would seem that Joseph's body, or at least his grave, has been found several times. In fact, burials suggested to be that of Joseph of Arimathea are so numerous as to present the problem of exactly which one was correct. There have been at least three occasions on which remains allegedly belonging to Joseph and/or his companions have been found at Glastonbury, one of which actually led to the veneration of his remains in the crypt beneath the Lady Chapel.

No matter how convincing the placement, description, or tone, such discoveries are always met with the same rebuttal: "I'm sure they found an actual burial, but you can never know if it was really Joseph or just *somebody's* bones dug up and put on display as a publicity stunt." To find if Melkin's prophecy actually led to the discovery of Joseph's venerable bones, let us track the history of his grave back to the beginning. If Joseph arrived in Britain around A.D. 66 as tradition states, he most likely died in the last quarter of the first century. It was left to his companions to bury him in whatever manner they felt most appropriate. Although we would at first assume that a first-century Jew would have been buried some distance from a place like a church, we must remember that this burial was not taking place in first-century Palestine. If Joseph was being buried in ground that he had sanctified by building his church, it is possible that those who remained wanted to separate him from the mass of pagan dead that lay buried beyond the confines of his church.

In so doing, they may have chosen to bury him in the consecrated earth beneath his church, thus in a small way putting him in a special place of honor which, for as long as the church stood, would never be disturbed or defiled.

Melkin, writing of this tradition in the sixth century, demonstrates quite clearly that this knowledge was accepted as truth in the time of Arthur. Later, under the date of 720 in the Chronicles of Helinand (roughly contemporaneous with the building of Ine's stone church), another British soothsayer is mentioned in relation to the Grail. Some time later, entering into the debated medieval period, William of Malmesbury writes about other sources which he chooses not to cite, but he does at least suggest that Glastonbury was founded by unnamed individuals that could go back to the time of Christ Himself. Outside of Melkin's writing, the first mention of Joseph's burial and tomb can be found not in history but in literature. In the later Grail romance called the *Perlesvaus*, Joseph's tomb features prominently in the discovery of the Holy Grail. Being in close proximity to both the Grail Castle and Perceval's family castle, Joseph's tomb is described as being placed in a small chapel between the castle and the wild woods beyond. Therefore knowledge of the tradition stating Joseph of Arimathea's remains lie buried somewhere in a place of honor at Glastonbury must have existed by the early thirteenth century, when the *Perlesvaus* was written.

Then in 1345 when John Blome embarked on his expedition to find the grave of Joseph, he did so prompted by "ancient writings" apparently suggesting it was somewhere at Glastonbury. Although the results of his dig are uncertain, another mention of this expedition, this time including an end to the story, was written a few decades later by a monk of Lincolnshire called R. de Boston, who turns out to be one Roget of Boston, a monk at Spalding Priory in Lincolnshire. He states that the remains of Joseph of Arimathea and his companions were found in Glastonbury. Many who read this citation claim that Roget was in error, and that he actually meant to say the remains of Joseph and his companions were *sought* at Glastonbury. While it is true that Joseph's remains were sought, this specific example presents an interesting as well as valid question. Why is it assumed he meant *sought* instead of *found*? Conversely, it has been said that Roget of Boston may have simply assumed the remains were found since someone had gone looking for them. However, this assumption raises a similar question. Why is it thought that Roget assumed the remains were found? If either of these were true, Roget of Boston would seem to be a rather sloppy historian.

To disprove these assumptions, let us first remember that Spalding Priory was founded by Crowey Abbey, famous for its histories. Why would a monk who served at a priory of a parent church famed for its in-depth and reliable histories be either foolish enough to simply misspeak the account or careless enough to assume its outcome? It could be that both are correct—that John Blome's attempt met with less than desired results, as witnessed by the lack of acclaim following this expedition, and that R. de Boston was correct in writing that the remains of Joseph and his companions were found at Glastonbury. Evidence supporting this supposition can be found within the confines of Glastonbury Abbey, specifically in the Old Cemetery to the south of the Lady Chapel. During the abbacy of Walter of Monington, when John Blome conducted his search, there existed a small chapel on the south boundary of the Old Cemetery. Later called St. Michael in the Cemetery, this small chapel was described at the time as being "ancient and ruinous"—a similar description given to the two obelisks or pyramids also found in the Old Cemetery and described by William of Malmesbury. The *Magna Tabula*, a great book retelling Glastonbury's legendary past, states that several decades later Walter of Monington's successor, John Chinnock, rebuilt and rededicated the chapel to all the holy dead whose relics lay beneath its altar, chief among which were those belonging to Joseph of Arimathea.

How does this relate to John Blome's expedition and Roget of Boston's assessment of its outcome? It provides a way for both accounts to be correct. If Blome went to Glastonbury Abbey looking for Joseph's remains due to reading about "ancient texts" outlining their location, he surely had a copy of these texts, which almost surely contained the prophecy of Melkin, to guide his efforts. When he searched near the southern corner of the Lady Chapel (the site where the chapel of wattles mentioned in the prophecy once stood), he likely found nothing, or at least nothing indicating that he had found the body of Joseph himself. It is even possible that he dug at several other locations in the grounds which he thought might have matched the description, also finding nothing. It is also possible that he requested to dig inside the Lady Chapel itself, but since he was under the strict condition that he was to dig only where permitted by the monks and where it would not disturb any of the buildings, his request was likely refused.

Having no success and loath to return empty-handed, it is likely at that point that Blome was shown the "ancient and ruinous" chapel at the far southern boundary of the cemetery. Given its decrepit state, he may have been given permission to dig there without fear of damaging the already ruined structure, or else the monks may have simply removed a few of the bones allegedly held therein, and told of their story. Then, uncertain as to the success or failure of his own endeavor, Blome returned to give his uncertain findings to the king. Some years later, as a result of this expedition, Blome's account was likely read by the monks at Spalding Priory who, upon reading of the chapel in the cemetery, surmised that these were indeed the bones of Joseph and his companions, and set the account down in one of their histories. Unfortunately, this reconstructed chain of events is entirely speculative and cannot be backed up by any strict evidence. It is, unfortunately, only my theory. It does, however, answer several lingering questions and connects archeological evidence at Glastonbury with two seemingly disparate historical accounts in a way that makes sense.

Then there is the account from the early fifteenth century, which may also recount the discovery of Joseph's grave site. A letter written from King Henry V to the abbot of Glastonbury in 1420 and Abbot Frome's reply regarding excavations undertaken in the abbey's cemetery and beneath the Lady Chapel the previous year may shed some light upon the ruined little chapel and its contents. According to this letter, Glastonbury monks dug in the Old Cemetery and beneath the Lady Chapel in 1419. In the southern cemetery (to the south of the Lady Chapel), they found three burials — a single articulated body furthest to the north, another articulated body furthest to the south, and in between, one coffin containing the bones of twelve individuals packed so tightly together that once removed, they could not be returned to their original coffin. Each of these coffins were described as being "ancient." The two individuals were described as having remains of flowers and herbs laid around their bodies, with a wooden rod laid under their bodies.

As if these three discoveries were not intriguing enough, the true gem was found inside the Lady Chapel. One last ancient coffin was found, containing one articulated body. What made this one remarkable is that it was the most highly decorated and ornamented among them all. Draped with rich linen fabric, this burial was obviously someone of high standing, especially when one considers the pride of place it occupied under the south side of the altar. The letter said that when this burial was found, it was so obviously important that they placed that coffin into another coffin or tomb described as a "stone box" so that it might be further investigated. Although not specifically named as the tomb of Joseph of Arimathea, it soon became the centerpiece of Joseph's veneration at Glastonbury.

This account surely sounds dubious to the modern mind. The aspects that especially stand out are the twelve bodies in one coffin and the burial inside the Lady Chapel obviously intended to be identified as Joseph of Arimathea. The latter matches the description in the prophecy of Melkin so perfectly as to sound too good to be true. Just as Melkin stated, this coffin was found near the southern corner of what was the wattle church present at the time of Melkin's alleged writing. Additionally, the rich ornamentation mentioned seems curious for such an old burial. Turning to the outside burials, the bodies of "12 individuals" are clearly reminiscent of Joseph's twelve companions who followed him to Britain from Judea. Considering all this, the two single burials seem out of place, but they too are curious. Who were they? If this was a hoax, why were they included, and why did they bound the coffin of the twelve bodies?

The strangely overt reference to the Joseph tradition at Glastonbury led many to believe that this was a hoax of some kind, most likely a money-making scheme organized between King Henry V and the abbot of Glastonbury. Unfortunately, it would appear the plan never came to fruition. King Henry died in 1422, shortly after the correspondence was written, leading to the abrupt cancellation of an otherwise masterful plan. There appears to have been no further planning on the official level between the discovery and King Henry's death. The only result of this excavation was the creation, or more correctly the adaptation, of an underground chapel into the first chapel devoted to Joseph of Arimathea.

The crypt at Glastonbury, which was created below the Lady Chapel around A.D. 1500, was apparently not the first place set aside to venerate the relics of the great abbey's legendary patriarch. The crypt proper was really only an expansion of a smaller space that already existed, roughly situated in the "St. Joseph's Chapel" area of the crypt, at its far eastern end. This is actually reflected in the architecture visible at Glastonbury Abbey today. When the Galilee was initially built at the end of the thirteenth century, this excavation had not yet taken place. As a result, the southern wall was only broken by the Great Door that led from the Galilee into the southern Old Cemetery. The door was later bricked in, apparently enclosing the Galilee completely.

However, on the southern wall of the Galilee today, one can see where there was once a doorway, further to the west from the Great Door, that is curiously covered by an exterior wall. This can be confirmed as an exterior wall because there are windows at the top allowing light into the crypt below. These windows are definitely more recent than the door because when the crypt was built, the floor levels of both the Lady Chapel and Galilee were raised by about a foot. Visitors to the abbey today can walk to the elevation in the Galilee where it joins the Lady Chapel and notice that the top of the window set into this exterior wall is visible above what used to be the floor level of the door. Therefore, this door was clearly built into the southern wall between the late 1200s when the Galilee was built and the 1500s when the crypt was created.

What makes this doorway so important is that it was quite possibly the way one might have originally accessed the first chapel of St. Joseph of Arimathea. When one realizes that the existing narrow door and stairs in the south wall of the Lady Chapel that once led into the crypt would have led nowhere prior to the creation of the crypt, there can be only one conclusion. If there existed an underground chapel of St. Joseph that predated the crypt, the now covered doorway in the Galilee would have been the only way down to it. Therefore, we must conclude that something happened between roughly A.D. 1300 and 1500 that prompted the doorway and passage down to an underground chapel to be built. Looking at a list of construction and renovation performed on the abbey between these times, one finds nothing having to do with the area around the Lady Chapel between the joining of the Lady Chapel and Galilee and the creation of the crypt, so one must wonder about the reason for this doorway's relatively short-lived use.

The question then becomes, which came first: St. Joseph's Chapel, built to house the hoaxed remains, or the remains which caused the chapel to be built. This sort of "chicken or egg" debate can never be answered, but the validity of the letter's description of the discovered remains sounds convincing from a forensic standpoint. The letter describes all but the mass burial of the twelve as bones lying "in the manner of death," which one can justly take as meaning fully articulate skeletons, as a body would naturally decay. The single coffin containing multiple individuals is obviously a reburial, and considering the other two individuals found in the cemetery were described together with the mass burial, it would seem to imply they were found in close proximity to one another, as a burial cluster. This suggests that that all three of these remains were reburials, not original burials. However, even these were described as having fluids present in the coffins that can be associated with natural decay, so it is likely that these individual burials were reburied in their original coffins, unlike the mass burial of the twelve.

The letter also states that the bodies were found with wooden rods under their bodies. This further suggests an account of an actual burial instead of a simple fabrication in light of similar descriptions of coffins discovered in the crypt in 1825. When mud and rubble was being cleaned out of the crypt, several coffins were found containing full skeletons complete with evidence of straw pillows, and other plant material indicative of herbs and flowers that had been placed in the coffins. In addition to these, each body was found to have an ash rod, nearly the length of the coffin, placed underneath it. It has been thought that these were ceremonial staffs akin to the crosier used to mark rank in the church. When this evidence is taken together with the quite authentic descriptions of the remains (instead of the "miraculous" manner in which some saints' bodies are found "undefiled" or "rosey-fleshed"), the supposition that the account given in the letter from Abbot Frome to King Henry V was merely a hoax or a publicity stunt must necessarily be questioned.

When these remains were placed in a stone box for later study, they did not simply sit in a dark, forgotten room only to be lost to history. The discovery of these remains arguably launched the "Joseph Mania" later ascribed to Abbot Beere and his age. Simply put, these remains and the tomb into which they were placed became one of the few pieces of evidence firmly linking the tradition of Joseph of Arimathea to history. In fact, what endures from the discovery of these remains, which for all the reasons listed above were most likely those of Joseph himself, can still be seen, touched, and possibly even one day investigated more fully. All one must do to journey to the final resting place of this last relic of Joseph at Glastonbury, and possibly that of what could be called the historical Holy Grail, is to cross the High Street in Glastonbury to the north of the abbey ruins.

The parish Church of St. John the Baptist now holds the tomb that was once the center of what some have called the cult of Joseph of Arimathea in Great Britain. Dated to the fourteenth or fifteenth centuries by the decorative carvings on the sides, this stone tomb can tell the modern investigator quite an elaborate story, the beginnings of which we have already seen. Although few know much about the strange stone sarcophagus in the north chapel of St. John's Church, most agree that it came originally from Glastonbury — some part of a monument to St. Joseph, they usually say. As was the case with many leftovers of the Dissolution, this tomb's path is something like that of a lost dog looking for a home.

According to tradition, the tomb once stood in the Chapel area of the crypt beneath the Lady Chapel, an object of veneration to countless pilgrims to the abbey. It had the curious feature of a mechanism that raised the silver coffin in which the saint's bones were placed from the stone tomb so that the visiting pilgrims might see them. Allegedly, many miracles took place before these remains including cures and surely many holy visions. However, when the Dissolution took place, a great many relics and other treasures were stripped from the great churches, abbeys, and cathedrals throughout the empire only to be added to the royal treasury if they were deemed of value, or tossed upon the rubbish heap if they were not. It is entirely likely that whatever remains the coffin once housed met with the latter fate.

However, seen as of no value in itself, and probably too large to be troubled with, the great stone tomb was left in its former place of honor to rot with the rest of the ruins. The presence of this tomb was witnessed by several pilgrims to the abbey, both before and after the Dissolution. Among these pilgrims, John Ray witnessed the tomb in the ruined remains of the chapel on June 22, 1662, only to remove them to St. John's later that year. This act was allegedly done to protect it from further desecration and damage, effectively hiding it in plain sight. Then in the early twentieth century, the stone tomb was moved from the church cemetery to inside the church and its present place in what used to be called St. Katherine's Chapel in the north transept. Photographs from this time obtained from the Glastonbury Antiquarian Society show the same tomb from different angles both outside in the churchyard and inside where it now rests.

12. Making a Case for Glastonbury

When it was relocated inside the church, it was examined at some length for the first time. It was noticed that it was more than simply weathered; it was damaged. As one may witness today, several pieces of the elaborate carvings have been broken off, and stand in stark contrast to the relatively new appearing carvings on the other tombs present in St. John's church, such as that of John Camel just across the aisle. The stones appear to have been very roughly removed, causing the fastening pieces that held the individual blocks together to be broken. In addition, it was found that there were remains of metalwork around the top edge resembling a metal grate, possibly once allowing pilgrims to affix devotional offerings upon it. The lid is notable for featuring a roughly rectangular indentation that is reminiscent of the stories about the silver casket which was raised and lowered into its resting place in the stone tomb.

Although this tomb in St. John's does not bear an inscription that reads "property of Joseph of Arimathea," it does have the next best thing. Besides the beautiful quatrefoils and other delicate carvings on this tomb, at one end there is another sort of inscription. A shield inscribed with the symbol of the caduceus emblazoned in the center can be found flanked by the letters "J" and "A." The caduceus could have many meanings since it is the symbol for Mercury, but one apt meaning that could hearken back to Joseph is to recall that Mercury was known as the messenger of the gods.

The inscription "J A" of course makes one think of *Joseph d'Arimathie*—Joseph of Arimathea. It has been posited, however, that "J A" simply stands for John Allen, whose tomb some say this is. One might then wonder if there was a John Allen of note in the region who might have been the true owner of this tomb. Although there is a John Allen, a priest and martyr, who died in 1538 because he did not agree with King Henry VIII's Acts of Supremacy, it should be noted that he was executed in the city of Tyburn near Birmingham quite some distance north, apparently having little or nothing to do with Glastonbury. Although it is certainly possible that there is some other John Allen to whom this tomb could belong, this theory is as conjectural as the theory that it belonged to Joseph of Arimathea. In addition, several questions remain unanswered. Why would John Allen's tomb have started its life in the crypt at Glastonbury Abbey? If this were any other man's tomb but Joseph's, even that of a wealthy patron of St. John's Church, why would it be moved from St. John's churchyard inside to the north transept? Why would it have an indentation in the top and signs of a metal grate around the edge? Finally, why would it have the symbol of the caduceus between his initials? While such symbols might be common in the eighteenth century forward for Masons and the like, such group symbolism was not used at the time the tomb was created.

Regardless of whether we can agree that this is Joseph of Arimathea's tomb, we can say with some certainty that this was believed to be an actual relic of Glastonbury's legendary founder. It is hard for us to believe such a claim today, but at the time, such was accepted as indisputable fact. While we can't be as driven solely by trust and faith today, we can rely on the evidence at hand—the same sort of evidence that has led to theories and conclusions accepted as credible in other matters. The pure fact of the matter is that if the preceding were presented as a scientific theorem, it could never be accepted, because what we have isn't fact; it's circumstantial evidence and theory. However, if we continue in the theme of a court trial in which this chapter is framed, it is quite a different matter. We still cannot definitively place Joseph of Arimathea at Glastonbury beyond a reasonable doubt, so if our goal had been to place Joseph at the scene of the crime, so to speak, our case would be unwinnable.

However, if our goal is to prove that there's more to the Grail legend than simple medieval fantasy, the evidence presented in this book more than does that. Our goal was to call into question the assumption that there is nothing further to investigate regarding Joseph of Arimathea and the Grail at Glastonbury. If one is honest and proceeds without preconceived notion, the volume of evidence suggesting Joseph was in fact present in Glastonbury in the first century is sufficient to create a reasonable doubt in the assertion that it is all just a quaint yarn woven for the tourist trade. We began our investigation by seeing the difference between trying to validate the medieval stories of floating goblets, magic castles, and questing knights and trying to prove that a first-century Jew from Israel traveled to Britain carrying some type of vessel. I believe we have successfully proven this as possible.

To prove the possibility of the Joseph tradition at Glastonbury, we asked three questions. First, is it possible that a man from Judea came to Britain in the first century? The answer is yes; there was significant travel between the Mediterranean countries and Britain throughout history. Second, is it possible that this traveler brought with him something from his homeland? Again, the answer is yes. If someone came from the Classical world to this new, frontier island, it is not only possible but probable that he carried some possessions from the land he had just left. Third, is Glastonbury the sort of place where such a world traveler would come? Absolutely. The Somerset region of England was rich in resources and was a fair land in which to settle, farm, and make a new life. If we accept the date of around A.D. 66 as the time when Joseph came to Britain, we must remember that Rome had begun its colonization of Britain in 55 B.C., over 100 years before. To Joseph in his time, Britain may have seemed much like the Americas were to seventeenth and eighteenth-century Europe—the New World, a virgin territory in which one might start

12. Making a Case for Glastonbury

over. A wild, untamed country to be sure, but a place far from everything he knew, far distant from the pains of the past.

While it is elementary to say something could have happened, it is a different matter to say that it did. Unless you witness an event yourself, you can never be certain of any event, and sometimes not even then. Since no one today was alive to follow Joseph, to stow away aboard his ship, and match his footsteps to see if they did end up on England's pleasant pastures green, there is no way to have that assurance. There can be no proof, because except for personal observation, the very term "proof" degrades into "evidence." Therefore, we must rely on evidence supporting or refuting a claim. In our case, we must see if there is sufficient evidence to say that it is likely Joseph was present at Glastonbury in the first century. Judging from the earliest written accounts suggesting the church's foundation by disciples of Christ, as well as an early written account mentioning Joseph and his burial site in some detail, paired with historical attempts to use these writings to locate his grave or tomb, there seems to be sufficient evidence, albeit circumstantial, to suggest that Joseph was actually at Glastonbury.

Although there will always be skeptics, regardless of whatever evidence is presented, the Joseph traditions at Glastonbury now appear more likely to be based in history instead of simply in medieval romance. While it is still far from certain, evidence presented here does suggest, if not prove, that Joseph was the founding member of the church that became the once great Glastonbury Abbey. In so doing, we open up the greatest locked door standing between history and the legend of the Holy Grail. If we accept the possibility that Joseph of Arimathea really did come to Britain and build his wattle church, how hard is it then to accept the possibility that he carried with him the cruets of the Grail legend? If Joseph left the Holy Land to start a new ministry abroad, and if he participated in the preparation of Jesus's body after the crucifixion, supplying his own tomb for the body, how likely is it that he actually carried with him one or two small vessels that held the blood of Jesus? This is the question that plagues anyone who has ever discovered the legend of the Holy Grail. You must ask yourself, do you believe the Grail actually exists?

Chapter 13

The Historical Grail

In keeping with the tradition of the Grail Quest, the previous chapter presented a question: Do you believe the Grail actually exists? In asking the question that must be asked, you have achieved the Grail. Your quest has ended.

* * *

There may be some of you who, upon reading this statement, find your intellectual egos bruised. How can such a claim be made? Nothing has been proven here! This is all just an entertaining way of masking the fact that, as ever, there is no proof the Grail ever really existed. To this I would most vehemently reply, you're right. Nothing new has been presented here. There is still no proof the Grail ever existed in reality. If this book has proven to be entertaining, I as the author am most pleased, although entertainment was not the goal, nor was masking a lack of evidence with suggestive stories and theories. My goal has ever been to make it clear that the supposition that there is no history, no evidence, and no reason to believe an object that could be called the Grail ever existed is entirely inaccurate. In fact, I would go one step further to say that to posit such a firm stance is nothing less than pride and intellectual laziness. I would never go so far as to say, "This is why the Grail was real, and it existed at Glastonbury, and there is no question of it," because to do this would be equally lazy and irresponsible. For the past twenty years, the theories I hold now have been formed simply by following where the history and evidence led me, unencumbered by the certainty that the entire Grail legend was nothing more than a myth. Instead, I simply chose to allow all options.

As mentioned in the previous chapter, scholars are limited in what they may set forth as their position on the matter. They can only base their stance on pure facts, because those are the defining parameters within which their discipline operates. The benefit of this is not cluttering the body of "truth" with what cannot be verified. But this limitation does not allow for possibility, and that is its greatest failing. I have spoken with some scholars who answer the difficult questions with statements such as, "It just is." I have also had the true pleasure of speaking with scholars who will tell you what they know, and when met with a question for which they have no answer or can't say with certainty simply reply, "I don't know." These are the truest form of scholar, and the real life "Grail Knights" who, instead of following what their mentors and teachers have told them, admit the limits of their own knowledge and, like Perceval before the Grail Procession, humbly asks, "What is it?"

Most human learning relies on leaps of faith. Sometimes those leaps result in a clumsy fall, but oftentimes the result is discovery that would never have been made otherwise, simply because someone dared to think, "What if?" What if the Grail were a real object? What if Joseph actually did bring it (or them) to Britain? What if he actually founded the church there? All intriguing questions, yet without anything to substantiate them you are left to the realm of fantasy and wishful thinking. Then one asks the final question, "What if there *is* evidence to substantiate these claims?" That is when you truly achieve the Grail.

We have seen evidence supporting the theory that Joseph of Arimathea came to Britain in the first century. As a result, we can say that it is equally likely that he did arrive in Britain with something that contained blood relics of Christ that would later be identified with the Holy Grail. The argument against this evidence can usually be boiled down to one of two statements. Either "You can't possibly believe the Holy Grail is real, can you?" or "There is no proof the Holy Grail was ever a real object." The first statement is an emotional response to the subject matter rather than an honest attempt to engage it, and is therefore irrelevant to this investigation. The second statement, while true, fails to understand its own limitations.

We have agreed that there is not proof, not just of the Grail, but in truth of anything we cannot witness for ourselves. Therefore the use of the word "proof" is irrelevant to this investigation. Instead, we have attempted to present *evidence* that, in absence of proof, must suffice in our decision-making process. With this in mind, let us now ask the question, "Is there evidence suggesting that there is a historical Holy Grail?" Before making a decision, we must abandon our preconceived notions and honestly consider the evidence. As with the Joseph tradition at Glastonbury, such an objective investigation leads to the conclusion that the Grail legend very likely began as a seed of real-world history. One of the biggest reasons why the Grail has never been seen as an historical object is due to its image as set forth in medieval literature. Seen as a classic chalice, golden and covered in precious jewels, the very picture is contrary to our understanding of what a vessel from the time of Christ would be. We would expect a very simple cup of wood, clay, or stone — the sort of humble trappings that are associated with Jesus and his teachings. However, more troubling than its appearance are the Grail's actions.

The Holy Grail is portrayed as a supernatural object, almost alive with magic. It is seen as a vessel held by the invisible hand of God Himself, bestowing boons of plenty upon the deserving knight. The most delectable food of the knight's choosing can be found within. It hovers in the air before the entire court only to vanish like a mystic vision. It gives health to the sick or wounded, and gives eternal life to whomever drinks from it. In some texts, the Grail seems to exist both in our reality and in an unearthly realm. The Grail seems to preside over Mass, containing the actual body of Jesus in the form of a youth, a child, an old man, or simply as a Mass wafer. Obviously the Grail is to Christ as the Ark of the Covenant was to God in the Old Testament. It is a container, itself beyond the physical bounds of earth but made of our own matter, in which the holy presence of God resides.

The Grail is apparently one of several divine relics one might find in the Grail Castle. Along with it are three other relics of equally magical ability. In this awe-inspiring procession are the Spear that pierced Christ's side on the Cross, a plate or platter used at the Last Supper, and the sword that beheaded John the Baptist. The legend of the Spear was well known throughout Christendom, but the dish used at the Last Supper seems almost redundant. In addition, the sword of John the Baptist seems strangely out of place with the other relics of Christ's Passion. Typically these relics are guarded by a league of holy, ancient, and worthy knights who, while part of the Fisher King's court, seem to be as enraptured by the relics as is Perceval. In at least one Grail text, these knights are specifically called Templars who all appear to be trapped in time much as the sacred relic they worship.

These characteristics strike the modern mind as those of a fictional object rather than an archeological one, and justifiably so. These traits were no doubt added by the medieval writer to illustrate the Grail's sacred nature. If such an object existed in reality, it would have been quite simply a vessel that was once used to hold a blood relic belonging to Jesus. Whether it was a cup or a vial, numbering one or two or more, the basic fact would be that the Grail was nothing more than a first-century version of objects we still have today. According to various traditions related to the Grail, it is likely that these vessels were of two forms — a larger, open vessel such as a small bowl or shallow dish, and a vial, much like a modern perfume bottle.

Starting with the second type, the perfume bottle form, we are reminded of Mary Magdalene and her pound of spikenard, which was likely just a box containing six small vials, or ampoules, of the costly oil. These vials were probably made of a semi-precious material such as the traditional alabaster or onyx, but could have also been made of glass depending on the wealth of the buyer. The form was varied and could have either been an elongated teardrop shape such as a Roman unguentarium or might have been short, round, and sitting atop a short foot like a dye or pigment jar. If these were the basis for the Grail of legend, they could have been used to collect the blood of Jesus as He hung on the Cross and when His body was being prepared for interment in Joseph's new tomb. However, it is more likely that these were used as secondary reliquaries, or vessels into which the blood was poured from another object such as a bowl or cup.

It is this type of object which most likely spawned the traditional image of the Grail as a cup. It may have been taken from the room of the Last Supper, the upper room of biblical narrative that served as Jesus's home away from home during his final trip to Jerusalem before his arrest, trial, and execution. The blood was seen as the seat of the soul to the first-century Jew, and as such it was required by Hebrew funerary law to collect all the blood that issued from the body while it was being prepared for its requisite year in a tomb. Once the body had decayed, the bones were placed inside a stone ossuary and reburied along with whatever grave goods remained in the tomb. Since Jesus's tomb was revisited a mere three days later, the blood contained in this vessel would have still been present. It is uncertain whether only one vessel was used for this purpose or two, because the collection of blood would have taken place both at the foot of the cross and in the tomb. For this reason, it is possible that one vessel contained the bloody dirt that formed at the foot of the cross while another was used to collect the fresh blood that flowed from the body as it was prepared in the tomb.

It has been suggested before that there is another relic, possibly the Nanteos Cup in Wales, that served as this additional cup or vessel that once contained the bloody dirt and was left in the tomb only to be discovered later, but the jury is still out on this alleged Grail contender. Tests show that the Nanteos Cup is nothing more than Wych elm, common to Britain, and was likely a simple medieval mazer. Though it now seems unlikely that this is a relic from the time of Jesus, one still wonders from where this tradition originated. The story goes that this relic was brought to Nanteos via the Ystrad Fflur (Strata Florida) monastery in Cardiganshire, Wales, by a number of Glastonbury monks fleeing persecution. In an attempt to protect their precious relic, which had supposedly been hidden in the walls of the abbey, they went to Wales for the relic's safekeeping, only to become the personal chaplains of the Powell family of Nanteos in Aberystwyth. When the last of the monks lay dying, he told the story to Mr. Powell, instructing him to guard their sacred relic "until the church shall claim her own." It is thought that this object of curiosity first appeared in the mid 1800s thanks to George Powell, the colorful owner of Nanteos Manor during the time, most likely resulting from archeological interest in the Strata Florida ruins. This damaged little wooden cup may not be the Holy Grail of legend, but the question still lingers — what led Mr. Powell to believe the Holy Grail could be found in Wales?

Returning to Glastonbury and its legendary founder, it is said that Joseph did not bring the Grail to Britain in the form of a golden chalice, a wooden bowl, or even as a single object at all. Joseph allegedly brought two "cruets," or small ampoules which contained the blood and sweat of Jesus and which later formed the basis of the Grail tradition in Glastonbury. If this is the case, the Grail legend as we know it today was created thanks to these secondary vessels that served as a type of personal reliquary. If we recall the story of Mary Magdalene and her sister Martha hosting a dinner in Jesus's honor a few days before the Last Supper, we discover a very telling formula which leads to the formation of these secondary Grails.

According to the Bible, Mary used a box of the costly scented oil called nard, or spikenard, to anoint Jesus's feet and later dried them off with her own hair as an act of devotion, leading the other disciples to rebuke her for wasting such wealth. The account is somewhat misleading. Called a "pound of nard," the box was probably not a box containing this amount of the oil, but a box containing several small vials of the oil, possibly sealed with wax. A friend and colleague named John Koopmans has pointed out that the first-century meaning of the amount mentioned, "a pound," would not yield the sixteen ounces with which we are familiar today. Measured in weight instead of volume, a Jewish pound of the day was only twelve ounces. This pound of nard would have been purchased in a box containing several scent jars or vials most commonly holding approximately two ounces each. This amount would have rendered six vials of two ounces, totaling the pound mentioned in the Bible.

Considering the fact that Mary used one of these for the act mentioned above, the rest were saved to be used later, most likely when the "three Marys" returned to the tomb only to find it empty. When the vials and their anointing oils were no longer needed for their original purpose, they could have been emptied and used to hold small amounts of blood which would have been distributed from the central relic, the cup or bowl used to collect the blood during the preparation of the body in the tomb. This means that five of these vials from the original six remained to be given to those who returned to the empty tomb.

It is interesting here to reiterate the legends associated with Joseph, Nicodemus, and Mary Magdalene in relation to the relics they allegedly possessed. We are familiar with the tradition of Joseph of Arimathea and his two cruets. If we believe that these are two of the five scent jars or ampoules that were once part of Mary's pound box of spikenard, we are left with three unaccounted for. Another "secret" follower of Jesus, Nicodemus, reputedly also possessed two vials of blood relics. According to legend, he carved the divinely inspired face of Jesus soon after the Crucifixion, later to be incorporated into the Volto Santo now found in Lucca, Italy. The nearby town of Luni possesses one of these two vials while the other was kept by Lucca where it was discovered on the Italian shores. These relics were found hidden in a compartment in the neck of the carving after it landed at Lucca — sent from Jerusalem on a boat with no sails, no rudder, and no oars. In addition we have the story of Mary Magdalene, who lived the remainder of her life as something of a hermit in the mountains of southern France. Her body was supposedly found with a similar vial, from which sprang the now famous tradition of Mary and her alabaster jar. It would therefore appear that all five of Mary's vials are accounted for, if not present. Mary kept one for herself, having previously used one to anoint Jesus's feet; two were given to Nicodemus to remain in Jerusalem until such time as they were endangered and sent to Italy; and lastly two were given to Joseph, most likely when he and Mary Magdalene parted company.

If their traditions are to be believed, the vials of blood belonging to Joseph, Nicodemus, and Mary all contained nothing but liquid blood, devoid of any other materials such as dirt or sand. It is probable that these vials, including Joseph's legendary two cruets, contained the mixed blood and other bodily fluids collected as the body was being prepared for entombment. This was the blood that ran from wounds, such as the spear entry wound in the side, instead of any blood derived from the dirt collected from the foot of the Cross. If there was another vessel containing bloody dirt from the site of Golgotha, it is uncertain whether or not it became integrated with the traditional Grail cycle.

The chalice that could be the origin of the historical Grail tradition can be seen by any tourist venturing to Valencia, Spain, but the fate of the five vials belonging to Joseph, Nicodemus, and Mary is not so certain. The earthly remains of Mary Magdalene and her alabaster jar allegedly were discovered in her hidden rock tomb under the present site of the Saint Maximin Basilica in France. The vials allegedly hidden in the carving known as the Volto Santo were divided between the towns of Lucca, where the Volto Santo can be seen today, and a neighboring town, Luni. Both vials belonging to Mary Magdalene and the vial found in Luni, Italy, are said to exhibit the same miraculous property: The small amount of blood found inside bubbled on occasion, testifying to its holy nature.

Although these nearly magical attributes stray back into the realm of mysticism and legend, these accounts do tell us what became of the cruets or alabasters belonging to Mary Magdalene and Nicodemus. We do not, however, have any indication of what became of the two cruets that Joseph brought to Glastonbury. The very idea of the Grail being lost comes from the fact that Joseph's vials, the objects that spawned the Grail legend, have never been found. Although there are several potential candidates for the lost cruets around the world, none have ever been shown to be the artifacts that once called Glastonbury home. One may wonder whatever became of these two important artifacts — the historical Grails at the heart of all the legendary accounts.

The only time Joseph's cruets were mentioned in any text outside the Grail romances is in the contentious prophecy of Melkin. The greatest bone of contention among scholars is that Melkin's writing was never mentioned or cited prior to John of Glastonbury's history of questionable reliability. However, it has been demonstrated quite clearly that there is every likelihood that these writings were in existence long before John of Glastonbury. If this text is to be believed, we discover that Joseph was in fact buried with his two cruets of white and silver. The prophecy clearly states,

> For Joseph has with him in his sarcophagus 2 white and silver vessels, filled with the blood and sweat of the prophet Jesus. When his sarcophagus is discovered, it will be seen whole and undecayed, and will be opened to the whole world.

Therefore we must realize that the cruets in question, Joseph's "Grails," last saw the light of day when they were interred with Joseph sometime in the first century. With this in mind, it is easy to see why the vials that inspired the Grail legend were seen as lost. Since no one really knew where Joseph's grave could be located, the Grail was similarly lost to history.

Since the church at Glastonbury never really possessed the Grail in the form of Joseph's two cruets, only knowing of their alleged existence, this would explain why they themselves never claimed to own the Grail, why they never listed it among their relics and holdings, and why they actually claimed their association with Joseph and not the Grail as the center of their monastic tradition. Although Melkin's writing demonstrates that these vessels were part of the foundation of Glastonbury's church, Joseph of Arimathea was clearly their most important ecumenical credential. When the search for Joseph's grave was undertaken, it can be assumed that a desire to find the Grail in the form of legitimate blood relics was part of the search. As it would seem that John Blome was aware of Melkin's writing, it must be assumed that he was also aware that the grave would contain these precious vessels.

We now understand where, in theory, the Grails could be found at Glastonbury, but since the assertion of this text is that Joseph's burial site was found in the fourteenth or fifteenth century, it does present a dilemma. Where are Joseph's cruets? If his body was found, so too presumably were the two vials containing the blood relics of Jesus. So what became of them, and why were they never written into the already legendary history of Glastonbury Abbey? Unfortunately, here there are more questions than answers.

The abbots of Glastonbury have in the past claimed the discovery of King Arthur's grave and that of his queen. They claimed the wattle church had been built by Joseph himself, possibly containing some mystery under the curious pattern built into its cobblestone floor. It was famed for its many relics and ancient texts, including an alleged charter written by St. Patrick. Therefore, it can be assumed that if they had discovered anything they could have matched with Melkin's cruets buried with Joseph they surely would have. Does that mean that they never actually found Joseph's burial, or does it mean that Melkin's prophecy is either incorrect or false?

This question can only be answered by examining the evidence we already have. It would seem that Melkin's writing was real and in existence for John Leland, John of Glastonbury, and John Blome to see and reference. Similarly, it would seem likely that the one burial that fits Melkin's description of where Joseph's body would be found was in fact that of Joseph of Arimathea. If the text can be believed, as I assert it can be, and Joseph's grave was found in 1419, as I assert it was, how can we reconcile these accounts with Melkin's prophecy regarding the presence of two cruets in Joseph's grave?

It is curious that no mention was ever made of these cruets being found, either in a grave that was discovered or kept as holy relics in their sacristy. If we accept the assertions given in the previous paragraph, we are left with exactly three options — the Grails either were never found, were lost, or intentionally hidden. If the cruets were never found, it could simply be that Melkin was mistaken. Writing several centuries after Joseph was buried, he could have been incorrect in his claim that the cruets would be found interred with Joseph's body. However, this seems unlikely since he was aware of where and how Joseph was buried. Making a mistake of this kind would suggest either the melding of written record and some kind of oral tradition, or misdirection on the part of his sources. If the Grails were discovered but later lost, they might never have entered into the stream of Glastonbury's historic traditions. This too seems unlikely for the obvious reasons. Such important, holy relics would have been treated with the utmost care and reverence, and surely would not have been accidentally discarded.

This suggests only one thing — the Grail was found at some point and was for reasons unknown left out of official records. Although this option seems most likely, it is also one of the most difficult to believe. If the Holy Grail, a relic of Christ's blood, had been found, it is difficult to think of a reason why Glastonbury Abbey would want to keep it a secret. One could argue that perhaps someone found the relics and didn't recognize them for the important artifacts they were. It is possible that by the time Joseph's grave was found in 1419, the Grail romances had already been written and in circulation for some two and a half centuries. For all that time, everyone had become familiar with the idea of a single Grail cup or chalice. Then when the tomb was discovered, two tiny vials may have been seen simply as grave goods — items that once contained oils or perfumes interred with the body. This sort of grave offering is well known in prehistoric graves in Britain, but was still a custom in the Middle Ages as well. It has already been mentioned that the translation of Melkin's writing is difficult at best, and surely would have been so then as well as now. If someone discovered the two cruets using Melkin's text as a guide, it is possible that the translation could have been made more in keeping with their medieval view of the Grail, such as "vessel of both white and silver." If this were the case, it is curious that they were not included in the details of the grave given in Abbot Frome's letter to King Henry V, although it could have been covered by the description of the finery and ornamentation found within.

There are many possible explanations for why these treasured relics might have been lost to history. It seems that their discovery would have warranted some kind of mention given their association with Melkin's prophecy and their connection to Joseph of Arimathea. Surely it would have survived in legend if not in written record. Although it is possible the cruets were in the rich burial found in the 1419 excavation, it is also possible that this burial had been found previously and that the cruets were removed. Therefore, we must ascertain if it was more likely that the relics described by Melkin, Joseph's two cruets of white and silver, were discovered during the time of King Ine when the bodies of the twelve individuals were uncovered, during the time of Dunstan when these remains were reburied and the chapel in the cemetery was built, or in 1419 when all four coffins were excavated.

If this coffin had been found in the early eighth century, it is possible that these two Roman scent jars or vials were removed. It is uncertain whether they would have been identified as Roman by the eighth century Saxons. Conversely, it is possible that these objects had been discovered at that time, and that they were fully aware that these were sacred objects, but that their meaning had been lost over time, the Roman relics simply becoming two items of unknown provenance and not associated with Joseph. This too seems unlikely since the time between Melkin's writing and the construction of the first stone church on the grounds was a mere 150–180 years. For this reason, it is unlikely that Joseph's coffin was found by King Ine. If Melkin's writings were used to discover the twelve bodies found outside the wattle church, Ine would have likely identified one of these twelve as Joseph, and considered his search over. In addition, had the two cruets been found at this time, they would have been immediately recognized, their discovery becoming an integral part of Glastonbury's mythical past.

In addition, let us recall the *Chronicle* written by Helinand of Froidmont. Listed under the year 720, the *Chronicle* speaks of a miraculous vision of a "hermit of Britain" regarding Joseph of Arimathea and his sacred vessels, resulting in a history written by this British hermit called *De Gradale*, or *Of The Grail*. In this entry, Helinand conjectures the Grail to be a bowl or shallow dish from the Last Supper due to the derivation of the word *greal* from the French. Although Helinand's history is intriguing, it is still unlikely that the cruets were found at this time if for no other reason than that if they had been found when Ine used Melkin's prophecy to find the graves, Helinand would not have gone to such lengths to derive his definition of the Grail from the French term for a serving dish. He would have simply provided a description of the objects found inside the coffin.

Second, it would seem very unlikely that this coffin was uncovered during Abbot Dunstan's time, as he seemed more interested in preserving the ancient dead than digging for them. The only thing that would tie Dunstan to the relics of Joseph of Arimathea is the construction of the small chapel later called "St. Michael in the Cemetery." Archeological evidence indicates that this chapel was constructed around the same time that Dunstan enclosed the old cemetery by a wall built to contain the fill dirt used to raise the ground level in the cemetery by as much as 2 meters. However, there is again no evidence, written or archeological, that suggests Dunstan found the interior coffin containing the remains of Joseph or his two cruets. If these relics were found and placed inside his chapel in the cemetery, this chapel would have become the beating heart of the entire monastic complex, and it would have never been allowed to fade from memory, much less allowed to become "ruinous" even into the fourteenth century.

I maintain that this chapel was intended to contain some of the relics of what were seen as early church fathers found in twelve individual "cist" burials in the mid tenth century by King Ine using Melkin's prophecy as a guide, leading to the enlarging of his church and the construction of the atrium joining the stone church to the wattle church. Dunstan removed these relics from the single coffin containing the combined bones of the twelve individuals and then reburied it, redepositing the relics in his chapel to maintain the practice of their veneration. All the while, the coffin containing the actual bones of Joseph of Arimathea remained undisturbed due to their location under the oldest, most sanctified structure on the site, the wattle church, until they were finally discovered during the excavations in 1419.

When all these possibilities are weighed and considered, only one option emerges as the most likely. It is very possible that the two cruets mentioned by Melkin were indeed found with Joseph's body during the 1419 excavation, and were intentionally omitted from record. The reasons for this are a mystery, but there are several possibilities. First, consider the times in which the 1419 discovery took place. The Dissolution was more than a century away, but the seeds of reformation and iconoclasm had already been planted a few hundred years before in other countries. The mood amongst churches, especially very wealthy churches, was changing rapidly. It could have been decided to keep the discovery of Melkin's cruets of white and silver a secret for this reason.

It is also possible that if these relics were discovered, they were kept secret because their worth was too great to become widely known. Feuds among neighboring churches had taken place in the recent past, leading to a time of great struggle and hardship for the community at Glastonbury. If relics of great worth and importance such as these were uncovered, the abbot may have felt it prudent to keep the fact a secret. Ultimately it is impossible to know for sure why Joseph's cruets were never mentioned or listed among its sacred relics. We can assume that Melkin's writings did actually exist, and so, the cruets could be found in Joseph's tomb. We can also assume with reasonable certainty that the tomb was found, presumably with the relics intact. Whatever the reason may have been to keep them a secret, if they were still housed at Glastonbury when the Dissolution took place they were most likely cast aside, destroyed, became anonymous trinkets in the king's treasury, or were otherwise lost to history.

There is a possibility, however, that these two little vials did survive the heavy hands of the Dissolution. If we recall the theory that the Grail Castle of medieval romance actually referred to the Grail Chapel, or the church containing the Grail, we must also recall the tradition that when the Grail was recovered, many sacred relics housed in the Grail Castle were dispersed among other hermitages and churches across the country side. It is possible that this tradition foreshadowed events that would later befall Glastonbury, resulting in the dispersal of the most valuable relics among other holy houses in the region. It is interesting here to recall the story of the Nanteos Cup in Wales. It was said that monks from Glastonbury carried the wooden bowl that had been hidden in the abbey before the Dissolution to the Strata Florida to prevent its destruction. Further pursued, these monks sought refuge with the Powell family, later entrusting the relic to them for safekeeping.

It has been shown that the wooden cup, claimed to be a miraculous cure for many, is nothing more than a medieval bowl common to the area, most likely discovered by a nineteenth-century antiquarian digging in the ruins of Strata Florida. This would seem to remove the Nanteos tradition from this investigation of the Grail. Nevertheless, the question still lingers: what would lead anyone to think the Holy Grail could be found at Strata Florida? Is it possible that the story itself was legitimate, but the relic thought to be the Grail was not? If so, this could have been where at least one of Joseph's vials wound up after being removed from Glastonbury Abbey. A similar story might be found at Rosslyn Chapel in Scotland — another site associated with the Grail.

Rosslyn Chapel allegedly houses the true Grail, locked secretly inside one of the elaborately carved pillars standing before the high altar. Although metal detection conducted on this pillar shows no signs of any metal object within it, a small onyx vial hidden in a small compartment similar to that used in the Volto Santo would not be discovered in this manner. It is also possible that the Templars, with whom the Scottish Chapel is associated, were given at least one of these two relics to care for during these troubled times. If this did occur, it could explain why the modern order of Italian Templars and their leader, Rocco Zingaro, claimed to possess the true Holy Grail in the form of a small, Roman-style onyx scent jar quite similar to that allegedly found by Graham Phillips in Shropshire.

Phillips presents some intriguing research regarding what he believes to be the Holy Grail, but his trustworthiness as a historical Grail researcher has been brought into question by certain dubious claims in his books *The Search for the Grail* and *The Chalice of Magdalene*. For example, he makes the assertion that a "Marian Chalice" was mentioned by Olympiodorus, having been secreted away to Britain from Rome in A.D. 410. After having many people point out that there is no such reference, he recanted this point. In addition, he claims that a thirteenth-century French copy of the First Continuation of Chrétien's *Conte del Graal* contained a text called *La Folie Perceval*, major characters and plot events of which are reflected in the images found in the Tarot deck. Fortunately with the help of John Koopmans, it has been determined that there is no such reference in this text, and all efforts to contact Mr. Phillips for clarification have gone unanswered. Though these facts make it difficult to accept any of Mr. Phillips' findings, it is possible that he has actually happened across the traditions that hint back to one of the lost cruets of Joseph from Glastonbury. The story behind the Roman vial allegedly hidden and later found in Hawkstone Park does in some ways mirror that of the Nanteos Cup. If the object itself is not what the claims state it is, it does suggest that there did exist the tradition that something that could be called the Grail was there at one time. The "riddles" hidden in a nineteenth-century book called *Sir Gawain and the Red Knight* suggest someone at some point thought the small, broken onyx vial once hidden inside the base of a statue was the true holy relic. Therefore one must wonder why such a tradition exists in Shropshire at all. Is it possible that this is where one of Joseph's cruets ended its journey?

All of this is conjecture, of course, and in no way indicates whether, where, or when Joseph's cruets were found or deposited. If these Roman scent jars are the relics that inspired the Grail legend in Europe, the Grail is still lost, waiting to be discovered by some intrepid future researcher. We must remember that just because we don't have these two relics in hand, we cannot and should not conclude that they didn't exist. The enduring mystery of whatever became of Joseph's cruets only serves to keep interest in the Grail legend alive throughout the ages. However, since we now have substantial evidence suggesting Joseph was indeed at Glastonbury in the first century and that he was buried with two vessels containing blood relics acquired just after the Crucifixion, we are left with a new riddle to solve. If Joseph actually brought the "Grail" in the form of two cruets to Britain, where are they now?

Regrettably, we must now leave the present location of Joseph's Grails as a yet-to-be-solved riddle for future investigation and return to the evolution of the Grail legend. It remains a mystery how the two cruets mentioned by Melkin were lost to history. However, we can be sure that when the traditional Grail romances were written, the authors did not have in mind the image of a Roman scent jar or unguent flask. There can be little doubt that further information might have been found in the ancient texts held in Glastonbury's library, lost to the fire of 1184. In fact it was very fortunate that the story of the Grail left Glastonbury before the fire to gain a foothold among the poets and troubadours in the high French courts of Champagne. Otherwise the book might have been lost to the flames never becoming part of our culture.

It is clear that at the time the Grail romances were written, any historical factuality regarding Joseph and the two Roman scent jars had long since been forgotten, replaced by reconstructed history and legend. Therefore, it is no surprise that this is reflected in the literature — a Grail made of gold and magic, not alabaster and reverence. Taking the Grail stories by themselves, it would seem that their writers knew little to nothing about what the Grail actually was, and therefore replaced the holes with fantasy. This indicates that the actual relics that were the true Grails were not known, and thereby the Grail was seen as a lost relic to be sought and quested after.

As previously mentioned, this would mean the Grails either had been found some time before and forgotten (which seems very unlikely), or were yet to be found, most likely in the 1419 excavation. Even though the objects themselves were not in hand, the very placement of Chrétien's Grail story in England demonstrates that there was in fact a longstanding tradition that the Grail had been carried there after the Crucifixion. It was no coincidence that the father of the Grail romance, a French poet, placed the story of the Grail in the rival land of Britain. Many scholars over the ages have assumed that Chrétien took a Celtic tale and adapted it to suit a French noble court, but no one has ever asked why he didn't simply rewrite it based in his own land of France. Simply by stating the Grail was to be found in England, Chrétien illustrates that there was this tradition held in Britain long before the writing of his "originating" work.

Although Chrétien conceded that this holy relic was in the land of the legendary King Arthur, he could not provide any detail about the Grail itself. This is likely why the nature of this object, other than his description, was left so vague in his *Conte*. Quite simply put, he probably didn't know what else to say about it since there appeared to be no knowledge of it in England other than the fact that it once existed. The elaboration upon the true nature of the Holy Grail as we understand it came from his continuators, such as Robert de Boron. It was from writers such as this that we have derived our Christian significance for this previously enigmatic relic. It would appear that in the end, Chrétien was required to turn his gaze away from Britain toward Spain to get a clearer picture of his Grail.

The ending to Chrétien's Grail story was only written when Phillip of Flanders went on pilgrimage to Santiago de Compostella. In 1172, on his way to view the relics of St. James, Phillip almost certainly went to the mountain monastery of San Juan de la Peña near Jaca. There, he witnessed a cup that purportedly was the very same from which Jesus drank at the Last Supper, and was later used by the first popes in the Holy Land until it was sent to Spain by St. Laurence. He was surely shown the texts written long ago testifying to the authenticity of this relic, giving its pedigree all the way back to St. Peter. It is from here that Chrétien, through Phillip, likely derived his image of the Holy Grail as a golden chalice adorned with gems and pearls, kept in a far-off land in a secretive, protected citadel.

We know that the Santo Caliz currently in Valencia Cathedral was housed in San Juan de la Peña during the time of Phillip's pilgrimage. We also know that when the first-century relic first arrived at San Juan de la Peña, it was in the simple form of an agate cup without the elaborately ornamented base that would be added later. When it left San Juan de la Peña in the fourteenth century, it had been made into the dazzling medieval goblet we see today. Therefore, at some point during its time at San Juan de la Peña, the simple first-century agate cup became the Santo Caliz de la Cena.

Researchers such as Michael Hessemann have said that this transformation likely took place in 1135, the only time the sacred relic left the mountain monastery. It was at this time that King Ramiro II of Aragon allegedly commissioned his goldsmiths to create the golden base that now accents the red agate cup at the top. If this assessment is correct, Phillip of Flanders witnessed the Santo Caliz in all its medieval glory when he was on pilgrimage nearly forty years later. Although it is not specifically stated that Phillip went to San Juan de la Peña while on his way to Santiago de Compostella, the theory is actually corroborated by another writer who was Chrétien's contemporary and, some would say, his rival.

Wolfram von Eschenbach, the first German poet to write about the Holy Grail, included several apparent references to San Juan de la Peña in his Grail romance, *Parzival*. He claimed that the Holy Grail, a mysterious stone upon which mystical writing appears, was found in the mountain castle called Munsalvaesche where it was protected by none other than the Knights Templar. He wrote that the Grail Castle at Munsalvaesche was surrounded by many other hermitages and has the curious feature of "living water" inside the sanctuary in which Parzival's Moorish brother Feirefiz was finally baptized. If we had any initial doubts about San Juan de la Peña being the place where the Grail of legend could be found, Wolfram (who claimed a more in-depth knowledge of the source material also used by Chrétien) paints a very clear picture of the Spanish mountain monastery. In a wild area, as Wolfram described, the sanctuary in which the Santo Caliz was kept features a natural spring or "living waters," the cup does indeed have mysterious markings on the base (which were not added until medieval times), the Santo Caliz was in fact venerated by a group of Spanish "proto-Templar" knights, and San Juan is surrounded by many mountain hermitages predating the church itself. Most importantly, the mountain range which shelters San Juan de la Peña is known as San Salvador, or in the medieval Occitan language of the region, "Munsalvaesche."

To further illustrate the idea that San Juan de la Peña was the inspiration for the Grail Castle, another German writer named Albrecht von Scharfenberg, who continued the Grail writings began by Wolfram von Eschenbach, went one step further. He went into some detail describing the Grail Castle, which he actually calls the Grail Chapel, stating the place where the Grail was venerated was surrounded by twenty-two carved arches. Many assume this means that the building in which Albrecht's Grail was housed was surrounded by an arched courtyard or cloister, but in the chapel area in San Juan de la Peña, the area where the Santo Caliz was venerated, we find that the triple-arched altar area is built from twenty-two individual arches — three in the front, seven around the back wall of the center chamber, five around the back wall of the left and right chambers, and finally, two arches joining the center chamber to either side chambers, totaling twenty-two separate arches. This information taken together with Wolfram's description of the Grail Castle (or more correctly the Grail *Chapel*, as we have seen with the Glastonbury/*Perlesvaus* connection) and Chrétien's description of the Grail as a gold and jeweled chalice, leaves little question that the Santo Caliz and San Juan de la Peña served as a physical model on which to base the classical Grail Legend.

When the Santo Caliz was used to finalize the story of the Grail as it came from Glastonbury, the spread of sacred vessels from the Crucifixion across Europe came full circle. By the time the Grail romances were written, the idea of Joseph's Grail as two Roman scent jars had long since been forgotten, replaced by the vague notion of a rich medieval chalice. The audience for which Chrétien de Troyes wrote his *Conte del Graal* was more interested in being entertained by a good story than understanding the historical aspects of the mystical tale, and thus the legend of the Holy Grail was born. When the Santo Caliz was seen by Phillip of Flanders, medieval pilgrim and patron to Chrétien, a Grail more fitting medieval sensibilities became the image provided in these provocative stories of spirituality and high courtly behavior. The mysterious, mythical events that allegedly led to the foundation of the high mountain monastery of San Juan de la Peña likely contributed to the fantastic light in which the story was painted. Even the tradition that the Holy Grail came from the table of the Last Supper likely came from the Santo Caliz.

I assert that the red agate cup that now sits atop the gold and jeweled medieval reliquary in Valencia Spain is the one vessel among all contenders which can be most correctly called "The Holy Grail." This is likely the vessel that was used to catch Christ's blood while His body was being prepared for entombment in Joseph's donated tomb. Oddly enough, however, this is not the vessel that begat the Grail legend born of Arthuriana and medieval romance. The Grail that legend claims Joseph of Arimathea brought to England was actually two of the five cruets, or Judeo-Roman unguentaria, that were filled with blood from the Santo Caliz cup after the Crucifixion, and after the tomb was found empty. Thus from the *primary* Grail, the Santo Caliz, a set of *secondary* Grails were created, which included Joseph's cruets, those of Nicodemus, and the one carried to France by Mary Magdalene. The classic Grail story was based on the tradition that Joseph had in his possession at Glastonbury the Grail, a vessel that contained the blood of Jesus Himself. Since no relic could be found — or at least none known to the general public — the image of the Holy Grail, the magical golden goblet that floats, provides food to worthy knights, offers everlasting life, and finally departs this earth for lands unknown, was taken from the ornate golden chalice that the Santo Caliz had by then become.

The original purpose for this book was to illustrate that the Holy Grail could have been a real historical object, albeit through something of a roundabout method. If evidence could be presented that Joseph of Arimathea actually did come to Britain, then it would be only a small step further to demonstrate that he could have come to Britain while carrying two vessels that originated in Jerusalem — the two cruets that would eventually be changed into the single Holy Grail of legend. The traditions of Joseph at Glastonbury have always been seen as a quaint local legend with little to no basis in fact. However, it has been demonstrated that not only could it have been so, but that there actually exists evidence suggesting Joseph was at Glastonbury and did found the first wattle church on the site. By using Melkin's prophecy as a guide, we can see that not only was a burial found that was associated with Joseph of Arimathea, but also that the idea of Joseph being at Glastonbury went back much further than the medieval "cult of Joseph" that could be found there during the High Middle Ages.

Although it seems dangerous at best to base a theory on a character and text that many assume to be the product of John of Glastonbury's fertile imagination, Melkin's writings have turned out to be invaluable in demonstrating the flaw in the typical assumption that Glastonbury Abbey was a medieval "hoax factory." The prophecy of Melkin may not have been referenced by any writer before John of Glastonbury, but it seems obvious that it was a well-known text for centuries before this. It was seen by John Leland before and after the Dissolution. It was known by John Blome when he requested permission from the king to search for Joseph's grave site. It was likely used in the location of King Arthur's burial site. It was also very likely referenced in Helinand's *Chronicon* and his definition of the Grail. In fact, the text Helinand mentioned, the *De Gradale*, may have been written by Melkin himself, making this semi-mythical character the very first Grail Romancer. This one text links the ancient, legendary claims found at Glastonbury Abbey with the age in which histories, inventories of church holdings, and the earliest archeological digs took place, providing most of the knowledge of England's history that we possess today.

Conversely, physical remains found in the early fifteenth century which corroborate Melkin's prophecy provide a link between artifacts still in existence today to the golden age of Joseph's veneration at Glastonbury. In the nearby parish Church of John the Baptist, a stone tomb now sits that once formed the base of an elaborate reliquary from which either Joseph's coffin or a box covering his bones could be lifted into the sight of medieval pilgrims standing in the crypt of Glastonbury Abbey. Rescued from the ruins after King Henry VIII's forces ransacked the abbey, this tomb was conveyed to the parish church across High Street in hopes of saving the last remaining vestige of the great man who founded the community at Glastonbury. This medieval artifact reaches back from our modern day to join hands with Melkin's prophecy, allegedly written in the time of Arthur, both testifying to the true age and veracity of the Joseph tradition.

If it could be proven that Joseph actually founded the wattle church at Glastonbury, as it seems we have with reasonable certainty, how much harder would it be to say that he did actually bring the Holy Grail from the Crucifixion to Britain? Stripped of all its medieval fantasy, the Holy Grail is simply a vessel that once held the blood of Christ. It is known that first-century Jews collected the spilled blood of the recently dead to be interred with the body. Therefore, we see that such a vessel likely existed. If Joseph had in his possession this type of vessel, carried with him as a personal relic and link to his lost Master, he could have brought it with him from his native Palestine. Buried with him at the time of his death, Joseph's cruets became the stuff of legend, passed down through the ages, slowly eaten away by apathy and skepticism until Melkin's writing again inspired the quest to relocate both the relics and the man, returning both to their place as a legitimate part of Glastonbury's rich history.

Few ever think of the Holy Grail in terms of history. It is much more common to see it as an interesting and powerful theme driving a particular genre of medieval literature. If anyone ever makes the statement that the Holy Grail is a real artifact, that person usually watches an incredulous smile begin to stretch across the face of one to whom the statement was made. "You can't really believe the Grail exists!" "Everyone knows it's just a story." "There has never been any proof that the Holy Grail was anything other than fiction." Throw in a smattering of *Indiana Jones* references and utterings of "not scholarly research," and you have the modern Grail Quest in a nutshell. It was said in the beginning that there is no proof, not just of the Holy Grail, but in fact of anything. There can be no proof outside of mathematics and chemistry. However, to say there is no evidence that the Holy Grail ever existed outside of medieval romance is without question false.

There is ample evidence that the traditions of Joseph of Arimathea coming to Britain with the Holy Grail are indeed true. The tradition is older than the texts most cite to show it is not. An ancient text speaks of Joseph and the Grails, dating before the traditional body of Grail romances. A tomb exists in which the body thought to be that of Joseph was kept. Finally, a cup exists, albeit in Spain instead of England, that can be legitimately called the Grail from which several other "Grails" were spawned. The Holy Grail, words that have become synonymous with "the epitome," is the best example of the old adage, "the truth is stranger than fiction." The story behind the Grail is much stranger, grander, more elaborate, and much more circuitous than the Grail of legend. As is the course of any intellectual pursuit, the first and most important directive is to question, and in questioning, you begin to learn and understand. If you do not question, it is impossible to move closer to the truth. Therefore, in asking what the Grail is, you achieve it. Though it may take a lifetime or more to truly understand the Holy Grail, it takes but a moment of earnest investigation to see that it is much more than fiction.

I believe that most of those who were certain the Grail was just an old legend before reading this book still believe that. However, I do hope this text has forced them to admit, if only to themselves, that the case for the traditions of Glastonbury aren't perhaps as quaint and fanciful as they had originally perceived. After two decades researching this thesis, I would be most satisfied with a heart-felt "hmmm..." instead of a rousing chorus of agreement. My efforts go out to those who are just now beginning their study of the Holy Grail and have yet to form an opinion. Perhaps if I am very fortunate, these words will inspire some student writing a paper about the legend, or maybe even a wide-eyed lay-scholar who has just seen a documentary about the Grail and wishes to know more. Like the Grail itself, this interest appears and is present for all too short a time and is then gone, leaving the knight alone to search it out in the wild woods of history. After many a weary season has passed, he will doubtlessly find himself before the object of his fascination. Hopefully, when he is asked the vital question, "Who is served by the Grail?" he can rightly answer, "*I* have been," and perhaps even include a humble "Thank You."

Bibliography

Ashe, Geoffrey, Leslie Alcock, A. A. Ralegh Radford, and Philip Rahtz. *The Quest for Arthur's Britain*. London: Granada, 1971.
Bennett, Janice. *St. Laurence and the Holy Grail*. Ignatius, 2004.
Carley, James P. *Chronicle of Glastonbury Abbey*. British Archaeological Reports 47, 1978.
_____. *Glastonbury Abbey and the Arthurian Tradition*. Cambridge: D. S. Brewer, 2001.
_____. *Glastonbury Abbey: The Holy House at the Head of the Moors Adventurous*. New York: St. Martin's, 1988.
_____. "The Manuscript Remains of John Leland: 'The king's antiquary.'" *Text: Translations of the Society for Textual Scholarship* 2 Indiana University Press, 111–120, 1985.
Cline, Ruth Harwood. *Perceval, or, The Story of the Grail*. University of Georgia Press, 1985.
Duggan, Joseph J. *The Romances of Chretien de Troyes*. Yale University Press, 2001.
Early English Text Society. *The Famous Historie of Chinon of England together with The Assertion of King Arthure*. Oxford University Press, 1925.
Evans, Sebastian, *trans. The High History of the Holy Grail*. London: J. M. Dent, 1898.
The Gospel of Nicodemus
Guenon, Rene, and Henry Fohr. *Symbols of Sacred Science*. Sophia Perennis, 2004.
Harrison, Hank. *The Crown of Stars*. Arkives Publications, unpublished. PDF document — www.arkives.com.
Hearn, Thomas, *Joannis Lelandi Antiquarii de Rebus Brittanicis Collectanea*. Oxford, 1716.
Hessemann, Michael. "The Cup of Christ?" *Inside the Vatican Magazine,* March 2006.
The Holy Bible. King James Edition.
Hopkinson-Ball, Tim. *The Rediscovery of Glastonbury*. Gloucestershire: Sutton, 2007.
Lefevere, Andre. *Parzival*. New York: The Continuum, 1991.
Lewis, Rev. Lionel Smithett. *St. Joseph of Arimathea at Glastonbury Or the Apostolic Church of Britain*. Kessinger, 2003.
Loomis, Roger Sherman. *The Grail: From Celtic Myth to Christian Symbol*. Princeton University Press, 1991.
Malmesbury, William. *Chronicle of the Kings of England*. 1090–1154.
_____. *De Antiquitate Glastonie Ecclesie*. Circa 1129.
Matthews, John. *Sources of the Grail: An Anthology*. Floris Books, 1996.
McCash, June Hall Martin. "Marie de Champagne and Eleanor of Aquitaine: A Relationship Examined." *Speculum: A Journal of Medieval Studies* 54, No. 4, October 1979.
Perring, Dominic. *The Roman House in Britain*. London and New York: Routledge, 2002.
Potter, T. W., and Catherine Johns. *Roman Britain*. Los Angeles: University of California Press, 1993.

Rahtz, Philip, and Lorna Watts. *Glastonbury: Myth and Archaeology*. Gloucestershire: History Press, 2009.
Rich, Vincent, *The International Lead Trade*. Cambridge: Woodhead, 1994.
Robertus de Boston. *Chronicon Angliae Petriburgense*. J. A. Giles, ed. London: D. Nutt, 1845.
Smith, Lucy Tulmin. *The Itinerary of John Leland In or About the Years 1535–1543*, Volumes 1–5. Carbondale: Southern Illinois University Press, 1964.
Willis, Rev. Robert. *The Architectural History of Glastonbury Abbey*. Cambridge and London: Deighton, Bell, 1866.

Index

Alfonso I, King 217, 219
Ambrosius Aurelianus 95
Aristobulus 109, 233
Arviragus 110

Badon Hill 76
Beckery 29, 44–45, 75–78, 116, 180
Beere 44, 50, 143, 247
Blome, John 117–120, 125, 133–134, 148, 241–244, 258–259, 268
Bond, Bligh 49–50, 137
Boston, Robertus de 118, 134, 243–244
Bran/Bron (the Blessed) 95–101, 105
Bride's Mound 78, 180

Cadbury 157–158
Caer Worgorn 94–95
Cahuz 179–181
Camlann 78
Caractacus/Caradawc/Caradog 95–96
Cenacle 214–215
Chinnock 48, 131–133, 186, 244
Constantine 26, 28, 55; Cystennyn Llydaw 95
Cor Tewdws 94–95
Croyland Abbey 118–119
Culhwch and Olwen 18

Deruvian 26, 28, 75, 124
Dunstan 29–30, 39, 42–43, 121–125, 129–133, 169, 261

Edward III 117, 119, 134, 143
Eleanor of Aquitaine, Queen 40, 173–174, 191–193
Elucidation 175–176
Eschenbach, Wolfram von 197, 201–212, 217–219, 222–223, 266

Eucharist 17, 64, 190, 212, 215–216, 219, 223

Fisher King 18, 98–100, 108, 172, 181–185, 194, 205–206, 254
Flegetanis 202–203
Flower of Life 83
Fouke Fitz Waryn 172, 181
Frome 119–125, 134, 143, 245–247, 260

Gawain 17, 177, 181, 196, 263
Geoffrey of Monmouth 38, 78, 161, 164, 197
George and Pilgrim Inn 46
Germanus, Bishop 94–96
Gildas 92–96, 100–101, 161, 240–241
Guinevere 17, 38, 42, 87, 121, 178–179, 207

Harod 62
Helena 26
Helinand 102–103, 126, 240, 243, 261, 268
Henry of Blois 3, 27, 31, 167–179, 187, 190–191, 194, 220–222
Henry II, King 37, 102, 167, 174, 176, 190–194, 222
Henry V 245–247, 260
Henry VIII 43, 46, 146, 151–154, 162–163, 242, 249, 268
Herlewin 30, 169, 177
Holinshed 146–147

Ilid/Illid 96–97, 99, 101, 105
Illtud/Illtyd 92–96, 100

John of Glastonbury 19–20, 40, 89–91, 101–105, 117, 148, 162, 164–165, 227, 234, 239, 241, 258–259, 268
John of Taunton 36

Index

Kabbalah 82–82
Kyot 197, 202

Lake Village 24–25, 46, 70, 157, 181, 234
Lancelot 17, 19, 177, 190, 207
Lapis exilis 205, 216–219; Lapsit Exillis 201, 203, 205
Last Supper 11, 17, 54, 212, 215, 221, 223, 254–256, 261, 265, 267
Laurence, Saint 212, 216, 265
Leland, John 2, 20, 38, 43, 47, 90, 101–105, 145, 148–165, 187, 239–242, 259, 268
Llandaff 90–91
Llanilltud Fawr 93–94
Llantwit Major 92–97, 100–101, 105
Lucius, King 26

Maelgwyn 91, 240
Maglocunus 90–93
Magna Tabula 48, 131, 244
Marie de Champagne 167, 170–174, 190–193, 198, 221
Mary Magdalene 16, 45, 49, 61, 65, 232–233, 254–258, 263, 267
Merlin 17, 90, 102, 149, 161–164
Mithras/Mithraism/Mithraic Zodiac 80–81, 237
Mordred/Modred 38, 174, 178
Munsalvaesche 203–209, 217, 223, 266

Nanteos 184, 255, 262–263
Nicodemus 13, 60–64, 232, 256–258, 267

Parzival 197, 201–212, 217–219, 266
Paulinus 29, 79, 94, 127–128
Pelagius 94
Perlesvaus 107–108, 172–187, 195–196, 203, 206, 243
Phagan 26–28, 75
Phillip of Flanders, Count 2, 167, 170–173, 190–191, 195–198, 211–213, 220–222, 265–267

Philospher's Stone 201, 204–205, 216, 219
Pilate 13, 58–64, 179, 230–232

Ramiro, King 218–219, 265
Ramsey Psalter 39–41
Ray, John 146–147, 248
Rigaldus de Berbezillo 193–194
Rigaut de Barbezieux 193–194, 221
Robert de Boron 64, 98, 196, 232, 265

St. Asaph 91
St. Bridget 45
St. David 36, 47, 72, 94
St. Michael in the Cemetery 127, 131, 133, 186, 244, 261
St. Patrick 26–27, 48, 75, 94–95, 119–124, 164, 259
San Juan de la Peña 199, 207–223, 265–267
Santiago de Compostella 198–199, 213, 220–222, 265–266
Santo Caliz 3, 199, 211–224, 265–267
Scharfenberg, Albrecht von 212–212, 218
Selwood 46
Simon of Zelotes 109
Spalding Priory 118, 148, 243–244
Spoils of Annwn 18, 100
Stoke-sub-Hamdon 38–39
Strata Florida 184, 255–256, 262–263

Thomas Hearn 43, 161, 164
Thurstin 30, 169, 177
Tree of Life 82–83, 88, 237

Uther Pendragon 95

Vesica Pisces 83
Virgin Mary 20, 31, 51, 87, 112, 180, 232

Whiting 43–50, 109–110, 159
William of Malmesbury 26–31, 69–88, 116, 132, 159, 168–170, 179, 197, 235–239, 243–244

www.ingramcontent.com/pod-product-compliance
Ingram Content Group UK Ltd.
Pitfield, Milton Keynes, MK11 3LW, UK
UKHW041929140426
5217IPUK00014B/391